John of the Cross as a young nurse's aide in the Hospital of the Conception, Medina del Campo, a hospital for patients suffering from contagious diseases, particularly syphilis. Engraving from a Spanish edition of the *Works of St. John of the Cross*, published in Seville, Spain, 1701.

"I am very happy with the publication of this timely, necessary, and urgently needed book. A magnificent work by my brother and friend Daniel Chowning, who not only offers a wise and profound reflection on the healing power of contemplation in John of the Cross, but does so as the fruit of a lifetime of experience and as an authentic and faithful witness with his life to what his writing conveys. It is a very necessary and recommendable reading in order to heal the wounds of our times with the most effective medicine distilled in the writings of John of the Cross: contemplation as a way to learn to love and to let oneself be loved."

— Father Miguel Márquez, superior general of the Discalced Carmelite Order

"Coming from decades of careful study of the texts and the living out of their meaning, the author offers a comprehensive, eminently accessible, and reliable interpretation of John of the Cross's teaching. He opens a contemplative pathway to understanding and entering into the challenging, transformative, lifelong process of growing union with God that gradually breaks our enslavement to disordered desire. Fr. Chowning makes noteworthy use of John's texts. For example, he interweaves the wonderful theology present in *The Romances* into the flow of his major writings. While the insights of contemporary psychology illuminate this study, the author rightly stresses John's emphasis on God's faithful, self-communicating, healing love."

— Constance FitzGerald, OCD, Carmelite Monastery, Baltimore

"*Healed by Love* is a clear presentation of a frequently misinterpreted spiritual master. It is an insightful interpretation of the spirituality of St. John of the Cross regarding spiritual healing. Chowning provides both an in-depth diagnosis of our spiritual sickness and an analysis of the process of healing and transformation according to the great Spanish Carmelite mystic. It will find an eager reception among both scholars and the general audience alike."

— Marc Foley, OCD, author of *The Dark Night: Psychological Experience and Spiritual Reality*

"In this beautiful and very readable book, Fr. Daniel Chowning has distilled the teaching of St. John of the Cross for a new generation, linking it with his own personal, pastoral, and psychological insights. Under St. John's guidance all are encouraged to surrender to the process of healing and transformation in Christ. It is a contemplative journey that leads to freedom and the integration of the whole person. Chowning's writing is the fruit of many years of studying and teaching the Carmelite saints, and I was hooked from page one. Be enthused, inspired, and challenged to make the journey of contemplative love a way of life 'costing not less than everything.' It's never too late to set out."

— Sr. Elizabeth Obbard, Carmelite nun of Quidenham Monastery, UK, and spiritual writer

"Because sin, both original and personal, causes all our human brokenness, only God can truly heal us and restore us to our lost wholeness. As St. John of the Cross teaches, God heals and restores us through contemplation as he communicates himself directly to our souls when we dispose ourselves to receive this divine grace by daily living the Gospel. Drawing on his years of extensive research into the life and writings of the sixteenth-century doctor of the church and of providing spiritual guidance for numerous persons within the Carmelite tradition, Fr. Chowning clearly explains the divine psychotherapy by which God purifies us of our sins, unites us with His will, and transforms us into new persons in Christ Jesus. All who long for their own healing and especially those in healing ministries—physicians, psychotherapists, confessors, spiritual guides—will welcome *Healed by Love*."

— Kevin Culligan, OCD, charter member of the Institute of Carmelite Studies and the Carmelite Forum

"Remarkable for its depth and clarity, *Healed by Love* is a carefully crafted guide to John of the Cross's spiritual path toward healing through contemplation: God's gift, our response. In the unfolding of the journey, the book makes John's writings accessible to today's searching hearts. Fr. Chowning demonstrates that John of the Cross knew the human heart well: its longings, its challenges, and its graced capacity for transformation into the love for which it was created."

— Patricia Kieler, SDS, spiritual director

"Today it seems as if all creation is crying out for healing. In this new work, the author explores in depth the central message of St. John of the Cross that 'healing and transformation come from opening ourselves more and more to God self-communicating love through prayer and contemplation.' In the process, Fr. Chowning also provides us with a very accessible and engaging introduction to the mystical doctor himself. At a moment when our world and our hearts often feel so broken, this book is especially timely."

— Steven Payne, OCD, The Catholic University of America

"There is a longing in every human person to be loved, healed, and restored. For centuries the wisdom of St. John of the Cross has enlightened our path on this journey of transformation in love. Yet, in our own day, we need masters to once again teach us how fundamental St. John's teachings are for our times. This book is a masterpiece of Fr. Daniel Chowning's scholarship, prayer, and integration of this mystical doctor's teaching. Anyone seeking God's healing and transformation will find in this book an abundant source of wisdom and encouragement leading them to greater freedom and love in Christ."

— Mother Gloria Therese Laven, OCD, superior general, Carmelite Sisters of the Most Sacred Heart of Los Angeles

Healed by Love

Contemplation as a Path of Healing
according to St. John of the Cross

Daniel Chowning, OCD

LITURGICAL PRESS
Collegeville, Minnesota

litpress.org

Cover art: Detail of Jesus healing from a fresco in St. George Church, Antwerp, Belgium. Getty Images.

Unless otherwise noted, Scripture quotations are taken from the New Revised Standard Version Updated Edition. Copyright © 2021 National Council of Churches of Christ in the United States of America. Used by permission. All rights reserved worldwide.

Where noted, Scripture texts in this work are taken from the *New American Bible, revised edition* © 2010, 1991, 1986, 1970 Confraternity of Christian Doctrine, Washington, DC and are used by permission of the copyright owner. All Rights Reserved. No part of the New American Bible may be reproduced in any form without permission in writing from the copyright owner.

Excerpts from *The Collected Works of St. John of the Cross*, translated by Kieran Kavanaugh and Otilio Rodriguez (Washington, DC: ICS Publications, 1991). Used with permission.

© 2025 by Daniel Chowning, OCD
Published by Liturgical Press, Collegeville, Minnesota. All rights reserved. No part of this book may be used or reproduced in any manner whatsoever, except brief quotations in reviews, without written permission of Liturgical Press, Saint John's Abbey, PO Box 7500, Collegeville, MN 56321-7500. Printed in the United States of America.

Library of Congress Cataloging-in-Publication Data

Names: Chowning, Daniel, author.
Title: Healed by love : contemplation as a path of healing according to St. John of the Cross / Daniel Chowning.
Description: Collegeville, Minnesota : Liturgical Press, [2025] | Summary: "In Healed by Love, Carmelite Friar Daniel Chowning, urges those in need of healing to seek refuge in the spiritual doctrine of St. John of the Cross"—Provided by publisher.
Identifiers: LCCN 2024045593 (print) | LCCN 2024045594 (ebook) | ISBN 9798400800122 (trade paperback) | ISBN 9798400800139 (epub) | ISBN 9798400801952 (pdf)
Subjects: LCSH: Spiritual healing—Catholic Church. | Contemplation. | John of the Cross, Saint, 1542–1591.
Classification: LCC BT732.5 .C496 2025 (print) | LCC BT732.5 (ebook) | DDC 248.3/4—dc23/eng/20241213
LC record available at https://lccn.loc.gov/2024045593
LC ebook record available at https://lccn.loc.gov/2024045594

*To my Carmelite brothers of the Province of the
Immaculate Heart of Mary and the
Carmelite Sisters of the Most Sacred Heart of Los Angeles*

Contents

Introduction 1

Chapter 1
St. John of the Cross as Healing Minister 9

Chapter 2
Created for Love 27

Chapter 3
The Pathology of the Soul 53

Chapter 4
A Dysfunctional Manner of Loving 73

Chapter 5
The Path of Healing: Jesus the Divine Physician 107

Chapter 6
The Divine Therapy 119

Chapter 7
Sitting in the Fire 143

Chapter 8
The Theological Life: A Path of Healing 163

Chapter 9
Hope: A Green Coat of Mail 179

Chapter 10
Red Toga of Charity 189

Chapter 11
Healed by Love 199

Conclusion
Contemplative Love 219

Introduction

"If I but touch his cloak, I will be made well," thought the woman in Mark's Gospel who suffered for twelve years from hemorrhages, had endured much from physicians, spent all her money, and felt no better. She had heard about Jesus' healing powers. He was her last resort. With audacious courage and faith she touched Jesus despite the law that forbade physical contact with him because to do so would render him impure. Surrounded on all sides by the pressing crowd, Jesus asked, "Who touched me?" Her touch was different. Imbued with faith, it released healing energy from him. Realizing that she was healed, she fell down before him, told him the whole truth. Jesus said to her, "Daughter, your faith has made you well; go in peace, and be healed of your disease" (Mark 5:28-34).

This desperate woman in search of healing represents every one of us who longs for healing, inner freedom, and transformation. The Gospels are full of stories of people who longed to touch even the fringe of Jesus' garment to be healed of physical, spiritual, and mental suffering.[1] Those with leprosy, blindness, and other disabilities; tax collectors, prostitutes, and those marginalized from temple worship sought Jesus to touch the tassel of his cloak or to be touched by him. Their very infirmities were a springboard to an encounter with him and to experience God's surpassing love for humanity.

Healing is at the heart of the Good News of Jesus Christ. In his book *Jesus of Nazareth*, Pope Benedict XVI reminds us that Christianity is

---

[1] "And wherever he went, into villages or cities or farms, they laid the sick in the marketplaces and begged him that they might touch even the fringe of his cloak, and all who touched it were healed" (Mark 6:56).

a "therapeutic religion."² Healing is an essential dimension of the apostolic mission and Christian faith in general. Jesus exercised an intense ministry of healing that continues today in the church and in our world whenever people long to "touch" God's garment with their desires and openness to God's love.

One of the major signs of our times in our Western culture is the search for healing, which is intimately related to the thirst for a deeper spiritual life. Venture into any major bookstore, or search on the internet, and you will discover a vast amount of literature on spirituality and healing and the various approaches to the healing of the mind, body, and spirit. For instance, we find books on faith and healing; meditation and healing; the therapeutic effects of bodywork such as massage, yoga therapy, psychotherapeutic healing; and even art and music therapy.

There is a wide range of research and literature on the therapeutic effects of meditation. For instance, Professor Herbert Benson, MD, a cardiologist and associate professor emeritus of medicine at Harvard Medical School, became a pioneer in the field of the therapeutic effects of meditation when he introduced to patient care a method of meditation called the "Relaxation Response."³ Much of the Buddhist literature, especially mindfulness meditation, encompasses the healing dimension of spiritual practice and has entered into field medicine, pain management, and psychotherapy.

---

[2] Pope Benedict XVI, *Jesus of Nazareth: From the Baptism in the Jordan to the Transfiguration* (New York: Doubleday, 2007), 176.

[3] Dr. Herbert Benson, MD, *The Relaxation Response* (New York: William Morrow, 1975); *Beyond the Relaxation Response* (New York: Times Books, 1984). Dr. Benson founded the Benson-Henry Institute for Mind Body Medicine, which studies the inseparable connection between the mind and body and the complicated interactions that take place among thoughts, the body, and the external world. Mind-body medicine integrates modern scientific medicine, psychology, nutrition, exercise physiology, and belief to enhance the natural healing capacities of the body and mind. See Daniel Goleman and Joel Gurin, eds., *Mind-Body Medicine: How to Use Your Mind for Better Health* (New York: Consumer Reports Books, 1998), 3–18.

Two institutes of forgiveness, the Stanford Forgiveness Project and the International Forgiveness Institute at the University of Wisconsin, have been established in the United States and have researched extensively the therapeutic effects of forgiveness.[4] There is solid scientific evidence that forgiveness is good for one's physical, mental, and spiritual well-being.

Bill Wilson, one of the founders of Alcoholics Anonymous, recognized that sobriety can only be maintained by working a spiritual program based upon traditional spiritual values. Although expressed in nonsectarian and universal religious language, the Twelve Step program advocates liberation from addictions and healing for people who surrender to a transcendent power and commit themselves to an interior life based upon principles of humility, faith, hope, love, and a meditative life.

Health care professionals look to major world religions for enlightenment regarding the total health care of the human person. An example of this took place in December of 1995 when 950 physicians, nurses, social workers, hospital chaplains, theologians, psychologists, educators, and other health care professionals gathered in Boston, Massachusetts, for a conference on spirituality and healing. Harvard Medical School's department of Continuing Education and the Mind/Body Medical Institute at Boston's Deaconess Hospital sponsored the conference.[5] This meeting was significant and reflected the growing interest in the relationship between spirituality and healing. Health care professionals recognize that the total health of the human person includes attending to the mind and spirit as well as the body. For this

---

[4] Robert D. Enright, *Forgiveness Is a Choice* (Washington, DC: American Psychological Association, 2001); Dr. Fred Luskin, *Forgive for Good: A Proven Prescription for Health and Happiness* (San Francisco: HarperCollins, 2003). See also Kevin Culligan, OCD, "Prayer and Forgiveness: Can Psychology Help," in *Spiritual Life* 48 (Summer 2002): 78–87. Reprinted in *Spiritual Life*/online 3 (Fall 2017): 95–106.

[5] For a full report on this conference, see Kevin Culligan, OCD, "Spirituality and Healing in Medicine," *America* 175, no. 5 (August 1996): 17–21.

reason, they look to the mystics of the world religions for further enlightenment on the total health of the human person.⁶

According to the World Health Organization, health is more than the absence of physical illnesses. Health is a state of well-being experienced on the psychological, moral, and physical level. Spirituality, therefore, is an integral part of the healing process because God is the very ground of our being. We are wired for God. There has been extensive research on the curative power of faith and meditation for physical and psychological healing, pain and stress management, grief, and addictive behavior.

My purpose in writing this work is to present the doctrine of St. John of the Cross through the lens of the healing and transformation of the human person. We all long for physical, psychological, and spiritual healing. When we look at our world of war; violence; human trafficking; addictions to drugs, alcohol, sex, pornography, prestige, and comfort; as well as the psychological illnesses that burden so many people, young and old, we realize how much our world is desperate for healing and transformation.

My understanding of the Carmelite saints such as St. John of the Cross, St. Teresa of Avila, and St. Thérèse of Lisieux is that their spirituality is born from their own personal journey of healing and transformation. They write about the beauty and dignity of the human person created in the image and likeness of God, yet in need of healing and transformation due to the effects of original, personal, and even generational sin. Each of these Carmelite mystics explored the depths of their own humanity as a dwelling place of God, yet they were aware of their own brokenness and fragility. Through a life of prayer and contemplation they experienced God's self-communicating and transformative love that healed them and transformed them into instruments of God's love to others, to the church, and to a world in need.

---

⁶ The Benson-Henry Institute for Mind Body Medicine at Massachusetts General Hospital continues to research and offer yearly programs on the relationship between spirituality and healing. For more information, see https://www.massgeneral.org/psychiatry/treatments-and-services/benson-henry-institute.

Several years ago, a friend gifted me with an icon of St. John of the Cross with these words from *The Spiritual Canticle* inscribed upon it: "The love of God is the soul's health." These words express in the most profound and simple way my personal experience as a Carmelite friar, as well as the heart of the doctrine of St. John of the Cross: God's love for us, our radical need for healing and transformation, and God's love as the source of our healing. "The soul does not have full health until love is complete. Sickness is nothing but the lack of health, and when the soul has not even a single degree of love she is dead. In the measure that love increases she will be healthier, and when love is perfect, she will have full health."[7]

John of the Cross has something important to say about God, the human person, and our search for healing and transformation. How does John of the Cross understand the spiritual and psychological ills of the human person? What is healing for him and how do we come to healing? Although he lived more than four hundred years ago, what guidance can he offer our contemporary search for healing? These are fundamental questions we hope to answer in our study.

I will begin with a brief overview of John's life and how the ministry of healing, both physical and spiritual, was an important one in his youth, as well as his life as a Carmelite friar. Witnesses testify that John had a charism for caring for the sick. Although John does not write about physical healing in his writings, the themes of healing and transformation are fundamental to his entire doctrine. For John of the Cross, our understanding of sickness and health depends upon our conception of the human person and our life's vocation. Therefore, we must explore John's theology of the human person. Since John's anthropology is complex, we will reflect on our divine vocation to union with God through love, the very purpose of our existence: the mystery of God as self-giving love who desires to share life with

---

[7] John, *CW*, *The Spiritual Canticle*, Stanza 11, no. 11. References to the works of St. John of the Cross are taken from *The Collected Works of St. John of the Cross*, trans. Kieran Kavanaugh and Otilio Rodriguez (Washington, DC: ICS Publications, 1991).

human beings, the Christological foundation of the creation of human beings, and the psychological structure of the human person.

Having examined John's understanding of the human person and our vocation to union with God through love, we want to explore John's understanding of the pathology (the sickness) of the human person. Due to original and personal sin, we experience a "sickness" on the ontological level of our being. In order to understand this "sickness" we will study main texts from *The Ascent of Mount Carmel* and *The Dark Night of the Soul* where John analyzes the disorders of the human person that necessitate the purifying and healing process that takes place in the dark night of the sense and spirit.

The analysis of the disorders of the human person will lead us into an exploration of contemplation as a path of healing through the dark night of sense and spirit. What is the dark night of sense and spirit? How does contemplation heal us? Since modern psychology cannot but influence mystical theology, we will draw upon the insights of modern psychology in order to understand the path of purification through the dark night of sense and spirit as relevant to a contemporary understanding of transformation of the human person.

We will also discuss the importance of the three theological virtues of faith, hope, and charity as fundamental Christian healing attitudes as we journey through the therapeutic dark night. The inflow of God's self-communicating love that comes to us in prayer and contemplation will have therapeutic effects on our personality. Although ultimate healing will only take place when we are finally and completely united to Christ in eternal life, John of the Cross provides a portrait of what he considers a healthy and loving personality in many of the texts where he describes the fruits of God's transforming love in the life of the person who has arrived at union with Christ.

In the final chapter, I will conclude with how I believe John's doctrine corroborates with and contributes to the work of health care professionals regarding spirituality and healing, and with his understanding of healing in relationship to the contemporary interest in meditation and healing. I will also present implications of his doctrine for pastoral care in the church as well as our political and social structures. Finally, for John of the Cross as for Jesus, our Healer and Savior, we undergo healing in order to become healers, that is, to radiate God's love to all of humanity by our daily acts of love and service to all our brothers and sisters who long for God's healing love.

Chapter 1

St. John of the Cross as Healing Minister

WHY ARE WE ATTRACTED to the Carmelite mystics, particularly St. Teresa of Jesus, St. John of the Cross, and St. Thérèse of Lisieux, each of whom holds such a strong attraction for people? From my conversations with people drawn to the mystics, there are two primary sources of their attraction. The first is that the mystics awaken within us our desire for God, a desire God has planted deep within our hearts. The mystics are men and women who have had immediate and direct experiences of God's loving presence that transformed their lives. They are witnesses to the reality of God's self-communicating love.[1]

Secondly, the mystics speak to our search for healing and transformation. We all search for healing, conversion, interior renewal, deeper love, greater psychological and emotional freedom, and an expanded consciousness. For me, the experience of our mystics and their teaching act as a healing balm for the sick soul and a beacon of hope for all who hunger and thirst for more authentic love and freedom, and a deeper friendship with God for whom we were created.

---

[1] Bernard McGinn, *The Foundations of Christian Mysticism*, vol. 1 of *The Presence of God: A History of Western Christian Mysticism* (New York: Crossroad, 1991), xvii.

In her book *Mysticism*, Evelyn Underhill describes the mystics as "pioneers and explorers of humanity."[2] They are men and women who live their humanity to the full. Drawn by the Spirit, they courageously journey into the deeper regions of the spirit where God dwells. Their inner journey leads them up the mountain heights and down to the lowest valleys of their humanity. They become conscious of their human dignity as creatures created by God out of love and for love. They become aware of their woundedness and poverty as creatures who stand in need of God's healing and transformation.

In this interior adventure, they not only encounter God and experience God's self-communicating love but grow in understanding of humanity. The self-knowledge they gain and the transformation they undergo inspires them with profound insight into human nature and God's love for all humanity. In encountering God and their deeper selves, they come to understand the longings, desires, sufferings, and joys of humanity. By their lives they witness to the power of God's transforming love at work in our minds and hearts, dispelling the interior darkness that prevents us from embracing the light of God's unconditional love, freeing us from addictive behavior, purging our selfishness, awakening us to the awesome beauty of God's creation, opening our eyes to the dignity of each person, and enlarging our capacity to love others and creation as God loves. In John's Gospel, Jesus proclaims the Good News in this way: "I came that they may have life and have it abundantly" (John 10:10). This is healing: life in abundance. God calls us to a life beyond guilt, fear, hatred, suffering, pain, poverty, and even death.

Transformation is a mystery. In *The Living Flame of Love*, John of the Cross tells us that "transformation of the soul in God is indescribable."[3] At the end of *The Living Flame of Love*, when he writes about how God breathes the Holy Spirit in the soul, he confesses his incapacity and reluctance to speak about it. He prefers silence before

---

[2] Cited by John Welch, *When Gods Die* (New York: Paulist Press, 1990), 30. See also Evelyn Underhill, *Mysticism* (New York: E.P. Dutton, 1961), 414.

[3] John, *CW*, *The Living Flame of Love*, Stanza 3, no. 8.

the mystery. This is why our saints resort to poetry and metaphors to speak of the mysterious healing process that takes place in our lives under the influence of God's grace. In *The Interior Castle*, Teresa explains the journey of deepening union with Christ as a process of dying and rising analogous to a silkworm that undergoes a mysterious metamorphosis in a cocoon and emerges as a butterfly. Fire that penetrates a log of wood and gradually transforms the log into fire is just one of the many metaphors John uses to describe the process of deepening union with God through love. The "dark night" is a metaphor for the healing and transformation of the human person at the deepest level of our being.

John's major pastoral concern is, first of all, to make us aware of the mystery of God's incomprehensible love for us. God is passionately in love with humanity. God's love is so genuine that there is "neither the affection of a mother, with which she so tenderly caresses her child, nor a brother's love, nor any friendship comparable to it."[4] The purpose of our creation is love. "Love is the end for which we were created."[5] God created us out love and for love, created us to share in God's divine life. God is like the "Hound of Heaven"[6] who relentlessly seeks us in order to unite himself with us and makes us partakers of divine life. "What God seeks, he being himself God by nature, is to make us gods through participation, just as fire converts all things into fire."[7] We tend to think we are the ones seeking God first; rather, it is God who seeks us first. "It should be known that if a person is seeking God, the Beloved is seeking that person much more."[8]

However, despite our deepest desires, we are humanly incapable of responding fully to God's call to intimate friendship due to original sin and our historical woundedness and sinful patterns. To adapt the words of St. Paul, "We do what we do not want to do" (see Rom 7:15-16). This is why John's doctrine is like a healing balm for the wounded

---

[4] John, *CW*, *The Spiritual Canticle*, Stanza 27, no. 1.
[5] John, *CW*, *The Spiritual Canticle*, Stanza 29, no. 3.
[6] See Francis Thompson's poem "The Hound of Heaven" (1890).
[7] John, *CW*, *The Sayings of Light and Love*, no. 107.
[8] John, *CW*, *The Living Flame of Love*, Stanza 3, no. 27.

soul. He ministered to people who were searching for deeper intimacy with God yet experienced their incapacity to love God and others as they desired. In their search for God they encountered various trials and temptations on the spiritual, moral, and temporal levels that confounded and dismayed them. As one Carmelite scholar expressed it: "The entire work of St. John of the Cross is only the description of how the Holy Spirit takes charge of the crippled and impure creature, in view of transforming his doubly deficient activity and leading him to a divine way of thinking, loving and acting."[9]

When we consider John's life and writings we discover a profound sensitivity toward the poor, the sick, and spiritual seekers who suffer from life's various temptations, trials, and sufferings. John writes to provide consolation and guidance in the midst of life's obscure trials and sufferings.

> A deeper enlightenment and wider experience than mine is necessary to explain the dark night through which a soul journeys toward that divine light of perfect union with God that is achieved, insofar as possible in this life, through love. The darknesses and trials, spiritual and temporal, that fortunate souls ordinarily undergo on their way to the high state of perfection are so numerous and profound that human science cannot understand them adequately. Nor does experience of them equip one to explain them. Only those who suffer them will know what this experience is like, but they won't be able to describe it.[10]

John witnesses to God's passionate love for humanity and how God's merciful loving "gaze" descends upon what is broken, poor, and infirm and transforms it into beauty, into a partaker in divine life.[11]

---

[9] P. Lucien-Marie de St. Joseph, OCD, "Dynamisme de l'Amour," *Études Carmélitaines* 25 (1946): 173.

[10] John, *CW, The Ascent of Mount Carmel*, Prol.

[11] "By the eyes of the Bridegroom she refers to God's mercy: He descends in mercy on the soul, impressing and infusing his love and grace in her, making her beautiful and lifting her so high so as to make her a partaker of his very divinity (2 Pt. 1:4)." John, *CW, The Spiritual Canticle*, Stanza 32, no. 4. See also *The*

He believes that God performs marvelous deeds in our lives if we open to the presence of God, who comes to us in prayer and in the events of daily life, both joyful and painful.

John's Life—A Brief Biography

John's sensitivity and care for the sick, poor, and those who struggle spiritually has its roots in his childhood marked by poverty and deprivation. John of the Cross (Juan de Yepes) was born around 1542 in Fontiveros, Spain. We are unsure of the exact date of his birth due to a fire in 1546 that destroyed a major part of the church where baptismal records would have been stored.[12] He was the third son of Gonzalo de Yepes and Catalina Alvarez, both orphans, who were poor and made their living by weaving cloth.[13]

Spiritual Canticle, Stanza 23. "Beneath the apple tree, there I took you for my own, there I offered you my hand, and restored you where your mother was corrupted."

[12] Emilio J. Martínez González, *Tras las huellas de San Juan de la Cruz: Nueva biografía* (Madrid: Editorial de Espiritualidad, 2006), 29.

[13] The biographical information about John of the Cross is taken from the following sources: Silvano Giordano, *God Speaks in the Night: The Life, Times, and Teaching of St. John of the Cross*, trans. Kieran Kavanaugh (Washington, DC: ICS Publications, 2002); and José Vincente Rodríguez, *San Juan de la Cruz: La biografía* (Madrid: San Pablo, 2012).

Regarding Gonzalo de Yepes, the father of John of the Cross, hagiographers have presented Gonzalo as an orphan from Toledo who was adopted by noble Toledan relatives who owned a successful cloth business. As he grew up he became a merchant in the business. In his business travels he met Catalina Alvarez, also an orphan, who made her living by silk weaving. They fell in love and married. Because Gonzalo married out of his social class, which was socially unaccepted at that time, he was disinherited by his adopted family and fell into poverty and was forced to learn Catalina's trade. It is not possible to enter into the different historical polemics of Gonzalo de Yepes's family origins. According to Teófanes Egido, historians know little other than Gonzalo's name and that he was married to Catalina Alvarez. Hagiographers do not know whether he was the agent of his father or his uncles, or whether he lived with merchants or Toledan clerics, nor do they know anything about his origins. He died in 1545. (Cf. Egido, "Contexto histórico de San Juan de la Cruz," in *Experiencia y pensamiento en San Juan de la Cruz* [Madrid: Espiritualidad, 1990], 335–77.) See also Rodríguez, *San Juan*

Poverty, illness, and death cast their shadow over John's life as a young boy. Even though sixteenth-century Spain is often referred to as the "golden age," life for the lower classes was not so golden. Despite the economic expansion due to the discovery of America, a massive part of the population suffered poverty and indigence.[14] Sixteenth-century Spain endured years of bad harvests, droughts, and epidemics that caused poverty, misery, and hunger. "One could not find bread or food for any amount. And when one could get some barley bread, one considered oneself lucky."[15]

John's father, Gonzalo, died shortly after John's birth. Luis, John's brother, died of malnutrition. Gonzalo's death left Catalina a widow in dire poverty and alone to raise her two living sons: Francisco, the eldest, and Juan. Desperate to feed and clothe them, she took them to Medina del Campo, a thriving merchant town of the sixteenth century known for its charitable organizations. There she hoped to find work as a cloth weaver. She also employed herself as a wet nurse to earn a bit of money. John was nine years old when he arrived in Medina del Campo.

John lived in Medina for thirteen years. These were formative years for John. Fearing that she could not provide sufficiently for her young son, Catalina placed him in a school called La Doctrina, a charitable organization for poor and orphaned boys. The organization was partly a reformatory to prevent delinquency, and it taught the boys the catechism, reading and writing, and how to serve as acolytes at Mass and funerals. They also learned trades.[16]

---

de la Cruz, 67–84; and Balbino Velasco, *San Juan de la Cruz: A las raíces del hombre y del carmelita* (Madrid: Editorial de Espiritualidad, 2009), 55–78.

In addition to being poor, Gonzalo de Yepes and Catalina Alvarez were orphans. We are not historically sure, but both decided to settle in the village de Fontiveros, a fact that would later serve to give rise to a fanciful reconstruction of Juan de Yepes' genealogy. See Juan Antonio Marcos, "San Juan de la Cruz y Su Ambiente de Pobreza," in *Actas del Congreso Internacional Sanjuanista*, II, Historia (Avila: Junta de Castilla y León, 1993), 144–45.

[14] Marcos, "San Juan de la Cruz y Su Ambiente de Pobreza," 143.
[15] Giordano, *God Speaks in the Night*, 67–84.
[16] Rodríguez, *San Juan de la Cruz*, 97.

John was bright and learned quickly. His goodness and piety became evident, so he was assigned as an acolyte to the convent of the Magdalena nuns. It seems he had some training in carpentry, tailoring, and painting, but he excelled more with books than with manual labor.

Later on, Don Alonso Álvarez de Toledo, a generous and noble man inspired by divine grace, donated a large part of his inheritance to serve the sick and the poor. He became the administrator of the Hospital of the Conception known as *"las bubas."* One of the fourteen hospitals in Medina del Campo, *las bubas* was established to care for patients suffering from contagious diseases, particularly syphilis. The hospital was referred to as *las bubas* because of the soft tumors in the groin area caused by syphilis, which was widespread at the time.[17] Don Alonso hired John to work as a nurse's aide and alms seeker for the sick poor of the hospital. Having been born poor and reduced to mendicancy, John knew firsthand the suffering caused by poverty and illness, so he had no problem begging on the street for the hospital's poor patients. He also begged for the poor boys of La Doctrina.[18] For John, the sick and the poor were the same: the sick who are poor, and the poor who are sick, especially those suffering from syphilis, the most feared and forsaken because of the danger of contagion and people's repugnance. This experience taught him compassion and tenderness for those in extreme suffering.[19] From the very beginning, the works of mercy occupied a privileged place in John's life. His experience in *las bubas* taught him many lessons about wounded human nature due to the effects of original sin and disordered desires for pleasure. He intuited that the human heart tends to search for pleasure and love in all the wrong places by the fact that syphilis was spread through prostitution.

---

[17] José María Javierre, *Juan de la Cruz: Un caso límite* (Salamanca, Spain: Ediciones Sigueme, 1992), 133.
[18] Giordano, *God Speaks in the Night*, 41.
[19] Rodríguez, *San Juan de la Cruz*, 102–3.

Whether they were men or women whom John nursed and begged for, they were patients suffering as a consequence of displaced desires for pleasure, happiness, and love—what John describes as "disordered appetites" in Book One of *The Ascent of Mount Carmel*.

Begging alms for the sick poor was often an unpleasant experience, especially in a society where there was a great abyss between social classes; the higher society looked down on the poor, servants, and lower classes. It was a society where babies were often shamefully left abandoned at the doors of churches and monasteries, and where beggars roamed the streets, at times even maiming themselves to elicit pity from passersby.[20]

A page in *The Ascent of Mount Carmel* captures this observation:

> Joy in sweet fragrance foments disgust for the poor (which is contrary to Christ's doctrine), aversion for servants, submissiveness of heart in humble things, and spiritual insensitivity, at least in the measure of appetite.
>
> Joy in the delights of food directly engenders gluttony and drunkenness, anger, discord, and lack of charity towards one's neighbor and the poor, as toward Lazarus on the part of the rich man who ate sumptuously each day [Lk. 16:19-21].[21]

John also learned different healing methods employed at that time, such as "the cautery," which was a way of healing wounds by fire.

> To understand the nature of this wound, which is addressed by the soul, it should be known that the cautery of material fire always leaves a wound where it is applied. And it possesses this property: if applied to a wound not made by fire, it converts it into a wound caused by fire. Whether a soul is wounded by other wounds of miseries and sins or whether it is healthy, this cautery of love immediately effects a wound of love in the one it touches, and those wounds not deriving from other causes become wounds of love.[22]

---

[20] Giordano, *God Speaks in the Night*, 43.
[21] John, *CW*, *The Ascent of Mount Carmel*, Book 3, chap. 25, nos. 4–5.
[22] John, *CW*, *The Living Flame of Love*, Stanza 2, no. 7.

Don Alonso not only recognized John's devotion to the poor sick but also his intellectual capacity for study. Recognizing John's piety and his intellectual gifts, Don Alonso probably hoped that John would study theology, be ordained to the priesthood, and become the hospital's chaplain. He gave John permission to study Latin and the humanities at the Jesuit college recently established in Medina del Campo. In addition to his care for the sick and begging for alms for the hospital's patients, John attended classes at the Jesuit school. Bright and gifted in language, he took courses in grammar, rhetoric, and philosophy. He attended classes in between his hospital duties and studied late into the night. Thus, John was no stranger to the struggle of trying to work and obtain an education at the same time. These years of caring for the sick poor, and having to work and study, profoundly influenced his life. He embraced this experience and revealed an amazing strength of character for a man of his young age. This gave him a compassionate heart and understanding of human nature and the disorders of the heart that engender suffering.

However, John felt called to the Carmelite Order. In February 1563, John entered the recently founded Carmelite Monastery of Santa Ana and was given the name Friar John of St. Matthias. He made his profession in 1564 and moved to the Monastery of San Andrés in Salamanca, where he continued his studies in the monastery and at the University of Salamanca.

Even as a student friar in Salamanca he continued to serve the sick poor. The friars of San Andrés ministered to patients in the hospital of Santa María la Blanca afflicted by "*mal gálico*," a bacterial infection spread by sexual contact, and syphilis.[23]

John was ordained to the priesthood in Salamanca in 1567 and celebrated his first Mass in Medina del Campo. Shortly after his ordination, he passed through a vocational crisis and seriously considered transferring to the Carthusians. The exact cause of his crisis is unclear. It seems that it had little to do with the religious lifestyle of the monastery but more from the intellectual atmosphere of the University

---

[23] Rodríguez, *San Juan de la Cruz*, 149–50.

of Salamanca.[24] During a visit to Medina del Campo that same year, he met Teresa of Jesus, who was making her second foundation in Medina. He shared his Carthusian aspirations with her. Impressed by his sincerity and spiritual longings, she begged him to wait. She had recently founded a new style of Carmelite life in 1562 that mirrored the first hermits on Mount Carmel: a life of solitude, silence, and unceasing prayer lived within community. She hoped to extend her reform to the friars. She promised him a monastery where he could realize his aspirations for a more contemplative lifestyle.

On November 28, 1568, the first Sunday of Advent, John donned the new habit of the Discalced Carmelites in the new monastery of Duruelo, a small hamlet not far from Avila, and took the name of John of the Cross. Thus began his new life in the Teresian Reform. Novices began to arrive. Early on, John took on the ministry of novice master and trained the novices in the vision of religious life envisioned by Teresa. John served the new community as a formator to some degree throughout his religious life.

In 1571, the provincial of the Calced Carmelite friars appointed Teresa prioress of the Incarnation monastery where she had lived the first twenty-seven years of her religious life before the foundation of St. Joseph's monastery in 1562.[25] Teresa faced some major challenges. There were 130 nuns in the community. The community was poor and in debt, and food was so scarce that bread and water had become the primary sustenance. In order to satiate their hunger, many of the nuns would leave the enclosure for periods of time to live with their families. Furthermore, secular women and relatives of the nuns were entering and leaving the enclosure under the pretext of bringing food and donations. These situations led to disturbances within the community and a decline in religious observance and the life of prayer.

---

[24] González, *Tras las huellas de San Juan de la Cruz*, 74–81.
[25] St. Teresa was given permission from the general of the order to begin a reform community in 1562. Her desire was to restore the eremitical spirit of the first Carmelite hermits in 1206–1209 in the Holy Land. St. Joseph's monastery was St. Teresa's first foundation in 1562.

Teresa was also concerned about the spiritual depth of the community. She discerned a serious lack of prayer and spiritual formation. With wisdom, tact, and gentleness—not to mention courage and reliance on God's grace and the help of the Blessed Virgin Mary—Teresa set out to address the alimentary and economic problems of the community as well as the spiritual crisis. She realized that good confessors were crucial to initiate and bring about reform, so she requested that the Discalced friars, in particular John of the Cross, be appointed the community's confessors. In 1572, John of the Cross and another Discalced friar, began their ministry as confessors to the Incarnation monastery. John was thirty-two years old.[26]

Initially, some of the nuns were suspicious of John, but his patience and intuitive understanding of the feminine spirit won their confidence.[27] Teresa was fifty-seven years old, and although much older than John and of a very different personality, she opened her heart and soul to him. He was a great support to her. They shared the same spiritual longings and ideals. It was evident that John had a special gift in directing souls. Teresa "confessed that in all the directors she had dealt with she had not found anyone who could tell her in substance what she was trying to communicate from her first word."[28] Teresa received the grace of spiritual marriage on November 18, 1572, in the presence of John while receiving communion from him. Once when they were reflecting together on the mystery of the Trinity, both fell into a rapture.

Not only was John renowned as a good confessor, but he was also known as an exorcist. It was during his period as confessor to the nuns of the Incarnation monastery that he was asked to intervene in the case of a possessed nun, Doña Maria de Olivares, an Augustinian in the monastery of Our Lady of Grace. The process of exorcism was

---

[26] Nicolás González y González, "Fray Juan de la Cruz, confesor del monasterio de la Encarnación, de Avila," in *Juan de la Cruz, Espíritu de llama*, ed. Otger Steggink (Rome: Institutum Carmelitanum, Pok Pharos Publishing, 1991), 130.

[27] Efrén de la Madre de Dios and Otger Steggink, *Tiempo y Vida de Santa Teresa* (Madrid: Biblioteca de Autores Cristianos, 1996), 210.

[28] Efrén and Steggink, *Tiempo y Vida de Santa Teresa*, 530.

a fierce battle that lasted eight months. The case was eventually presented to the Inquisition in Valladolid.[29]

Two other the exorcisms took place during this period. One was of another nun in Avila. The other was a young girl from a small village who was brought to the Incarnation on a Sunday to be delivered from an evil spirit. Upon hearing two nuns praying, the evil spirit cried out and John prayed the prayers of exorcism and she was delivered.[30]

For John of the Cross, the five years as confessor to the nuns of the Incarnation was a period of growth in human and spiritual maturity. They gave him a wealth of experience in the direction of souls and an understanding of the pathologies of the soul.

A major event took place in John's life on the night of December 2, 1577. A group of Calced friars broke into the hermitage where John was staying, blindfolded him, and took him on horseback to the Calced monastery in Toledo. It would take us too far afield to discuss all the reasons for his kidnapping. Basically, it was a juridical problem and a fierce opposition to Teresa's reform movement. The superiors of the Calced friars considered John a rebellious friar because of his involvement with Teresa's reform.

John was imprisoned in the prison cell of the Toledo monastery for nine months. This was one of the darkest periods of his life. The monastery prison cell had once been a latrine. It was so tiny that he could hardly lie down. The only light came through a slit in the wall high up. There was no heat against the frigid Toledo winter, nor relief from the summer's stifling heat. John endured extreme deprivation. He was not allowed to say Mass or receive visitors. Three times a week he was taken to the refectory where he was humiliated and publicly beaten in attempts to force him to renounce the reform. He bore the marks of those beatings for the rest of his life. But he stood his ground and refused to abdicate before the superiors, who tried to persuade him by offering him a position as a prior, a gold cross, and other worldly positions. John was a free man, a man of integrity who refused

---

[29] José Vicente Rodríguez, "Juan de la Cruz: exorcista en Avila," in *Juan de la Cruz, espíritu de llama*, ed. Steggink, 250–64.

[30] Rodríguez, "Juan de la Cruz: exorcista en Avila," 260–61.

to be seduced by positions of honor, prestige, and comfort. He was a man of one ideal—to love and serve God.

What is so amazing is that in the midst of such darkness, mistreatment, and deprivation, he composed some of the most beautiful lyrical and mystical poetry of sixteenth-century Spain. It was as though the deprivation emptied him out of all false securities, and a world of spiritual beauty opened up within him. Having asked for paper and pen from one of the most benign of his jailors, he composed *The Spiritual Canticle*, *The Romances on the Gospel*, and *Song of the Soul That Rejoices to Know God through Faith*. His jailors could not rob him of his love for God or his interior freedom and dignity.

By August 1578, he was so weak that he knew he had to escape. He managed to tie blanket strips together to make a rope. Then, one night, he was able to escape through a window. He made his way to the convent of the Discalced Carmelite nuns.

John's Toledo experience marked the beginning of a new stage in his life's journey. Following his escape, he was sent to the south of Spain, to Andalusia. The ten years he lived there were the most active and fruitful of his Carmelite life. He was confessor to Carmelite nuns, spiritual director of both religious and laity, founder of some monasteries, superior, and vicar provincial. He wrote all his major works during this Andalusian period in the midst of his administrative duties. It is speculated that he traveled twenty-seven thousand kilometers during his life.

John's early career as a nurse's aide and alms seeker for the sick profoundly shaped his religious life. There was something charismatic about his attentiveness to the sick. Throughout his religious life, service to the sick had a privileged place in his ministry. There are extensive and impressive testimonies of his service to his sick brethren.

"When one of his friars was sick, he cared for him with a mother's heart, remaining with him, pampering him, making his bed, keeping him clean and often feeding him himself," reads one account.[31] Another goes into further detail:

---

[31] Giordano, *God Speaks in the Night*, 41.

> He had great charity especially for the sick, and he sought to care for and indulge them without concern about the cost, and he went himself to help them pass the time and acted as child when this was necessary in order to bring some alleviation. He enjoyed having music played for the sick when it was helpful to them. He didn't want them to lack anything that was necessary or any comfort. When he saw they had no appetite, he would suggest to them as many kinds of dishes he could think of to see if any would appeal to them. Even if he doubted whether they would really eat something, he procured it for them.[32]

In 1580 the entire community in Baeza was struck by the pandemic of the universal flu. John was absent at the time. When he heard that the whole community was sick, he immediately returned and nursed them himself, preparing their meals, making their beds, and attending to their various needs. He used different therapies to cheer his sick brothers. He would tell them jokes and prepare a friar's favorite dish to increase his appetite. He also hired musicians to play for them.[33] He refers to therapeutic means of caring for the sick in *The Dark Night*:

> Since the soul, as it were, is undergoing a cure to regain its health, which is God himself, His Majesty restricts it to a diet, to abstinence from all things, and causes it to lose its appetite for them all. This effect resembles the cure of sick people when esteemed by members of their household: They are kept inside so that neither air nor light may harm them; others try not to disturb them by the noise of their footsteps or even whisperings and give them a very delicate and limited amount of food, substantial rather than tasty.[34]

He cared not only for the physically ill, but for the spiritually ill as well. His ministry as a confessor and spiritual director gave him a wealth of experience and insight into the infirmities of the soul. There was a young woman from Avila whom people called "Robert the

---

[32] Giordano, *God Speaks in the Night*, 205–6.
[33] Giordano, *God Speaks in the Night*, 41.
[34] John, *CW*, *The Dark Night*, Book 2, chap. 16, no. 10.

devil" because of the devilish and mischievous things she did. She was encouraged to confess to John of the Cross at the Incarnation monastery. Despite her fears, she presented herself for confession. When she expressed her hesitation to confess to him because of his reputation of holiness, he replied: "I am no saint; but the more the confessor is holy, the gentler he is and less scandalized by others' faults because he knows better the human condition."[35]

In cases of scrupulosity and particular temptations, he knew the right word and medicine to prescribe. For instance, for Brother John of Saint Anne, who struggled with terrible worries about predestination, John helped him overcome them and become less self-preoccupied.[36]

To a Carmelite nun struggling with scrupulosity, he wrote: "If you could put an end to your scruples, I think it would be better for the quietude of your soul not to confess these days. But when you confess do so in this manner." He advised her what to confess and what not to confess, encouraging her to keep her focus on God's love for her instead of her disturbing memories.[37]

To another nun overly anxious about how she may have offended the major superior, he wrote: "In reading your letter I felt sorry for your affliction, and I grieve over it because of the harm it can do to your spirit and even your health. But you ought to know that I don't think you should be as afflicted as you are . . . Be courageous, my daughter and give yourself to prayer, forgetting this thing and that."[38]

John's ministry as spiritual guide extended to people from all vocations and walks of life: married and single laypeople, cloistered Carmelite nuns, friars, and the wealthy and educated as well as the poor and simple. Such a rich variety of human experiences gave him a keen insight into the human condition. For this reason John writes of the human person as created for union with God through love, as

---

[35] Cited in Rodríguez, *San Juan de la Cruz*, 249.
[36] Giordano, *God Speaks in the Night*, 204.
[37] John, *CW, Letters*, 20.
[38] John, *CW, Letters*, 22.

a dwelling place of the Trinity yet wounded and in need of a healing that only God can provide. From a moral and ontological perspective, the human person is in need of healing, blessed but broken.

In 1588, John was transferred back to Castile to be prior of the monastery in Segovia. There, he helped build the monastery with his own hands. He exercised an extensive ministry of spiritual direction to religious and laity, to professors, and to simple people who came seeking his spiritual wisdom.

Soon a persecution was launched against him because he stood against Fr. Doria's harsh treatment of P. Jerome Gracian, to whom Teresa had entrusted the success of the reform of the friars, as well as Fr. Doria's efforts to control the communal and spiritual life of the Carmelite nuns. As a result, Fr. Doria planned to exile John to Mexico. In 1591, John's health began to fail. He was sent back to Andalusia to a small contemplative community called La Peñuela where he gave himself up to prayer, working in the garden, and exercising his ministry as spiritual director. But all was not comfort and joy, as new trials awaited him. A certain friar, Juan Evangelista, whom John had once corrected, held a bitter grudge against him. He set out to assuage his vindictive nature by doing all he could to destroy John's reputation.

In September 1591, John fell ill with a fever. He moved to the monastery in Ubeda. The prior, P. Cristósomo, who had also been corrected by John years earlier, resented having this sick friar in his community. John accepted the mistreatment with patience and no complaint. John's charitable acceptance of everything eventually won over the prior, and he finally became one of his admirers.

An inflammation in John's leg worsened, and gangrene set in. Finally, on December 13, 1591, the end drew near. John prepared himself for death. At midnight the bells rang for Matins. John asked why they were ringing. When they told him they were ringing for Matins, he said, "Glory be to God for I shall say them in heaven." He kissed the crucifix and prayed: "Into your hands, O Lord, I commend my spirit." He breathed his last breath. He was forty-nine years old.

A letter John wrote in response to a Carmelite nun in Segovia distressed over the persecution against him reveals the depth and health of his soul. "Do not let what is happening to me, daughter, cause you any grief, for it does not cause me any. What greatly grieves me is that the one who is not at fault is blamed. Men do not do these things, but God, who knows what is suitable for us and arranges things for our good. Think nothing else but that God ordains all, and where there is no love, put love, and you will draw out love."[39]

These words are an eloquent testimony to the life and spiritual health of John of the Cross—who responded in love to every circumstance in life, good or bad, joyful or painful. "Where there is no love, put love, and you will draw out love."

---

[39] John, *CW*, *Letters*, 26.

Chapter 2

Created for Love

JOHN OF THE CROSS exercised a ministry of healing in accordance with the Gospel: "Cure the sick; raise the dead; cleanse those with a skin disease; cast out demons" (Matt 10:8). He was born in poverty and deprivation and experienced sickness and death at an early age with the death of his brother, Luis, and his father, Gonzalo de Yepes. His thirteen years in Medina del Campo introduced him to healing ministry in the hospital of *las bubas*, where he served as a nurse's aide and alms seeker for victims of syphilis, a dreaded disease rampant in the sixteenth century. He continued his healing ministry as a Carmelite friar, nursing his brothers in community, and practiced the ministry of inner healing as a confessor, spiritual director, and even an exorcist. Witnesses testified that John had a charism for caring for the sick. This charism extended to the deepest sickness of all—the sickness of the soul, afflicted by disordered self-love and attachments. His main pastoral concern was to guide people through the trials and sufferings of life to find true peace and spiritual healing. To understand health for John, we need to explore his anthropology, how he understands the human person and the purpose of our creation.

Even though John had a charism for ministering to the sick, he does not discuss physical healing in his writings. He has a broad understanding of health. For John, health is a process of psychological and spiritual integration, equilibrium, and wholeness.[1] Essentially, health is a matter of love. The perfection of love constitutes the full health of the human person. The more we grow in love, the healthier we become because love alone is the reason for our existence. "After all, this love is the end for which we were created."[2] "The love of God is the soul's health, and the soul does not have full health until love is complete. In the measure that love increases she will be healthier, and when love is perfect she will have full health."[3] Love has an energizing force that unites the human personality. The more we grow in love, the more we reach the fullness of our destiny, which is to participate in divine life, the essence of which is a relationship of self-communicating love. For John, therefore, health must be seen in relation to God's original plan in creating human beings. Why did God create us? What is the purpose of our existence? What gives meaning to our life? What is our mission on this earth? These questions lead us to explore one of the richest elements of John's doctrine—one that is often overlooked—his understanding of the human person and our divine vocation to union with God through love.

In a letter addressed to a young woman aspiring to become a Carmelite nun, John synthesizes with profound simplicity the meaning and purpose for which God created us. "May God ever grant you, my daughter, his holy grace so that in all things you may employ yourself in his holy love and service, as is your obligation, since that is why he created and redeemed you."[4] John encouraged the young aspirant to surrender her entire being to God, that is, to direct all the energies of her body and soul to the service and love of God and neighbor. All her works were to be performed in love; all her joys lived in love; all her sufferings borne in love; all her relationships grounded in love. In other words, she was to strive with God's grace to live the great commandment of love: "You shall love the Lord your God with all

---

[1] Federico Ruiz, *Místico y maestro San Juan de la Cruz* (Madrid: Editorial de Espiritualidad, 1986), 272.
[2] John, *CW*, *The Spiritual Canticle*, Stanza 29, no. 3.
[3] John, *CW*, *The Spiritual Canticle*, Stanza 11, no. 11.
[4] John, *CW*, *Letters*, 12.

your heart and with all your soul and with all your mind" and "your neighbor as yourself" (Matt 22:36-39; see also Deut 6:5 and Lev 19:18). According to John, the great commandment of love contains all we need to do to live an integrated, healthy, and whole life.[5]

When John writes "so that in all things you may employ yourself in his holy love and service, as is your obligation, since that is why he created and redeemed you," he may have in mind God's plan for us expressed in the notion of "original justice." John gives us an insight into the integral health to which we are called in those few texts where he refers to original justice.[6] However, we must not understand original justice as an expression of a perfect human state before original sin. The return to original justice is best understood as the gift of God's divine life given to human beings from the beginning of their appearance on earth, manifested in Christ, and coming to fullness only at the end of time. It expresses symbolically that "from the beginning human beings were created with a supernatural vocation to be children of God," and thus to be harmoniously and entirely directed toward God.[7] John's interest is always the integral wholeness

---

[5] John, *CW*, *The Ascent of Mount Carmel*, Book 3, chap. 16, no. 1.

[6] John, *CW*, *The Ascent of Mount Carmel*, Book 3, chap. 26, no. 5; *The Dark Night*, Book 2, chap. 24, no. 2; *The Spiritual Canticle*, Stanza 26, no. 14. In *The Spiritual Canticle*, Stanzas 28, 37, 38, and 39, the perfection of love is understood as a process of integration of the whole person (senses, spirit, and body) where one's whole person is directed towards the love and service of God (*The Spiritual Canticle*, Stanza 28). There is no longer interior division or fragmentation. The soul returns to the "other day," the day of original justice, that is, the state of peace and happiness for which God created us before original sin. God predestined us to share in the fullness of divine life. "Neither eye has seen, nor ear heard, nor has it entered into the human heart, what God has prepared for those who love him" (1 Cor 2:9). See Eulogio Pacho, "La antropologia sanjuanistica," in *Estudios sanjuanistas* II (Burgos, Spain: Monte Carmelo, 1997), 84.

[7] Juan L. Ruiz de la Peña, *El don de Dios: Antropología teológica especial* (Santander, Spain: Editorial Sal Terrae, 1991), 160–64. Ruiz de la Peña writes of the Christological dimension of the notion of original justice. "If earlier we said that paradise is the symbol of God's gift of grace to humanity, we can now specify with greater precision: paradise is the symbol of the Incarnate Word, 'the veiled image of Jesus Christ himself'"; in him we have been chosen "before the foundation of the world" (Eph 1:4-5); by him and for him we have been created

of the person. Our person and all our actions are to be integrated into a life of love. He expresses this vision in *The Spiritual Canticle*. After having passed through the purification of her whole person—body, soul, sense, and spirit—the soul lives in intimate communion with God. Her entire being is directed toward God.

> Now I occupy my soul
> and all my energy in his service;
> I no longer tend the herd,
> nor have I any other work
> now that my every act is love.[8]

This intimate friendship with God is to be the source of the interior integration, harmony, and peace that is reflected in our relationships with God, others, and the world. When we are rooted in love, the ground of our being, we experience well-being and peace with God, others, and creation, even if physical illness may remain part of our experience.

Longing for Love

John of the Cross understands the deepest longings of the human heart. One of his primary observations is that we possess an inherent yearning for God. Deep within our heart is an innate and insatiable longing to love and be loved. This yearning for love is the driving force that propels us toward God. John provides the key to understand this driving force: "The soul's aim is a love equal to God's. She always desired this equality, naturally and supernaturally, for lovers cannot be satisfied without feeling that they love as much as they are loved."[9] Deep within our being is etched a "natural" and "supernatural" long-

---

(Col 1:16). The incarnation is not primarily a mystery of redemption and reconciliation; it is a mystery of divinization, of which the creation of man in the image of God (Gen 1:26) constitutes its first outline. That is why it could be said, with as much beauty as precision, that "when the clay was being molded, Christ, the future man, was in mind" (*El don de Dios*, 162–63).

[8] John, *CW*, *The Spiritual Canticle*, Stanza 28.

[9] John, *CW*, *The Spiritual Canticle*, Stanza 38, no. 3.

ing to love as God loves. This is the overwhelming and remarkable reality about God: there is no selfishness or competition with God's love. God desires to share with us the fullness of divine life. "With God, to love the soul is to put her somehow in himself and make her his equal."[10] God loves us and ardently desires that we come to know ourselves as loved and to share divine life. Whether we are conscious of it or not, buried in our hearts is an innate desire to love as God loves. This seems like an impossible dream and unimaginable aspiration, but God is the Creator of this desire. Our thirst for love is so profound, compelling, and ardent that we never feel satiated, even by those whom we love most and who love us unconditionally.

God: A Mystery of Self-Communicating Love and Goodness

John of the Cross traces the origin of our desire for love back to the Trinity and God's purpose in creating human beings. In his poem *The Romances*, he sings of God's loving plan to create human beings capable of knowing and loving God and participating in the very life of the Trinity.[11] John contemplates the Trinity as a Family of love, a mystery of self-communicating love and goodness who shares life.

> Three persons, and one Beloved
> among all three.
> One love in them all
> makes of them one Lover,
> and the Lover is the Beloved
> in whom each one lives.

---

[10] John, *CW*, *The Spiritual Canticle*, Stanza 32, no. 6.

[11] *The Romances* is one poem comprised of 310 verses. It is considered a general prologue to all John's works. It is John's contemplative reflection on the prologue and chapter 17 of John's Gospel. The poem recounts the story of salvation from the predestination of humankind to the birth of Christ. It contains some major themes John develops in his later works, i.e., union with God through love, the incarnation, and the central role of Christ in our journey toward union with God through love. It is a fundamental text for understanding the purpose of creation and the incarnation according to John of the Cross.

> For the being that the three possess
> each of them possesses,
> and each of them loves
> Him who bears this being.
> Each one is this being,
> which alone unites them,
> binding them deeply,
> one beyond words.
> Thus it is boundless
> Love that unites them,
> for the three have one love
> which is their essence;
> and the more love is one
> the more it is love.[12]

The God that John presents is a God whose essential nature is self-giving love. "The more love is one, the more it is love." Later on in his works, he will use these same terms of intra-Trinitarian love to explain our relationship with God, which is born from God's love and its continuation through us.[13]

Our Divine Vocation: Union with God through Love

It is from this understanding of God that John views creation and human destiny. Our origin is in our Triune God whose intimate nature is love. God's purpose in creating us is not simply because, being God, God wills to create beings outside himself; rather, God created us in order to enter into a communion of life with us, to draw us into God's family circle, into the trinitarian life which is a dynamic relationship of self-giving love. If God has predestined us to a life of intimate communion with God, then God has structured us in such a way that we can fulfill our divine vocation. What gives us the capacity to enter into a personal relationship with God is that God created

---

[12] John, *CW*, *Poetry*, *The Romances*.
[13] Federico Ruiz, "Metodo e strutture di antropologia sanjuanista," in *Temi di antropologia teologica*, ed. Ermanno Ancilli (Rome: Teresianum, 1981), 416.

us in God's image and likeness. We were created in the image of love, created to give and receive love, to know and love God, to participate in an intimate friendship with God, others, and creation.¹⁴

Predestined in Jesus Christ

For St. John of the Cross, our destiny to union with God through love is profoundly marked by the mystery of the incarnation of Jesus Christ.¹⁵ Only in light of the incarnation can we understand the beauty and dignity of the human person, created in the image and likeness of God, as well as our sublime vocation to loving union with God. For our Carmelite mystic, the incarnation of Jesus Christ not only restored humanity to our original nature but gives us the possibility of realizing the fullness of life for which God predestined us from all eternity.

From the beginning, God's desire was to create someone or something in the image and likeness of his Son. "Whoever resembles you most satisfies me most, and whoever is like you in nothing will find nothing in me."¹⁶ John of the Cross sees creation as the result of God's loving gaze. God looked at all he made with the image of his Son and thus communicated to creation natural being and graces and clothed it with beauty.¹⁷ All creation reflects the image of the Word of God.

---

¹⁴ Ciro Garcia, *Juan de la Cruz y el misterio del hombre* (Burgos: Editorial Monte Carmelo, 1990), 58–59. That we were created in the image and likeness of God follows the teaching in *Gaudium et Spes*, no. 12: "For sacred scripture teaches that women and men were created 'in the image of God,' able to know and love their creator, and set by him over all earthly creatures that they might rule them" (in Austin Flannery, ed., *Vatican Council II: Constitutions, Decrees, Declarations; The Basic Sixteen Documents* [Collegeville, MN: Liturgical Press, 2014]).

¹⁵ Secundino Castro, "La experiencia de Cristo, foco central de la Mística," in *Experiencia y pensamiento en San Juan de la Cruz*, ed. Federico Ruiz (Madrid: Editorial de Espiritualidad, 1990), 172. See also Secundino Castro, *Hacia Dios con San Juan de la Cruz* (Madrid: Editorial de Espiritualidad, 1986), 17–26.

¹⁶ John, *CW*, *The Romances*, Stanza 2, nos. 61–64.

¹⁷ Drawing upon Pauline theology, John expresses this clearly in Stanza 5 of *The Spiritual Canticle*: "It should be known that only with this figure, his Son,

Not only did God endow natural being and beauty to creation with the image of his Son, but when the Word became flesh in Jesus Christ, he entered fully into the flesh and blood of humanity and imparted to us supernatural being, elevating us and bestowing upon us sublime dignity.[18]

Thus, God's desire from the beginning is to exalt humanity and to raise us to a likeness of love. "The property of love is to make the lover equal to the object loved."[19] God fulfilled this desire by entering fully into human existence and becoming one with us in all things except sin (Heb 4:15). By his double nature as God and human, Jesus came to affirm that we were created to share in divine life. In the incarnation of Christ, God creates the possibility for the deification of humankind. God became man so that man might become God, proclaimed Irenaeus and Athanasius.[20]

> He would make himself
> wholly like them,
> and he would come to them
> and dwell with them,
> and God would become man
> and man would be God,
> and he would walk with them

---

did God look at things, that is, he communicated to them their natural being and many natural graces and gifts, and made them complete and perfect, as is said in Genesis: God looked at all things that he made, and they were very good (Gen. 1:31)."

[18] John, *CW*, *The Spiritual Canticle*, Stanza 5, no. 4. "Not only by looking at them did he communicate natural being and graces, as we said, but also with the image of his Son alone, he clothed them in beauty by imparting to them supernatural being. This he did when he took on our human nature and elevated it to the beauty of God, and consequently, all creatures, since in human nature he was united with them all."

[19] John, *CW*, *The Spiritual Canticle*, Stanza 28, no. 1.

[20] St. Irenaeus wrote this in *Against Heresies*, 3, 19, 1. St. Athanasius has a similar quote in his treatise on the incarnation. In *The Romances*, there is no other motivation for creation and the incarnation than the deification of humanity. John does not talk about guilt or reparation, nor restoration. It is equality of love between God and humans, the bride and bridegroom, that prevails.

and eat and drink with them,
and he himself would be with them
until the consummation of the world.[21]

In becoming human, God shared our existence down to the concrete realities of daily life such as eating and drinking. In becoming one with us to this extent, Christ not only communicated divine life to the minutest realities of daily existence, but also revealed the deepest meaning of our humanity. Now the possibility exists for us to know in "flesh and blood" what it means to resemble God and to participate in divine life.

> He would take her
> tenderly in his arms
> and there give her his love;
> and when they were thus one,
> He would lift her to the Father
> where God's very joy
> would be her joy.
> For as the Father and the Son
> and he who proceeds from them
> live in one another,
> so it would be with the bride
> for taken wholly into God,
> she will live the life of God.[22]

The incarnation of Jesus Christ, his life, death, and resurrection have left an indelible imprint on human nature. An irrevocable union has taken place between God and humankind. God has presented himself to humanity as the norm of an authentic human and holy life. He has shown us that we are only truly human in the measure that we are united to God in Christ Jesus. We now bear a sketch of Christ within us. Our calling is to complete this sketch within us, that is, to grow in the likeness of Christ. Until this sketch is completed through

---

[21] John, *CW*, *The Romances*, 4.
[22] John, *CW*, *The Romances*, 4.

loving union with God, we will never know complete health and ultimate satisfaction of heart.[23]

Created to Be the Spouse of Christ

To explain our divine vocation to an intimate communion of life with God, the most intimate of all the images that John of the Cross uses is the spousal metaphor. It expresses in the most profoundly human way the mystery of God's loving relationship with humanity. Inspired by the Song of Songs and following a long tradition of its mystical interpretation beginning with Origen, John sings in *The Romances* God's purpose in creating humanity. We were created to be "the spouse of Christ."

> My Son, I wish to give you a bride who will love you.
> Because of you she will deserve to share our company, and eat
>   at our table,
> The same bread I eat,
> That she may know the good I have in such a Son.[24]

Many people today find it difficult to relate to the nuptial image. For many, the spousal image seems overly sexualized, especially for men who find it strange to relate to Christ as their bridegroom. For some women, the marital analogy speaks of male dominance and all the complications of marriage. For others, the spousal language is reminiscent of an outdated, sentimental spirituality of the past. Other models of our relationship with God resonate more with modern psychology and our contemporary conception of the spiritual life—for instance, God as friend, disciple, teacher, or companion.

---

[23] "It should be known that love never reaches perfection until the lovers are so alike that one is transfigured into the other. And then the love is in full health. The soul experiences within herself a certain sketch of love, which is the sickness she mentions, and she desires the completion of the sketch of this image, the image of her Beloved, the Word, the Son of God, who, as St. Paul says, is the splendor of his glory and the image of his substance (Heb. 1:3)." John, *CW*, *The Spiritual Canticle*, Stanza 11, no. 12.

[24] John, *CW*, *The Romances*, 3.

Nevertheless, the spousal imagery has deep scriptural roots. Salvation history is a divine love story between God and Israel. The covenant on Mount Sinai meant more than words inscribed on stone tablets; the covenant by which God established a special relationship with Israel was a wedding, a marriage between God and God's people. "God desired to be united to his creatures in an everlasting relationship, so intimate, so permanent, so self-sacrificial and life-giving that it can only be described as a marriage between the Creator and creatures, between God and human beings, between YHWH and Israel."[25]

In the Old Testament, God expresses his passionate love for Israel by calling himself the bridegroom. "For your Maker is your husband; / the LORD of hosts is his name" (Isa 54:5). The prophet Hosea recounts Israel's adulterous infidelity, yet Yahweh had bound himself to Israel, led her into the desert, and entered into a marriage with her, a sign of a renewed covenant. The prophet Jeremiah refers to Yahweh as the bridegroom of Israel.[26] Since the Middle Ages, the Song of Songs has been one of the mystics' favored texts to interpret and ponder on the intimate relationship between God and the human person. The Song of Songs is the love story between God and the soul and their journey towards a marriage, the spiritual union between God and the human person. St. Teresa of Jesus wrote a commentary on the Song of Songs, and John's *Spiritual Canticle* was inspired by the Song of Songs.

God has created us to be the spouse of Christ and all that this signifies: the hunger to love and be loved, intimate love between Christ and the human person, a mutual sharing and surrendering of one's life and goods, friendship, faithful companionship, and partaking in the banquet of love with the Trinity. The spousal imagery awakens us to God's love affair with humanity, God's passionate love for

---

[25] Brandt Pitre, *Jesus the Bridegroom: The Greatest Love Story Ever Told* (New York: Image, 2014), 8.

[26] "The word of the LORD came to me, saying: Go and proclaim in the hearing of Jerusalem, Thus says the LORD: / I remember the devotion of your youth, / your love as a bride, / how you followed me in the wilderness" (Jer 2:1-2).

us, and our response. For John of the Cross, God has predestined us to be "a spouse," companion, partner, and friend, and to share in the intimate communion of life which is the essence of Trinitarian life.

Union with God through Love

The spousal analogy brings us to the central theme binding all of John's works: *union with God through love*. By virtue of our creation God has destined us to a life of loving union with God, other people, and creation.

"Union of the soul with God through love" is the foundation, the goal, and the binding force of all John's works. He expresses it with precision in the opening words in the Declaration to *The Ascent of Mount Carmel*: "The following stanzas include all the doctrine I intend to discuss in this book, *The Ascent of Mount Carmel*. They describe the way that leads to the summit of the mount: that high state of perfection we here call union of a soul with God." John's understanding and treatment of union grow from rich biblical and theological roots.[27]

In many contemporary spiritual authors the notion of union with God through love is often absent or, if present, easy to miss in its depth and richness. We are more accustomed to expressions such as *sanctity*, *holiness*, and *perfection*. Although John uses the term *perfection* in his writings, he prefers *union*. Perfection connotes a state of completion within the subjective self. Perfection is closed, subjective, and static. On the other hand, union is dynamic and relational. It implies gratuitous gift, outreach, communion, inclusivity, transformation, mutual self-surrender, likeness, and equality.[28] Therefore, we are talking about a dynamic, intimate relationship between God and the human person, in which each surrenders to the other.

---

[27] Federico Ruiz, *Místico y maestro San Juan de la Cruz*, 2nd ed. (Madrid: Editorial de Espiritualidad, 2006), 90.

[28] Ruiz, *Místico y maestro*, 91.

We yearn for God, but the awesome truth that we easily forget is that our yearning for God is a faint echo of God's longing for us! God is like the "Hound of Heaven" searching and pursuing us in and through the byways of life. "It should be known that if anyone is seeking God, the Beloved is seeking that person much more."[29] "In this interior union God communicates himself to the soul with such genuine love that neither the affection of a mother, with which she tenderly caresses her child, nor a brother's love, nor any friendship is comparable to it."[30]

In its deepest sense, "union of the soul with God through love" expresses God's love affair with humankind, our longing for God, and the divinization process to which we are destined by our very creation. God, who created us out of love and for love, passionately desires us and has destined us to share divine life. Jesus expressed this desire to his disciples the night before his passion and death: "I pray not only for them, but also for those who will believe in me through their word, so that they may all be one, as you, Father, are in me and I in you, that they also may be in us . . . And I have given them the glory you gave me, so that they may be one, as we are one, I in them and you in me, that they may be brought to perfection as one" (John 17:20-23, NABRE).

Union with God through Love: A Present Reality

To appreciate the richness and depth of John's understanding of our divine vocation to union with God through love, we need to consider several dimensions of union with God. To begin with, our call to union with God is not a distant goal, something we hopefully arrive at after a lifetime of spiritual practice and growth in love. Rather, union with God is a *present reality*. We are already united to God "substantially" by virtue of our existence. God is the ground of our being. If this substantial union failed we would cease to exist.

---

[29] John, *CW*, *The Living Flame of Love*, Stanza 3, no. 28.
[30] John, *CW*, *The Spiritual Canticle*, Stanza 27, no. 1.

God loved us into existence and sustains our existence.[31] We live in God like fish who live in the ocean. We can never be separated from God.

We were created in the image of God. Woven into the very fibers of our being is a living image of our triune God, a God of loving relationship. We were created in the image of Love, created to give and receive love, to know and love God, and to share in an intimate relationship with God, other people, and creation. This "imprint" of God within the deepest recesses of our being is what is most authentic to our human nature and makes it possible for us to enter into this dynamic, loving friendship with God.

God's indwelling presence, our natural union with God, is a reality John never ceases to impress upon us. "The soul's center is God."[32] God is the "substance" of the soul.[33] To say that God is the center and substance of our soul means that God dwells in the marrow of our being where we are pure capacity and receptivity for God.[34] We are made for God. The human person is created with an infinite capacity to receive God's knowledge and love. We are pure capacity for God and are propelled toward God. St. Augustine expressed it well: "You have made us for yourself, O God, and our hearts are restless until they rest in You."[35]

John draws upon the metaphor of a stone to illustrate this truth. When a rock is in the ground it is, in a fashion, in its center, even though not in its deepest center. It possesses the power, strength, and inclination to always go more deeply and reach its ultimate and deep-

---

[31] John, *CW*, *The Ascent of Mount Carmel*, Book 2, chap. 5, no. 3.

[32] John, *CW*, *The Living Flame of Love*, Stanza 1, no. 12.

[33] John, *CW*, *The Living Flame of Love*, Stanza 4, no. 3.

[34] The "substance of the soul" means the center or deepest part of our being where we are pure capacity, receptivity for relationship with God. "O Bridegroom Word, in the center of and depth of my soul, which is its pure and intimate substance, in which secretly and silently, you dwell alone" (John, *CW*, *The Living Flame of Love*, Stanza 1, no. 4). Cf. Eulogio Pacho, "Alma humana," *Diccionario de San Juan de la Cruz* (Burgos, Spain: Editorial Monte Carmelo, 2000), 60–72.

[35] St. Augustine, *The Confessions*, Book 1, no. 1, trans. Maria Boulding, OSB (New York: New City Press, 2014), 39.

est center. If no obstacle hinders it, it will arrive at its deepest center.[36] Just as a stone gravitates toward its deepest center in the earth, so we are propelled toward God who lives hidden in our depths. For John, therefore, the spiritual journey is an ever-deepening openness, response, and movement toward the core of our being where our loving Creator dwells. Since God is the hidden ground of our being, it is there, in our depths, that we are to seek God.

> It should be known that the Word, the Son of God, together with the Father and the Holy Spirit, is hidden by his essence and his presence in the innermost being of the soul.
>
> Oh, then, soul, most beautiful among all creatures, so anxious to know the dwelling place of your Beloved so you may go in search of him and be united with him, now we are telling you that you yourself are his dwelling and his secret inner room and hiding place. There is reason for you to be elated and joyful in seeing that all your good and hope is so close as to be within you, or better, that you cannot be without him. *Behold*, exclaims the Bridegroom, *the kingdom of God is within you* [Lk. 17:21]. And his servant, the apostle St. Paul, declares: *You are the temple of God* [2 Cor. 6:16].[37]

Our unceasing natural union with God has profound implications. First of all, we are never separated from God. We come from God and are enfolded in God. No place, or time, or occupation; no trial, or illness, or failure, or sin can separate us from God's presence. John stresses that God is never absent, even from a person in serious sin, and how much less from a person in grace.

Furthermore, because God dwells in the core of our being, we can never evaluate or judge our relationship with God solely by feelings of consolation or desolation. Our spiritual experiences, theological knowledge, and feelings, or lack thereof, are never a barometer of God's presence or absence.[38]

---

[36] John, *CW*, *The Living Flame of Love*, Stanza 1, no. 11.
[37] John, *CW*, *The Spiritual Canticle*, Stanza 1, nos. 6–8.
[38] John, *CW*, *The Spiritual Canticle*, Stanza 1, no. 4.

Finally, God's indwelling presence is the source of our beauty and dignity. We are more than the shape of our body, the color of our hair and eyes, the clothes we wear, our material possessions, our family background and education, our sinful or emotionally wounded history. God loves us; we are temples of the living God. If love is woven into the very fibers of our being—if we were created out of love and for love—love, therefore, is not something accidental to our nature; love is at the source of our being. Love is what most defines us and is the energy that directs our lives.[39] Love is the ground of our being and essential to our nature. Our true self is rooted in Love. "After all, this love is the end for which we were created."[40]

If our essential nature is embraced and sustained by God's ever-present and gracious love, then we can say that we have everything we need within us. John hopes to awaken our consciousness to this sacred and awesome treasure we possess within the depths of our being:

> What more do you want, O soul! And what else do you search for outside, when within yourself you possess your riches, delights, satisfaction, fullness, and kingdom, your Beloved whom you desire and seek? Be joyful and gladdened in your interior recollection with him, for you have him so close to you. Desire him there; adore him there. Do not go in pursuit of him outside yourself. You will only become distracted and wearied thereby, and you shall not find him, or enjoy him more securely, or sooner, or more intimately than by seeking him with you. There is but one difficulty: Even though he does abide within you, he is hidden. Nevertheless, it is vital for you to know his hiding place so you may search for him with assuredness.[41]

Union of Likeness

The union with God that interests John most is the union with God that *does not* always exist. Created in God's image, our divine

---

[39] Secundino Castro, "El amor como apertura transcendental del hombre en San Juan de la Cruz," *Revista de Espiritualidad* 35 (1976): 434.
[40] John, *CW, The Spiritual Canticle*, Stanza 29, no. 3.
[41] John, *CW, The Spiritual Canticle*, Stanza 1, no. 8.

vocation is to grow in God's likeness, which is a "likeness of love." Union of likeness is a dynamic and progressive process of transformation into divine life, or what we call divinization.[42] John believes that God desires that we "possess the same goods by participation that the Son possesses by nature," that we become "gods through participation, equals and companions of God."[43] To say that we are called to be "gods through participation, equals and companions of God" seems like an unimaginable vocation. This union is "supernatural," that is, it is the fruit of God's transforming grace. It exists when our will and God's will are in conformity. This supernatural union is God's self-communication to us that transforms us at the deepest level of our being—the spiritual level—and thus enables us to love as God loves. It means loving God, others, and this world with the mind and heart of God. It means radiating God's love in this world.

How can we limited human beings love as God loves? John gives us an inkling into the nature of this equality of love in *The Spiritual Canticle*:

---

[42] "To understand the nature of this union, one should first know that God sustains every soul and dwells in it substantially, even though it may be that of the greatest sinner in the world. This union between God and creatures always exists. By it he conserves their being so that if the union should end they would immediately be annihilated and cease to exist. Consequently, in discussing union with God we are not discussing the substantial union that always exists, but the soul's union with and transformation in God that does not always exist, except when there is likeness of love. We will call it the union of likeness; and the former, the essential or substantial union. The union of likeness is supernatural; the other, natural. The supernatural union exists when God's will and the soul's are in conformity, so that nothing in the one is repugnant to the other. When the soul rids itself completely of what is repugnant and unconformed to the divine will, it rests transformed in God through love" (John, *CW*, *The Ascent of Mount Carmel*, Book 2, chap. 5, no. 3).

Regarding "divinization," St. John of the Cross inherited the thinking of the Greek Fathers, in particular Pseudo-Dionysius, as well as the theology of grace of the Middle Ages. Cf. Henri Sansón, *El espíritu humano según san Juan de la Cruz* (Madrid: Ediciones Rialp, 1962), 143. Texts where John explains divinization include *Ascent of Mount Carmel*, Book 1, chap. 5, no. 7; *The Living Flame of Love*, Stanza 2, nos. 32–35.

[43] John, *CW*, *The Spiritual Canticle*, Stanza 39, no. 4.6.

> The soul loves God with the will and strength of God himself, united with the very strength of love with which God loves her. This strength lies in the Holy Spirit in whom the soul is thereby transformed, for by this transformation of glory he supplies what is lacking in her, since he is given to the soul for the sake of the strength of this love.[44]

Equality of love means that we become so transformed by God's Spirit of love that we become vessels of God's love through the power of the Holy Spirit. It is to this love that Jesus calls his disciples in the Gospels. The Gospels are full of examples in how we are to love as God loves. The Sermon on the Mount and other passages show us how:

> So when you are offering your gift at the altar, if you remember that your brother or sister has something against you, leave your gift there before the altar and go; first be reconciled to your brother or sister, and then come and offer your gift. . . . Love your enemies and pray for those who persecute you, so that you may be children of your Father in heaven, for he makes his sun rise on the evil and on the good and sends rain on the righteous and on the unrighteous. . . . Be perfect, therefore, as your heavenly Father is perfect. (Matt 5:23-24, 44-45, 48)

> Be merciful, just as your Father is merciful. (Luke 6:36)

Forgiveness is the fundamental teaching of Jesus:

> For if you forgive others their trespasses, your heavenly Father will also forgive you, but if you do not forgive others, neither will your Father forgive your trespasses. (Matt 6:14-15)

Jesus teaches us to feed the hungry, clothe the naked, and visit those who are sick and imprisoned:

> [J]ust as you did it to one of the least of these brothers and sisters of mine, you did it to me. (Matt 25:40)

---

[44] John, *CW*, *The Spiritual Canticle*, Stanza 38, no. 3.

> I give you a new commandment, that you love one another. Just as I have loved you, you also should love one another. By this everyone will know that you are my disciples, if you have love for one another. (John 13:34-35)

Jesus is the model of loving as God loves, a love that gives itself completely and is merciful, forgiving, and generous. He is our model and light.[45] Love, therefore, is the key to understanding the union of likeness to which we are destined. God's will is that we become loving people who love God, others, and creation as God loves. "Be merciful, just as your Father is merciful"; "Be perfect, therefore, as your heavenly Father is perfect" (Luke 6:36; Matt 5:48). Of course, it is only by the transforming and healing grace of God, the Holy Spirit, that we can love as God loves.

Among the evocative metaphors John employs to explain this transformative process, two stand out. The first is sunlight shining through a window.

John compares our soul to a window and the divine light of God's being to the sunlight that is ever shining within us. If the window of our soul is dirty and smudgy with sinful actions, addictions, selfish desires, and attachments, God's light is prevented from illumining and transforming the glass. However, the more the smudges are wiped away and the glass is cleaned, the more the sun's rays can shine through and transform it. If the window is totally cleansed, the sunlight will so transform and illuminate the glass that it will seem identical to the ray of sunlight shining through it. The window never loses its distinctness; it always remains a distinct glass pane, but it appears identical to the sunlight and participates fully in the light shining through it.[46]

If we reflect on this metaphor, we have a beautiful image of our task in life. God's indwelling presence is the divine light shining from the depths of our person. We possess the divine light within us.

---

[45] John, *CW*, *The Ascent of Mount Carmel*, Book 2, chap. 7, no. 9.
[46] John, *CW*, *The Ascent of Mount Carmel*, Book 2, chap. 5, no. 6.

However, our attachments, selfish desires, and sinful attitudes and actions are like smudges or a dirty film that prevent the light from radiating through us.[47] Just as sunlight so transforms a clean and pure window so that the glass seems to become one with the light shining through it, so we are called to become so transformed into God's love that there will be nothing in us to block the divine light of God's love shining from our depths. Our task in life is to do what we can to make space for God so that with God's grace we can wipe away the "smudges" and "smears" of our sinful actions, selfish desires, and attachments to created reality. "For to love is to labor to divest and deprive oneself for God of all that is not God. When this is complete the soul will be illumined by and transformed in God."[48] We can say that our vocation in life is to radiate the light and love of God to the world around us, to all those we meet and with whom we live—to be the light of Christ to others.

The second metaphor John uses to describe the transformation process is fire burning a log of wood. Fire and log become one. "What God seeks, he being himself God by nature, is to makes us gods through participation, just as fire converts all things into fire."[49] Just as fire converts everything it consumes into fire, God desires to transform us so that we will share the very properties of God's love and radiate the light and warmth of God's love to others.[50]

---

[47] It is interesting to note that in the first dwelling places of *The Interior Castle*, St. Teresa compares the human person (the soul) to a crystal capable of reflecting the brilliance of God's light shining within it. Serious sin is like placing a black cloth over the crystal. "The shining sun that is in the center of the soul, does not lose it beauty and splendor; it is always present in the soul, and nothing can take away its loveliness. But if a black cloth is placed over the crystal that is in the sun, obviously the sun's brilliance will have no effect on the crystal even though the sun is shining on it" (Teresa of Avila, *The Interior Castle*, Dwelling Places 1, chap. 2, no. 3; vol. 2 of *The Collected Works of St. Teresa of Avila*, trans. Kieran Kavanaugh and Otilio Rodriguez, 3 vols. [Washington, DC: ICS Publications, 1976–1985]).

[48] John, *CW*, *The Ascent of Mount Carmel*, Book 2, chap. 5, no. 7.

[49] John, *CW*, *The Sayings of Light and Love*, no. 107.

[50] We will return to the metaphor of fire and wood later on, but for the moment it is important to stress that the divinization process John describes does

Love, therefore, is the key to growing in intimate union with God. "Love produces such likeness in this transformation of lovers that one can say each is the other and both are one."⁵¹

The Structure of the Human Person

To appreciate the healing and transformation of the human person according to John of the Cross, it is essential to grasp his understanding of the psychological structure of the human person, which for the most part he has adapted from the scholastic framework of his day.⁵² One way to approach this seemingly complicated structure of the human person is to visualize the person as having two faces, or two major components, the sensory and the spiritual.⁵³

The exterior face is what John refers to as the "sensory" part of the soul (*el sentido*). It is also referred to as the exterior part and consists of the body and the external senses of sight, hearing, smell, taste, and

---

not infer some sort of "pantheism" or total absorption of human consciousness and individuality into the divine. John always protects the individuality and consciousness of the person in the transformation process. For instance, "Once transformed, the wood no longer has any activity or passivity of its own, except for its weight and its quantity that is denser than the fire. It possesses the properties and performs the actions of fire: It is dry and it dries; it is hot and it gives off heat; it is brilliant and it illumines; it is also much lighter in weight than before. It is the fire that produces all these properties" (*The Dark Night*, Book 2, chap. 10, no. 1). We see, therefore, that the wood still remains wood, although a transformed wood, and the window remains window, yet so polished and transparent that it appears to be light. Other texts where John uses the fire and log of wood to describe the transformation process: *The Dark Night*, Book 2, chap. 10, nos. 1–2; *The Living Flame of Love*, Stanza 19, nos. 19.22–23; 25.33.

⁵¹ John, *CW*, *The Spiritual Canticle*, Stanza 12, no. 7.

⁵² According to Henri Sansón, John's anthropology is a synthesis of Platonic and scholastic anthropology. For a more complete explanation, see Sansón, *El espíritu humano según San Juan de la Cruz*, 76–84. See also John Welch, OCarm, *When Gods Die: An Introduction to John of the Cross* (New York: Paulist Press, 1990).

⁵³ For my discussion of the psychological structure of the human person, I have relied upon the following study: Eulogio Pacho, "La antropología suanjuanistica," in *Estudios sanjuanistas* II (Burgos, Spain: Monte Carmelo, 1997), 43–86.

touch. It is through the external senses that we come in contact with the world. This sensory part also consists of our emotional life (feelings of joy, hope, sadness, and fear) as well as our desires (*apetitos*), that is, all that moves us toward what we like and away from what we don't like:

> The internal senses, imagination, fantasy, and sense memory, also form part of the external face in the measure that they depend upon the knowledge given them through the external senses.[54]

The internal face of the human person is the spiritual part (*el espíritu*). John often refers to *el espíritu* as the superior or rational part of the soul. The spiritual part is the seat of the spiritual faculties: the intellect, memory, and will. These faculties are those that enable us to know, to love, to choose, and to imagine. Being spiritual faculties, they make it possible for humans to participate in divine life.

John tells us that there is more to the human person than the internal and external faculties of the soul. There is a third element of the spiritual part of the soul that John refers to as "the center of the soul,"[55] or "the substance of the soul."[56] It is that place deep within us where we most reflect God, where we are made in the image and likeness of God. It is a dynamic center of human dignity because it is the dwelling place of God regardless of our moral condition. "It should be noted that the Word of God, the Son of God, together with the Father and the Holy Spirit, is hidden by his essence and his presence in the innermost being of the soul . . . It brings special happiness to a person to understand that God is never absent, not even from a soul in sin (and how much less from one in the state of grace.)"[57]

This means we are always in relationship (union) with God by our very existence.[58] There exists within us a place not touched by original

---

[54] Wilfred Stinissen, OCD, *La nuit comme le jour illuminé: La nuit obscure chez Jean de la Croix* (Toulouse: Éditions du Carmel, 2010), 12.
[55] John, *CW, The Living Flame of Love*, Stanza 1, no. 12.
[56] John, *CW, The Living Flame of Love*, Stanza 1, no. 9; Stanza 2, nos. 17, 21.
[57] John, *CW, The Spiritual Canticle*, Stanza 1, no. 8.
[58] John, *CW, The Ascent of Mount Carmel*, Book 2, chap. 5, no. 3.

sin. As we will discuss in the next chapter, original sin has wounded human nature, not corrupted it. The woundedness of human nature is that we are alienated from this deepest center, searching and pouring out ourselves in what can never ultimately satisfy our heart.

The Substantial Unity of the Human Person

A superficial reading of John's analysis of the structure of the human person can give one the impression that he dichotomizes the human person into body and soul, sense and spirit. Despite the divisions he makes, he understands the human person as an integral whole, "one suppositum," "whole harmonious composite."[59] He does not view the human person as a composite of body and soul, spirit and matter, considered as separate substances, nor does he believe that the human person is soul or body, or the sum of the two. Rather, he understands the human being as "incarnate or corporealized soul," as one unified reality we call the human person.[60] John's concern is always the integral wholeness of the human person. His reasons for analyzing the human person in terms of sense and spirit and the operations of the faculties (intellect, memory, and will) are primarily pedagogical and functional. He wishes to demonstrate how each part, the sensitive and the spiritual, has a role in the totality of the human person, and how we function under the influence of each part. The division he makes between sense and spirit allows him to explain the

---

[59] "One might, then, in a certain way ponder how remarkable and how strong this enkindling of love in the spirit can be. God gathers together all the strength, faculties, and appetites of the soul, spiritual and sensory alike, so the energy and power of this whole harmonious composite may be employed in this love. The soul consequently arrives at the true fulfillment of the first commandment which, neither disdaining anything human nor excluding it from this love, states: You shall love your God with your whole heart, and with your whole mind, and with your whole soul, and with all your strength (Deut. 6:5)" (John, CW, *The Dark Night*, Book 2, chap. 11, no. 4). See also *The Dark Night*, Book 1, chap. 4, no. 2; Book 2, chap. 1, no. 1; Book 2, chap. 3, no. 1; *The Spiritual Canticle*, Stanza 13, no. 4.

[60] Ruiz, *Místico y maestro San Juan de la Cruz*, 147–49. See also Ruiz, "Metodo e strutture di antropologia sanjuanista," 424.

conflict within us due to original sin and how God restructures us and brings us to wholeness through the dark night experience.

The substantial unity of the human person is one of John's fundamental teachings. To misunderstand this is to misinterpret his doctrine on the healing and transformation that take place through the journey of the dark night of sense and spirit. Although he expresses the unity of the person categorically, his images are even more expressive of the essential unity of the person. The image of the "*caudal del alma*" (the "energy of the soul") in *The Spiritual Canticle* and the image of the "city and its outskirts" are two examples. John explains the meaning of the *caudal del alma*:

> Now I occupy my soul
> and all my energy in his service;
> I no longer tend the herd,
> nor have I any other work
> now that my every act is love.[61]

One of the transforming fruits of union with God through love is that the whole person—body, senses, and spirit—is directed toward God. There is wholeness and harmony within the human person who directs their entire being toward loving and serving God.[62]

---

[61] John, *CW*, *The Spiritual Canticle*, Stanza 28.

[62] "By all her 'energy' she refers to all that pertains to the sensory part of the soul. The sensory part includes the body with all its senses and faculties, interior and exterior, and all natural ability (the four passions, the natural appetites, and other energies). All of this, she says she occupies, as she does the rational and spiritual part referred to in the preceding verse, in the service of her Beloved. By directing the activity of the interior and exterior senses toward God, her use of the body is now conformed to his will. She also binds the four passions of the soul to him, for she does not rejoice except in God or hope in anything other than God; she fears only God and has no sorrow unless in relation to him. And likewise all her appetites and cares go out only to God" (John, *CW*, *The Spiritual Canticle*, Stanza 28, no. 4).

In *The Ascent of Mount Carmel*, John speaks of reserving all one's strength for God. "For a treatise on the active night and denudation of this faculty, with the aim of forming and perfecting it in this virtue of the charity of God, I have found no more appropriate passage than the one in chapter 6 of Deuteronomy,

Another image John uses to explain the unity of the human person is "*ciudad y sus arrabales*," in English translated as "city and its outskirts."[63] In this text he describes the human person as a large city within which there are two parts: the interior part, equivalent to the center of the city, and the exterior part, referred to as the outskirts of the city. Just as a city is harmoniously composed of two parts, the center and its outskirts, so is the human person.[64]

Due to the substantial unity of the human person as an incarnate spirit, John affirms that there exists a natural relationship and intercommunication between the various dimensions of the human person. Neither the sensory nor the spiritual part can act in an autonomous and independent way. What is experienced by the spiritual part of the soul will have repercussions in the sensory part, and vice versa. For instance, spiritual experiences such as ecstasies, raptures, and deeper levels of contemplative prayer can impact the body. If the body is not prepared for such an experience, it can cause weakness or other physical effects. Likewise, a traumatic psychological or emotional

---

where Moses commands: You shall love the Lord, your God, with all your heart, and with all your soul, and with all your strength (Deut. 6:5). This passage contains all that spiritual persons must do and all I must teach them here if they are to reach God by union of the will through charity. In it human beings receive the command to employ all the faculties, appetites, operations, and emotions of their soul in God so that they will use all this ability and strength for nothing else, in accord with David's words: *Fortitudinem meam ad te custodiam* (I will keep my strength for you) (Ps. 59:10 [Ps. 58:10])" (John, *CW*, *The Ascent of Mount Carmel*, Book 3, chap. 16, no. 1).

[63] John, *CW*, *The Spiritual Canticle*, Stanza 18, no. 6.

[64] "The 'outskirts' of Judea (and Judea, we said, refers to the lower or sensory part of the soul) are the interior senses (memory, phantasy, and imagination) in which the forms, images, and phantasms of objects gather and reside. By means of these images the sensory appetites are moved. These forms are what she refers to as girls. When they are quiet and tranquil, the appetites are also asleep. These images enter the outskirts, the interior senses, through the gates of the exterior senses—hearing, sight, smell, and so on. They do so in such a way that we can call both the interior and exterior sense faculties 'outskirts,' for they are the districts outside the walls of the city. That part of the soul called the city is the innermost part, the rational portion, which is capable of communion with God; its operations are contrary to those of the sensory part" (John, *CW*, *The Spiritual Canticle*, Stanza 18, no. 7).

disturbance on the spiritual (psychological) level can have a debilitating effect on the body, and on the spirit as well. On the positive side, health in spirit can affect bodily health.

The implications of the interdependency and intercommunication of soul and body are profound and far reaching in terms of healing and transformation. John eliminates any radical dualism and sees the purification of the human person as an integral process of involving the whole person, body and soul, sensory and spiritual. It is the whole person who journeys to God. The purification of the dark night is a process of healing and transforming the whole person, sense, spirit, body and soul, uniting and integrating the whole person so they may be completely ordered toward God. The good news of God's healing and transforming love must touch our entire person, inside and out and from top to bottom. For St. John of the Cross, this harmony and integration has its origin in God's plan for humanity from the beginning when God created us.

Chapter 3

The Pathology of the Soul

ALTHOUGH WE WERE CREATED in the image and likeness of God, created for an intimate communion of life with God, others, and creation, all is not well. We are born into a broken world. We know from the violence, wars, and conflicts on all levels of life—political, religious and personal—that profound disorder and disharmony exist in human nature.

On the personal level, our emotional struggles, temptations, and sinful attitudes testify to the reality that there are two forces at war within us. The "flesh" militates against the spirit, the spirit against the flesh. As we read in the previous chapter, we are made for God and deep within our hearts is a desire to love God as God loves. Nevertheless, we tend to follow our own selfish desires and cravings instead of placing the love of God at the center of our lives. Other energies usurp our strength and weaken our efforts to forgive and to be as patient, generous, and compassionate as we desire. We displace our desires for love and happiness with substitutes that can never satisfy us: riches, sex, food, honors, and codependent relationships. We become easily dispersed, fragmented, and swept along by emotions such as anger, jealousy, and envy that go contrary to Gospel love.[1] To

---

[1] John, *CW, The Ascent of Mount Carmel*, Book 1, chaps. 6 to 10.1. Chaps. 6 through 10 of the first book of *The Ascent of Mount Carmel* analyze the way we are swept along by selfish desire (disordered appetites).

live selfishly, dispersed, and divided within ourselves leads to dysfunctional behavior, and eventually to a disintegration of the personality. All types of spiritual, emotional, and even physical illnesses are born from this interior warfare. We stand in need of a profound healing at the deepest level of our being.

John's optimism and hope for human nature is balanced by realism. Like all the mystics of the great world religions, he diagnoses a sickness on the metaphysical level of human beings that weakens our divine vocation and desire to love according to God's original plan. Human nature has been profoundly wounded by original sin. "For human nature, your mother, was violated in your first parents."[2] We are born into a world where sin has broken the harmony and peace God intended at our creation.

John describes the effects of original and personal sin as a disorder and interior conflict that has broken the harmony on all levels of loving union for which we were created: with God, others, and the world. John does not focus on the act of sin, but its effects.[3] It has weakened our freedom and subjects us to disordered desires, inclinations and attachments contrary to God's will.[4] As St. Paul says, "We do not do the good we want, but the evil we do not want" (see Rom 7:19). We "love in a base manner."[5] John compares the sickness of original, social, and personal sin to a dirty stain embedded on a piece of cloth that requires a strong lye to cleanse it.[6] Only God's grace can heal us of the deepest disorders of the human spirit. "Who can free themselves from lowly manners and limitations if you do not lift them to yourself, my God, in purity of love? How will human beings begotten and nurtured in lowliness rise up to you, Lord, if you do not raise them with the hand that made them?"[7]

---

[2] John, *CW*, *The Spiritual Canticle*, Stanza 23, no. 5.
[3] Federico Ruiz, *Místico y maestro San Juan de la Cruz*, 2nd ed. (Madrid: Editorial de Espiritualidad, 2006), 209.
[4] John, *CW*, *The Ascent of Mount Carmel*, Book 1, chap. 15, no. 1.
[5] John, *CW*, *The Dark Night*, Book 1, chap. 8, no. 3.
[6] John, *CW*, *The Dark Night*, Book 2, chap. 2, no. 1.
[7] John, *CW*, *The Sayings of Light and Love*, no. 26.

As we read in chapter 1, even though original sin has wounded human nature, there exists within us a sacred place, "the center of the soul."[8] John also calls it "the substance of the soul," which is not infected by original sin, where we are made in the image and likeness of God and where God dwells regardless of our moral state.[9] Our original woundedness is that we are alienated from our deepest Source of love and meaning and are conditioned to seek ultimate happiness in what can never ultimately satisfy our heart and give us true peace and happiness. For John of the Cross, the mystical journey is an interior journey to the center of our being, to our heart, where God dwells and where we come to know the Love that heals us and thus come to full health. There we will find our true self rooted in God's love. It is only through God's self-communicating love that we can make this journey.[10]

Pathology of the Soul

St. John of the Cross is a master diagnostician and physician of the human heart. William Thompson has called John a "pneumapathologist" because he has studied the sinfully dark side of humanity.[11] John's own faith journey and experience as a spiritual guide gave him insight into the sufferings, weaknesses, and temptations of the human spirit.

How does the "sickness of the soul" manifest itself? What are the disorders and conflicts that make us spiritually, emotionally, morally,

---

[8] John, *CW*, *The Living Flame of Love*, Stanza 1, no. 12.

[9] John calls this sacred center "the substance of the soul," where we are pure capacity for God. See John, *CW*, *The Living Flame of Love*, Stanza 1, no. 9; and Stanza 2, no. 17. See also John, *CW*, *The Spiritual Canticle*, Stanza 1, no. 8: "It brings special happiness to a person to understand that God is never absent, not even from a soul in mortal sin (and how much less from one in the state of grace)."

[10] Fernando Urbina, *La persona humana en San Juan de la Cruz* (Madrid: Ediciones, 1982), 219.

[11] William Thompson, "St. John of the Cross as Pneumapathologist: A Mystic's Hermeneutics of Suspicion," in *Fire and Light: The Saints and Theology* (New York: Paulist Press, 1987), 119.

and even physically ill? There are several key texts where John treats of the disorders of the human person to illustrate the necessity of God's purifying cure through the dark night as a process of healing and transformation. We will examine two specific texts: Book One of *The Ascent of Mount Carmel*, chapters 6–10, and Book One of *The Dark Night*, as well as selected texts from Book Two of *The Dark Night*. Although John analyzes the disorders of the human person in several places throughout his works, these texts bring into sharp focus the conflicts, spiritual illnesses, and interior fragmentation that cause us suffering. He gives us a diagnosis of our spiritual illness in order to stress the absolute necessity of God's therapeutic intervention. We can consider these texts as a sixteenth-century manual of the "maladies of the soul," or in psychological terms, a diagnostic manual of "dysfunctional behavior."[12] However, due to the vocabulary rooted in scholastic philosophy and theology, they are easily misunderstood if not interpreted correctly, so we must examine them carefully and try to grasp the essence of John's teaching.

The Enslaved Heart: Disordered Appetites

The first text where St. John of the Cross analyzes the pathology of the soul is Book One of *The Ascent of Mount Carmel*, chapters 6–11. He begins by analyzing the situation of beginners in the spiritual life who are enslaved by what he describes as "disordered appetites." The

---

[12] I have chosen these texts because they are the ones in which John impresses upon the reader the necessity of the dark night. Also, generally speaking, they are the ones that Sanjuanist scholars concentrate on in their analysis of the human disorders according to St. John of the Cross. For instance, Ruiz, *Místico y Maestro San Juan de la Cruz*; José Vincente Rodríguez, OCD, *San Juan de la Cruz profeta enamorado de Dios y maestro* (Madrid: Instituto de Espiritualidad a Distancia, 1987); Eulogio Pacho, *S. Juan de la Cruz, Temas fundamentales*, 2 (Burgos, Spain: Monte Carmelo, 1984); and José Damián Gaitán, *Negación y plenitud en San Juan de la Cruz* (Madrid: Editorial de Espiritualidad, 1995). I have borrowed the term "dysfunctional behavior" from Kevin Culligan's article, "St. John of the Cross and Modern Psychology," *Studies in Formative Spirituality* 13 (1992): 32.

people he describes are immersed in a world of dispersion and fragmentation, relating on the superficial level of life, enslaved by the pleasure principle. They are swept along by their emotions, selfish desires, and attachment to sense pleasure. The image of an "enslaved heart" appears throughout John's description of these beginners.[13]

The term *appetite* is central to the vocabulary of these chapters and is a common word in John's vocabulary, especially in *The Ascent of Mount Carmel*. However, *appetite* is rarely used today, so it is difficult to define it in contemporary psychological terms. Even in John's time it was not easy to translate, and John does not give us a clear definition. The way he uses it in these pages can be confusing.[14] Psychologically speaking, an appetite is an inclination toward something that is beneficial for human life. Appetite is not simply the tendency that drives us toward something we see as good for us, nor is it considered in the moral or spiritual sense as a fault or sin, because John uses the term both positively and negatively. He says we must have an "appetite for God,"[15] and an "appetite to imitate Christ."[16] Even though he fails to give a precise definition, he generally defines "disordered appetites" as selfish desires, the egotistical way we relate to God, people, material objects, and creation.[17] Because we were created by God out of love and for love, we possess an innate desire (appetite) for God. We long to love and be loved; we long for God. Our pathology is that our desire for God becomes disordered, misdirected away from God who alone can satisfy the human heart and toward created reality—material goods, riches, pleasures, sex, food, money—that fails to satisfy our longing for love and happiness. Thus, the problem is not an appetite itself, but disordered appetites, that is, those directed toward things other than God.

---

[13] John, *CW*, *The Ascent of Mount Carmel*, Book 1, chap. 4, no. 6.
[14] When John writes about the harm the appetites cause for us, it is important to remember that it is "disordered" appetites that damage the human personality.
[15] John, *CW*, *The Ascent of Mount Carmel*, Book 1, chap. 10, no. 1.
[16] John, *CW*, *The Ascent of Mount Carmel*, Book 1, chap. 13, no. 3.
[17] Ruiz, *Místico y Maestro San Juan de la Cruz*, 228.

Appetite, as John of the Cross presents it, is an irrational impulse that moves a person to satisfy his needs primarily in view of the pleasure he experiences in them. The one who is the slave of the appetites, eats, touches, sees, feels only for the satisfaction he finds; the true values for him are those that can give him this kind of satisfaction. For them he lives; they are, taken as a whole, the value to which he orients his whole existence. They are in practice his god. . . . Every appetite potentially becomes an idol: that is to say, a value that claims to be unique in determining the choices (decisions) of the person, at the expense of the person's free will.[18]

John often employs other terms to describe the phenomenon of the appetites: *affection, attachment, desire, longing, inclination, hunger, passion, vehemence, the force of passion, centering one's heart on someone or something,* and *lust.* These terms express a movement toward something we lack, a tendency or movement born from hunger and thirst for something we desire. The metaphor of hunger and thirst is frequent in John's writing because it expresses the urgency and torment of unfulfilled human desire.[19] John specifies that disordered appetites are those that are misdirected. They are best understood as restless cravings and desires for love, meaning, and satisfaction of heart that drive us to pour out ourselves in created reality in ways that rob us of the happiness and satisfaction of heart for which we long. Addictive behavior is one way to understand disordered appetites. We see the world of appetites manifested in addiction to food, alcohol, sex, pleasure, material possessions, power, control, and prestige. We can become slaves of our disordered appetites on many levels, some very subtle. We can become attached to the way we want things accomplished, to our own opinion and need to control others, to another person in a codependent way, to pleasing other people, to a particular duty, to a specific image of God, and even to spiritual consolations.

---

[18] Footnoted in Ruiz, *Místico y Maestro San Juan de la Cruz*, 229. Cf. F. Foresti, "Le radici bibliche della 'Salita del Monte Carmelo,'" *Carmelus* 28 (1981): 239.

[19] Victorino Capánaga de San Agustín, *San Juan de la Cruz: Valor psicológico de su doctrina* (Madrid: Editorial de Espiritualidad, 1950), 158–59.

We see the dynamic of disordered appetites in the "if only" situations in our lives: "If only I had a large house, I would be happy; if only this person would recognize me, I would be happy; if only the community would agree with my ideas, I would be happy; if only my prayer were more consoling, I would be happy." The "if only" wishes create a state of dependency upon something outside ourselves for emotional and spiritual fulfillment. In this sense, they constrict our heart and diminish our capacity to give ourselves freely. Disordered appetites, therefore, refer to a disordered way of loving, the selfish way we relate to God, others, and creation. Slavery to our disordered desires imprisons us on the level of how things feel and appear, in the world of likes and dislikes, pleasant and unpleasant. John describes the person enslaved by the appetites as "*el hombre sensual*," that is, the person who lives on the level of the senses, feelings, and appearances, rather than at the deeper spiritual level. For instance, we may go to prayer more for the spiritual consolations and delight we derive than to please God, or we may perform duties that are pleasurable but avoid unsatisfying tasks, or we may give generously to someone in order to receive something in return.

Contemporary authors have interpreted disordered appetites in psychological terminology. Fernando Urbina in his commentary on *The Dark Night* defines disordered appetites from Freudian terminology as "fixation." Other authors define it as addiction or codependency.[20] However we interpret disordered appetite, there is a

---

[20] Fernando Urbina, *Comentario a Noche oscura del espíritu y Subida del espíritu y Subida al Monte Carmelo de San Juan de la Cruz* (Madrid: Ediciones Marova, 1982), 33–34. Some authors translate "disordered appetite" as addiction and codependency. Cf. F. K. Nemick and M. T. Combes, *O Blessed Night, Recovering from Addiction and Attachment Based on the Insights of St. John of the Cross and Pierre Teilhard de Chardin* (New York: Alba House, 1991). In terms of addiction see Gerald May, MD, *Addiction and Grace: Love and the Spirituality of Healing of Addictions* (San Francisco: HarperCollins, 1991). In terms of "unredeemed" desire see Constance FitzGerald, OCD, "Impasse and Dark Night," in *Living with Apocalypse*, ed. T. Edwards (San Francisco: Harper & Row, 1984), 93–116.

volitional-affective quality to it since it is rooted in the will, the organ of love.

What concerns John is not love for created realities or people, but how we relate to them in possessive or selfish ways. The problem lies not in material things or people, but in the human heart when it inordinately desires to find ultimate satisfaction in created reality for selfish motives. "Since the things of the world cannot enter the soul, they themselves are not an encumbrance or harm to it; rather, it is the will and appetite dwelling within that causes the damage when set on these things."[21]

This becomes even clearer in chapter 1 of Book One of *The Ascent of Mount Carmel*, where John further nuances the type of disordered appetites to which he is referring. Not only are they *inordinate*, but they are *voluntary* and *habitual*. The object of desire is of little importance, whether it is a book, a pen, a piece of clothing, one's bedroom, a person, some "trifling" conversation, or some satisfactions in "tasting, knowing and hearing things." What concerns John is the manner in which we relate to those realities, relating to them solely for the pleasure and satisfaction derived from them. "It makes little difference whether a bird is tied by a thin thread or by a cord. Even if it is tied by thread, the bird will be held bound just as surely as if it was tied by cord."[22] Thus, the appetites impede our freedom.

A Disordered Way of Loving

John works from a Greek and Roman philosophical principle. Philosophically, two contraries cannot exist in the same subject, and love brings about an equality with the object loved. "For the property of love is to make the lover equal to the object loved."[23] This is a fundamental theme in John's system; to love the created and limited

---

[21] John, *CW*, *The Ascent of Mount Carmel*, Book 1, chap. 3, no. 4.
[22] John, *CW*, *The Ascent of Mount Carmel*, Book 1, chap. 11, no. 4.
[23] John, *CW*, *The Spiritual Canticle*, Stanza 28, no. 1.

is to become like it.[24] The inverse is also true: the more we love God, the more we are united to him and resemble him.

Not only does love brings about equality with the object loved, but it also subjects the lover to what it loves. One becomes enslaved by what one loves. "Love not only equates but even subjects the lover to the loved creature."[25]

Having established the principle that love brings about a likeness to the object loved, John surveys a wide range of human ideals and values and compares them to the greatness and supreme value of God.

> All the creatures of heaven and earth are nothing when compared to God. . . . All the beauty of creatures compared to the infinite beauty of God is the height of ugliness. . . . All the grace and elegance of creatures compared with God's grace is utter coarseness and crudity.[26]

A first reading of these comparisons without an understanding of the experience of God they reflect would lead us to believe that John is setting up an opposition between God and creation and denigrating created reality in writing that, compared to God, creation is "nothing," "ugly," and "crude." But this is far from his intention. God is not in competition with creation and human beings, for God is the Source of all that exists. These statements reflect the experience of a person

---

[24] "For a better proof of this, it ought to be kept in mind that an attachment to a creature makes a person equal to that creature; the stronger the attachment, the closer is the likeness to the creature and the greater the equality; for love effects a likeness between the lover and the loved" (John, *CW*, *The Ascent of Mount Carmel*, Book 1, chap. 4, no. 3).

[25] John, *CW*, *The Ascent of Mount Carmel*, Book 1, chap. 4, no. 3. In a footnote in *The Collected Works of St. John of the Cross*, Kieran Kavanaugh explains John's idea that love effects a union with the object loved: "This fundamental idea in John's teaching, that love effects the likeness between the lover and the loved, has its roots in the classic Greek and Roman poets and philosophers. Though John insists so much on the divine transcendence, a likeness or equality between God and humans can still be effected, not on the ontological level, but on the affective plane. When God loves humans, he makes them his equals in love" (p. 124).

[26] John, *CW*, *The Ascent of Mount Carmel*, Book 1, chap. 4, nos. 5–7.

who has glimpsed the infinite goodness and beauty of God. John wishes to communicate a message about God. God is the Source of all life, goodness, and beauty. God is All. God is Everything. No matter how good, wise, and beautiful the creatures of this world may be, nothing can be compared to the goodness, wisdom, beauty, and love of God who is the author of all that exists and upon whom everything depends. In light of God's tremendous love and goodness, all other things pale into insignificance without losing their value and worth. But isn't this how it is when two people fall in love? A man and woman fall in love, and as a result other men and women no longer attract their hearts as before. Their hearts are stolen. Yes, others are beautiful and good, but all other loves and attractions pale in relation to their beloved.

John has another reason for making such radical statements: ultimately, only God can satisfy the human heart because God created us for a communion of life with God. Although the world and creatures are beautiful and made by God, they cannot slake the deepest thirst of the human spirit. Anything less than the infinite fails to satisfy us.[27] Rather than placing our heart in the divine Source of love and meaning, and seeing creation in the light of God, we choose to center our hearts and affections in created reality that can never ultimately satisfy us. This is a message that resounds throughout John's works. It is a truth he learned early in life, having been born in poverty and misery. Experience taught him that so much of human suffering comes from not grasping the truth that, ultimately, only God can satisfy the human heart.

The "Pathologies" of the Soul

Chapter 6 of Book One of *The Ascent of Mount Carmel* takes us deeper into the pathology of disordered appetites and how they harm the personality. John's theory is that when we close ourselves from a loving relationship with God and relate to creation and others with

---

[27] John, *CW*, *The Living Flame of Love*, Stanza 3, no. 18.

selfish motives, when we choose to relate to creation apart from God, and when we depend upon creatures to satisfy our longing for love and meaning, we suffer spiritually and psychologically. John depicts the person enslaved by inordinate appetites as suffering from a debilitating spiritual illness.

> If you desire that devotion be born in your spirit and that the love of God and the desire for divine things increase, cleanse your soul of every desire, attachment, and ambition in such a way that you have no concern about anything. Just as a sick person is immediately aware of good health once the bad humor has been thrown off and a desire to eat is felt, so will you recover your health, in God, if you cure yourself as was said. Without doing this, you will not advance no matter how much you do.[28]

According to John, the disordered desires cause two principal kinds of harm: privative and positive. The privative harm is that they deprive us of God's Spirit in the sense that they limit our freedom and weaken our desire to make God the center of our life.[29] John employs an apt image, drawing from the book of the prophet Jeremiah: "[T]hey have forsaken me, / the fountain of living water, / and dug out . . . cracked cisterns that can hold no water" (Jer 2:13). Giving full rein to our disordered appetite is like trying to drink water from a leaking cistern. We never slake our thirst. John makes a comparison based upon Scripture. God, our Father, wants us to sit at the table as his beloved children and to share in his Spirit, but we choose the

---

[28] John, *CW, The Sayings of Light and Love*, no. 78.
[29] "To begin with, it is clear in speaking of the privative harm that a person by mere attachment to a created thing is less capable of God; and this, in the measure that the appetite has entity in the soul. For two contraries cannot coexist in the same subject, as the philosophers say, and as we also mentioned in Chapter 4. Since love of God and attachment to creatures are contraries, they cannot coexist in the same will. What has creature to do with Creator, sensory with spiritual, visible with invisible, temporal with eternal, heavenly food that is pure and spiritual with food that is entirely sensory, the nakedness of Christ with attachment to something?" (John, *CW, The Ascent of Mount Carmel*, Book 1, chap. 6, no. 1).

"crumbs" that fall from his table—that is, we choose to satisfy our cravings for love and meaning with creatures. Therefore, John compares the person enslaved by the appetites to "hungry dogs" lapping up the crumbs that fall from a dinner table.[30] A hungry dog lapping up crumbs from a dinner table symbolizes the indignity of the person who gives rein to disordered desires. Being a child of God, created in the image and likeness of God, and invited to partake of the banquet of the trinitarian life, they choose to reduce themselves to a life ruled by their addictions and anxious cravings for things that will never satisfy them. Because creatures are incapable of satisfying the hunger for love and meaning, they leave the person discontent, hungry, unsatisfied, and always wanting more and more and more. Just think of someone seriously addicted to drugs, alcohol, or sex, and how the addiction overpowers them and leads them to behave and live in such a way that undermines their human dignity and is destructive to their health and friendships.

Disordered appetites also cause positive harm. They cause various types of suffering. They "weary, torment, darken, defile and weaken" the person.[31] The verbs John employs to describe the harm caused by the appetites depict a state of suffering and ill-being. They indicate a "disease." The English word *disease* comes from the Middle English *disese* and Middle French, *desaise*, which means a lack of ease, uneasiness, trouble, and disquiet. Disease refers to a disturbance in the performance of the vital functions of the body, causing or threatening pain, illness, or disorder. However, disease is also applied figuratively to mind, moral character, and habits. It can refer to mental, emotional, and spiritual trouble.[32]

Weariness, torment, darkness, defilement, and weakness are symptoms of a disease or disorder within the person. What causes these symptoms? A selfish way of relating to creation based upon the pleasure principle, a closure of oneself to the divine Source of love and meaning. In chapters 6 through 10 of *The Ascent of Mount Carmel*,

---

[30] John, *CW*, *The Ascent of Mount Carmel*, Book 1, chap. 6, no. 3.
[31] John, *CW*, *The Ascent of Mount Carmel*, Book 1, chap. 6, no. 5.
[32] *Merriam Webster Medical Dictionary* (New York: McGraw Hill, 1996).

John illustrates the harm caused by disordered appetites through images and comparisons that deepen our insight into the roots of the sickness of the soul.[33] He provides various graphic examples of the damages disordered appetites cause us.

The first private harm is that they weary and tire us. When we are enslaved by disordered appetites we resemble little children, restless and hard to please, always whining for this thing or that, and never satisfied. Or we are like someone digging covetously for a treasure, who grows more and more exhausted. Or we are like a person with a fever whose thirst increases by the minute and who feels ill until the fever leaves.[34] The appetites also agitate and disturb us just as the wind disturbs water. We grow tired because we are like a famished person who opens their mouths to satisfy themselves with air. We are like a lover wearied and depressed when on the longed-for day the opportunity to meet his love is frustrated. I remember a woman confiding to me her addiction to shopping. She said, "My addiction to Kmart and Walmart is wearing me out. I'm so exhausted I can hardly keep up with my family duties."

In chapter 19 of Book Three of *The Ascent of Mount Carmel*, John gives examples of the harm caused to the personality by anxieties and agitation over temporal goods such as money. The anxiety and agitation caused by greed for money can lead to sadness, despair, and even suicide.[35]

---

[33] John's doctrine in chapters 6–10 of *The Ascent of Mount Carmel* is similar to chapters 16–45 of Book 3 of *The Ascent of Mount Carmel* where he treats the purification of the will. In chapters 19, 22, 25, 28, 31, and 41 of Book 3, he explains the *daños* (harms) that come to people when they direct the emotion of joy to objects rather than to God. John's theory is that disorder and interior conflict arise when we depend primarily on creatures for emotional and spiritual fulfillment. Such dependency results in all kinds of vices and evils that lead to suffering. Cf. Kevin Culligan, "St. John of the Cross and Modern Psychology," *Studies in Formative Spirituality* 13 (1992): 29–49.

[34] John, *CW*, *The Ascent of Mount Carmel*, Book 1, chap. 6, no. 6.

[35] There are "miserable souls who value earthly goods as their god and are so enamored of them that they do not hesitate to sacrifice their lives when they observe that this god of theirs undergoes some temporal loss. They despair and commit suicide for wretched reasons and demonstrate with their own hands the miserable reward that comes from such a god. Since there is nothing to hope for

Torment and affliction comprise the second harm caused by disordered appetites. John compares them to instruments of torture: "torture of the rack" and being "bound by cords."[36]

When we depend upon creatures for ultimate satisfaction we become like someone who falls into enemy hands. The tragic personality of Samson in the book of Judges illustrates how destructive and tortuous disordered appetites can be for us. They weaken, blind, afflict, enslave, and rob us of our dignity.

> Those who let their appetites take hold of them suffer torture and affliction like an enemy held prisoner. The Book of Judges contains a figure of this in the passage that narrates how the enemies captured mighty Samson, who was once the free, strong judge of Israel, and weakened him, pulled out his eyes, and chained him to grind at the millstone where he was grievously tortured and tormented [Jgs. 16:21]. This same thing happens to a person in whom the enemy appetites reside and triumph.[37]

John ends his explanation by extending a double invitation taken from Scripture. He speaks of God's compassion for those who seek to satisfy their hunger and thirst for love from creatures. He paraphrases Isaiah 55:1-2:

> Come to the waters, all you who experience the thirst of your appetites; and you who have not the silver of your own will and desires, make haste; buy from me and eat; come and buy wine and milk (peace and spiritual sweetness) from me without the silver of your own will, without paying with labor as you do for the

---

from him, he gives despair and death. And those whom he does not pursue right up to death, the ultimate injury, die from living in the affliction of anxieties and many other miseries. He does not permit gladness to enter their hearts or for any earthly good to bring them joy. Insofar as they are afflicted about money, they are always paying the tribute of their hearts to it. They cling to it unto their final calamity of just perdition, as the Wise Man warns: Riches are hoarded to the harm of their owner (Eccl. 5:12)" (John, *CW*, *The Ascent of Mount Carmel*, Book 3, chap. 19, nos. 9–10).

[36] John, *CW*, *The Ascent of Mount Carmel*, Book 1, chap. 7, no. 1.

[37] John, *CW*, *The Ascent of Mount Carmel*, Book 1, chap. 7, no. 2.

satisfaction of your appetites. Why do you offer the silver of your will for what is not bread (the bread of the divine Spirit) and waste the efforts of your appetites on what cannot satisfy them? Come, listen to me, and you will have the food you desire, and your soul will delight in abundance.[38]

What stands out in these scriptural texts is the sense of well-being that comes from God and the suffering and debilitation that come from depending upon created reality for ultimate spiritual and emotional fulfillment. "The creature torments while the Spirit of God refreshes."[39]

Blindness is the third harm. For John, blindness is the principal harm and origin of all the damaging effects that disordered desires create. Like "vapors" or a "cloudy mirror," they impede the light of natural wisdom, as well as a true vision of our dignity of being made in the image and likeness of God. We say that "love is blind." Romantic passion can blind us to the true personality of the one to whom we are attracted, oblivious to both their gifts and talents as well as their weaknesses and limitations. It is the same with any strong desire. How blind we can become when we're consumed by a desire for material possessions, money, pleasure, alcohol, or fame! Disordered appetites darken our reason and lead to all kinds of suffering and evil for ourselves and others. For instance, in chapter 25 of Book Three of *The Ascent of Mount Carmel*, John enumerates the harms caused to persons from inordinate absorption of various sensory pleasures and goods. For instance, the joy of superficial conversations can give rise to distraction of the imagination, gossiping, envy, and rash judgments. Inordinate desires for material possessions can lead to disgust for the poor (which is contrary to Christ's doctrine). Inordinate cravings for food lead to "gluttony, drunkenness, anger, discord, and a lack of charity for one's neighbor and the poor."[40] A good example is the damage that addiction to social media can effect: distraction of spirit,

---

[38] John, *CW*, *The Ascent of Mount Carmel*, Book 1, chap. 7, no. 3.
[39] John, *CW*, *The Ascent of Mount Carmel*, Book 1, chap. 7, no. 4.
[40] See John, *CW*, *The Ascent of Mount Carmel*, Book 3, chap. 25, no. 103.

indecency, impure thoughts, greed, lust, malicious gossip, and pornography. John makes an analogy of a moth so blinded by its desire for the beauty of light that it flies directly into a bonfire. With the darkening of our intellect, our will weakens and we are incapable of embracing God's will with pure love.[41]

Concerning the weakening of the will, John demonstrates how disordered appetites diminish our love of neighbor. For John, not only can we become attached to pleasures and material goods such as clothes, food, and money, we can also become attached to our good works and customs in such a way that we judge others who are different. Like the Pharisee we can boast that we are not like so-and-so, nor do we act like that person. "I thank you that I am not like other people: thieves, rogues, adulterers" (Luke 18:11). This can lead to judging others as evil and imperfect and can give rise to anger and envy when they receive praise and seem to have more value than we have.[42] We can also do good works with the intention of being praised by others, rather than performing them out of love for God.

John concludes his discussion of how our selfish cravings can blind us by reminding us that we cannot rely simply on the good intelligence we receive from God. King Solomon is an example. God graced him with great wisdom and he at first restrained his affections for women, but his desires eventually consumed him to the point that he built altars to his wives' false gods. His failure to deny his appetites darkened his intellect so that finally the light of God's wisdom was extinguished.[43]

We see therefore that the principal harm caused by disordered appetites is the inability to see the truth. We are surrounded by truth, immersed in the truth, but our inordinate desires for self-gratification cloud our vision and render us incapable of seeing the true nature of reality, God, and ourselves. Consequently, such obscurity is the source of much suffering and illness in our world.

---

[41] John, *CW, The Ascent of Mount Carmel*, Book 1, chap. 8, no. 3.
[42] John, *CW, The Ascent of Mount Carmel*, Book 3, chap. 28, no. 3.
[43] John, *CW, The Ascent of Mount Carmel*, Book 1, chap. 8, nos. 6–7.

Disordered appetites also defile and stain us, which is the fourth harm they engender within us. John's underlying thought when he describes how the appetites defile and stain us has a strong tradition in Christian theology even in the patristic period.[44] We were made in the image of God, thus created with sublime dignity and beauty. Disordered appetites defile our beauty and dignity when we give rein to them. "Strokes of soot would ruin a perfect and extraordinarily beautiful portrait, so too inordinate appetites defile and dirty the soul, in itself a perfect and extremely beautiful image of God."[45]

The implications of John's teaching are profound. We were created in the image and likeness of God, the image of Love. Our dignity and beauty lie in God's love for us, which is imprinted in the very fibers of our being. To follow our inordinate desires is to go contrary to our very nature as beings loved by God and created for a relationship of love. Such behavior leads to a denial of our dignity and consequently to a breakdown of the personality.

When our affections and thoughts are ordered toward the end intended by God, there is beauty and health. On the other hand, when our affections and thoughts depend upon creatures for ultimate emotional and spiritual satisfaction, there is disorder and ugliness. John tells us that love and a virtuous life beautify the personality, whereas centering our energy and affections on created realities robs us of our dignity and beauty as creatures created in God's image and likeness.[46]

---

[44] J. D. Gaitán, "San Juan de la Cruz y su 'Dichosa Ventura': Opción por Dios y purificación de los sentidos," *Revista de Espiritualidad* 45 (1986): 489–520.

[45] John, *CW*, *The Ascent of Mount Carmel*, Book 1, chap. 9, no. 1.

[46] "The variety of filth caused in the soul is both inexplicable and unintelligible! For were it comprehensible and explainable it would be surprising and also distressing to see how in the measure of its quantity and quality each appetite leaves a deposit of filth and an unsightly mark in the soul. It would be a surprise and a pity to observe how only one inordinate act can in its own way occasion innumerable kinds and various degrees of filth. The well-ordered soul of the just in a single perfect act possesses countless rich gifts and beautiful virtues. Each of these gifts and virtues is different and pleasing in its own way according to the multitude and diversity of the affections the soul has had for God. Similarly, in an inordinate soul the deposit of filth and degradation is as miserable and has the same variety as the variety of its appetites for creatures" (John, *CW*, *The Ascent of Mount Carmel*, Book 1, chap. 9, no. 4).

Division, dispersion, and *fragmentation* are the key words to describe the fifth harm caused by the appetites. When we are enslaved by disordered appetites we become like water poured out all over the place. "A person whose will is divided among trifles is like water that, leaking from the bottom, will not rise higher and is therefore useless."[47]

When our selfish cravings are dispersed and uncentered, there is no growth in virtue. We become like hot water that loses its heat when uncovered or aromatic spices that, when left unwrapped, lose the strength and pungency of their scent.[48]

John uses some powerfully descriptive metaphors to explain how disordered appetites weaken us, drain our strength, and divide us. They are like "shoots burgeoning about a tree, sapping its strength, and causing it be fruitless." Consequently, unmortified appetites stunt our growth and development. They are like "leeches always sucking blood from one's veins," thus draining our lifeblood and weakening us.[49] If they are not mortified, they eventually destroy the personality just as the offspring of vipers eat the entrails of their mother and finally kill her.[50]

John tells us that disordered appetites have the potential to weaken us psychologically and spiritually and provoke a pervasive disintegration that impacts our relationship with God, others, and creation.

> It is sad to consider the condition of the poor soul in whom they dwell. How unhappy it is with itself, how cold toward its neighbors, how sluggish and slothful in the things of God! No illness makes walking as burdensome, or eating as distasteful, as do the appetites for creatures render the practice of virtue burdensome and saddening to a person. Ordinarily, the reason many people do not have diligence and eagerness for the acquisition of virtue is that their appetites and affections are not fixed purely on God.[51]

---

[47] John, *CW, The Ascent of Mount Carmel,* Book 1, chap. 10, no. 1.
[48] John, *CW, The Ascent of Mount Carmel,* Book 1, chap. 9, no. 1.
[49] John, *CW, The Ascent of Mount Carmel,* Book 1, chap. 9, no. 2.
[50] John, *CW, The Ascent of Mount Carmel,* Book 1, chap. 10, no. 3.
[51] John, *CW, The Ascent of Mount Carmel,* Book 1, chap. 10, no. 4.

How often we see this in life when a person's disordered cravings for money, power, sex, fame, alcohol, material possessions, and pleasures eventually render them cold and insensitive to the needs of others, impervious to religious values, and even subject to depression. They become more and more alienated from their deeper true self and from a faith-filled relationship with God and others.

Conclusion

In Book One of *The Ascent of Mount Carmel*, St. John of the Cross gives us a perceptive analysis of the pathology of disordered appetites and the harm they cause us when we fail to restrain them. John depicts people enslaved by their appetites as selfishly pouring out their love and affection on created reality, hoping to derive love, meaning, and lasting satisfaction of heart. Instead of choosing to center their love and affection in God, they place them in creatures. As John stresses, the problem lies not in creation, but in the human heart and the way we relate to creation. By relating to creatures in a self-seeking and possessive way, we seek from creation something it can never provide. Only God can ultimately satisfy the longings of the human heart.

Enslavement to disordered desires harms the personality. Communicating this is John's main objective in Book One of *The Ascent of Mount Carmel*: unpurified disordered appetites "weary, torment, darken, defile and weaken" us.[52] The various types of harm caused by disordered appetites are symptoms of a sickness of the soul. The source of this sickness is a disordered way of loving that creates a disorder in the personality, worse even than physical illness.

---

[52] John, *CW*, *The Ascent of Mount Carmel*, Book 1, chap. 6, no. 5.

Chapter 4

A Dysfunctional Manner of Loving

BOOK ONE OF *The Dark Night of the Soul* is the second text where John diagnoses the "sickness of the soul." John describes the stage of the spiritual life when God begins his healing and transforming work through what he calls the passive night of the senses, that is, a period of growth and maturity in the Christian life when God begins to sever our disordered desire for sense-pleasure in our spiritual practices and also to sever our dependent relationships with created reality that usurp God's rightful place in our life.[1] John refers to "beginners" on the spiritual journey; however, these people are not beginners in the

---

[1] Although we will take up the theme of the dark night of sense and that of the spirit in a later chapter, it is helpful to briefly explain the meaning of the dark night of sense and spirit. The dark night symbolizes a process of transformation of the human person at the deepest level of our being that takes place in stages throughout life. We can say that it is a universal metaphor for healing and transformation. Because of the psychosomatic unity of our person (sense-spirit-body-soul) this transformation takes place in stages. It has an active dimension, that is, what we ourselves can do through our efforts to bring about purification, and a passive dimension: God's action. We passively allow God to purify us of what is impossible for us to change by our own efforts. The dark night of sense is a period of human maturity. Through the experience of aridity, deeper self-knowledge of our wounded personal history, sinful patterns, and imperfections, we move from a superficial love of God and neighbor to a more mature and authentic evangelical love and freedom from our attachment to sense-pleasure.

sense that they are recent converts to a serious Christian life. Rather, they are people who have undergone a conversion and live their spiritual life seriously. They are earnest in their prayer, and they strive to grow in self-knowledge and the evangelical virtues, and to free themselves from their disordered appetites and attachments. Like a loving mother, God "nurtures and caresses" the soul in the beginning with sensible consolations, which are necessary to engender enthusiasm and service. "It should be known, then, that God nurtures and caresses the soul, after it has been resolutely converted to his service, like a loving mother who warms her child with the heat of her bosom, nurses it with good milk and tender food, and carries and caresses it in her arms."[2]

In Book One of *The Ascent of Mount Carmel*, after John analyzes the harm engendered by our disordered appetites, he stresses that human willpower is insufficient to enter into the purifying path toward freedom from selfish desire. He emphasizes that "a more intense enkindling of another, better love, for Christ the Beloved is necessary for the vanquishing of the appetites and denial of this pleasure."[3] "The grace of God acts just as a loving mother by re-engendering in the soul new enthusiasm and fervor in the service of God."[4] John is wise; we cannot begin the journey of evangelical conversion without an experience of God's personal love for us that ignites our desire to respond to His love. We can compare it to the experience of two people falling in love. Without the fire of romantic love, the couple would not begin their journey toward marriage or persevere through the challenges of family life.[5]

The night of the spirit is deeper purification of the roots of our disorders and transforms us on the spiritual level of our being.

[2] John, *CW*, *The Dark Night*, Book 1, chap. 1, no. 2.

[3] John, *CW*, *The Ascent of Mount Carmel*, Book 1, chap. 14, no. 2.

[4] John, *CW*, *The Dark Night*, Book 1, chap. 1, no. 2.

[5] "The soul, then, states that 'fired with love's urgent longings' it passed through this night of sense to union with the Beloved. A love of pleasure, and attachment to it, usually fires the will toward the enjoyment of things that give pleasure. A more intense enkindling of another, better love (love of the soul's

John describes the spiritual life of these beginners. They give themselves enthusiastically to the life of prayer. Discursive meditation is delightful and easy for them, so they can spend long hours in prayer, even entire nights. "Penances are pleasures; fasts, happiness; and the sacraments and spiritual conversations are consolations."[6] Like the young rich man in the gospel, they are fervent and full of zeal for God; however, all is not well deeper within their spiritual life. There are levels of our psyche—past emotional wounds, selfish attitudes, personality characteristics and flaws—that may remain partly or completely unconscious. As we enter deeper into prayer, the Holy Spirit enlightens us to this inner world. This becomes clearer as John uncovers the motivation of these "beginners."

The problem with these beginners, as John perceives them, is "childishness," an egocentric behavior that he describes as a "base manner of loving."[7] We can translate John's description, "base manner of loving," as a dysfunctional or selfish way of loving.[8] The beginners are primarily motivated in their spiritual practices by the delights and

---

Bridegroom) is necessary for the vanquishing of the appetites and the denial of this pleasure. By finding satisfaction and strength in this love, it will have the courage and constancy to readily deny all other appetites. The love of its Bridegroom is not the only requisite for conquering the strength of the sensitive appetites; an enkindling with urgent longings of love is also necessary. For the sensory appetites are moved and attracted toward sensory objects with such cravings that if the spiritual part of the soul is not fired with other, more urgent longings for spiritual things, the soul will be able neither to overcome the yoke of nature nor to enter the night of sense; nor will it have the courage to live in the darkness of all things by denying its appetites for them" (John, *CW, The Ascent of Mount Carmel*, Book 1, chap. 14, no. 2). John emphasizes the importance of some experience of God's love in order to begin the spiritual journey in Stanza 1 of *The Spiritual Canticle*, where the soul is "wounded" by the Beloved and that begins the journey. The "wound" is a metaphor of an experience of God's love that initiates the journey toward union with the Beloved (John, *CW, The Spiritual Canticle*, Stanza 1, no. 1).

[6] John, *CW, The Dark Night*, Book 1, chap. 1, no. 3.

[7] John, *CW, The Dark Night*, Book 1, chap. 8, no. 3.

[8] John describes the egotistic way of loving as "base manner of loving" ("bajo modo de amor"). A more contemporary way of interpreting "base manner of loving" is dysfunctional way of loving.

consolations they derive from them rather than the desire to please God. "Since their motivation in their spiritual works and exercises is the consolation and satisfaction they experience in them, and since they have not been conditioned by the arduous struggle of practicing virtue, they possess many faults and imperfections in the discharge of their spiritual activities."[9] The key image to describe the immaturity and egotism of these beginners is that of a child being weaned from a mother's breast.[10] God must begin a process of purifying their desires and attachment to spiritual consolations much like a mother who must wean her child from her sweet breast so that the child can begin to walk on its own feet and put away the habit of childhood.[11]

Beneath the surface of their enthusiasm and search for God is an innate selfishness, much of which is unconscious. What makes their interior situation more serious than those John writes about in Book One of *The Ascent of Mount Carmel* is that the objects of their disordered desires are no longer riches, material possession, pleasures, food, sex, or honors; rather, they are pious observances, desires for sanctity, spiritual experiences, and immature images of God. The same disordered appetites and vices are at work yet camouflaged under the desire for perfection.[12] With profound psychological insight, John leads us into the deeper motivational level of the human person that requires the purification of desire. John's purpose in analyzing the disorders of these beginners is not to makes us feel guilty, but to show the absolute necessity of God's intervention to heal and transform us.

---

[9] John, *CW*, *The Dark Night*, Book 1, chap. 1, no. 3.

[10] The image of God's grace as a "loving mother" serves not only as a way of demonstrating the immaturity of beginners, but also as a way to illustrate how God educates us. God deals with us according to our nature. He first meets us at the level of the senses and then gradually weans us from sensory satisfaction to a more substantial and deeper relationship of love that is not dependent upon spiritual consolations and delights. This image is central to Book 1 of *The Dark Night*. It is an image of growth and maturity in the spiritual life.

[11] John, *CW*, *The Dark Night*, Book 1, chap. 1, no. 2; chap. 8, no. 3.

[12] Federico Ruiz, *Místico y Maestro San Juan de la Cruz*, 2nd ed. (Madrid: Editorial de Espiritualidad, 2006), 244. Cf. M. del Sagrario Rollán Rollán, *Éxtasis y purificación del deseo: Análisis psicológico existencial de la noche en la obra de San Juan de la Cruz* (Avila: Disputación Provincial de Avila, 1991).

The Seven Capital Vices: A Dysfunctional Manner of Loving

Before John discusses how God heals us in the transforming dark night, he analyzes the ways in which immature and unconscious selfishness may be manifested in our lives. To do so, he draws upon the traditional seven capital vices as a framework: pride, avarice, lust, anger, gluttony, envy, and sloth. The seven capital vices are unwholesome mindstates, emotions, and obsessive thinking patterns. They are the antipathy of mature love and humility.

Traditionally speaking, the seven capital vices are not sins in the sense of a conscious and voluntary sinful act. Rather, they are fundamental tendencies, afflictive thoughts, and emotions that lead to evil if not restrained.[13] These tendencies have their roots deep within our spiritual nature, beyond what we are conscious of, and this is why the grace of purification is necessary.

The Greek Fathers considered the capital vices as "sicknesses of the soul" contracted as a consequence of original sin.[14] Evagrius of Pontus in his writings and Jean Cassian in both his *Conferences* and *Institutes* described the capital vices as *"logismoi,"* understood as "thoughts" or "passions" (emotions) that afflict us. The Desert Fathers and Mothers knew well the human psyche and the thoughts and emotions that cloud our heart and reason. Coming from the desert experience, Cassian and Evagrius described the *logismoi* as eight in number: gluttony, fornication, avarice, anger, dejection (sadness), acedia (boredom), vainglory, and pride. Later on, Pope Gregory the Great changed eight capital sins into to seven sins. He combined vainglory and pride into pride, inserted dejection into acedia, and added the sin of envy. This is the list we know today.[15] The Greek Fathers analyzed the

---

[13] Aimé Solignac, "Péchés Capitaux," *Dictionnaire de Spiritualité*, XIII (1986), 1236.

[14] Jean-Claude Larchet, *Thérapeutique des maladies spirituelles* (Paris: Éditons du Cerf, 1997), 131.

[15] Lawrence S. Cunningham, *The Seven Deadly Sins: A Visitor's Guide* (Notre Dame, IN: Ave Maria Press, 2012), 2–4. See also Mary Margaret Funk, OSB, *Thoughts Matter* (New York: Continuum, 1998), 13–25. Funk's presentation of

logismoi minutely and concretely in order to prescribe the right remedy to regain one's health.

Like the Greek fathers, John analyzes these maladies of the soul.[16] Rich in psychological insight, his diagnosis of the seven capital vices reveals the moral and affective basis that underlies his teaching in *The Ascent of Mount Carmel*. However, when we read John's descriptions of the seven capital vices we must keep in mind that he analyzes them from a monastic environment, as present in people who are striving to live serious spiritual lives. Some of his examples may not apply to our concrete life situations, but a closer examination of the way the vices are manifested in our lives reveals that most apply to the spiritual life of serious seekers of God.

Pride

Although these beginners are fervent in their spiritual exercises, hidden within them lies a secret pride that leads to a pattern of behavior characterized by an exaggerated image of themselves and vanity in their spiritual life. In order to exalt and draw attention to themselves, their vanity leads them to speak of spiritual things in the presence of others and the desire to teach others rather than to be instructed. They condemn others who don't measure up to their expectations of holiness, and sometimes they give expression to this criticism like the Pharisee who despised the publican while he boasted and praised God for the good deeds he himself accomplished.[17]

---

thoughts is a helpful way to understand the seven capital vices and John's teaching on the seven capital vices of beginners.

[16] However, John admits that his analysis of these imperfections is not exhaustive. For instance, he writes concerning spiritual gluttony: "These people incur many other imperfections because of this spiritual gluttony, of which the Lord in time will cure them through temptations, aridities, and other trials, which are all a part of the dark night. So as not to be too lengthy, I do not want to discuss these imperfections any more, but only point out that spiritual sobriety and temperance beget another very different quality, one of mortification, fear, and submissiveness in all things" (John, *CW*, *The Dark Night*, Book 1, chap. 6, no. 8).

[17] John, *CW*, *The Dark Night*, Book 1, chap. 2, no. 1.

John's comparison of beginners to the Pharisee in the Gospel portrays the disorder underlying their behavior: an idealized self-image that leads to the condemnation and disparagement of others. This is what Jesus condemned in the Gospel story of the Pharisee and the publican. Apparently unconscious of his sinfulness and misery, the Pharisee exalted himself and condemned the publican who recognized his sinfulness and humbly acknowledged it before God. In exalting himself, the Pharisee separated himself from the rest of humanity. Not only does this show his lack of charity but, implicitly, it is a denial of his own sinful dark side. Thus do these beginners play the Pharisee. "Some of these persons become so evil-minded that they do not want anyone except themselves to appear holy; and so by both word and deed they condemn and detract others whenever the occasion arises, seeing the little splinter in their brother's eye and failing to consider the wooden beam in their own eye [Mt. 7:3]; they strain at the other's gnat and swallow their own camel [Mt. 23:24]."[18]

Their desire to be esteemed and praised, and their aversion to praising others, also manifest their selfish pride. They want others to recognize their spirit and devotion and even contrive to manifest it by movements, sighs and other ceremonies.

Underneath their pride system lies a deep insecurity: the fear of exposing the impoverished and sinful side of their personality for fear of shattering the image of holiness they have built for themselves and wish to convey to others. Fundamentally, they are afraid to present themselves before God in their truth, in all their poverty, woundedness, and imperfections. This is manifested in their relationship with their confessors and spiritual directors. For instance, they have a great fear of being questioned or criticized. If their spiritual director or superior questions their method of procedure or disapproves of their spirit, they go in search of another more to their

---

[18] John, *CW*, *The Dark Night*, Book 1, chap. 2, no. 2. It is worthy of note that John uses the biblical character of the Pharisee in chapter 28 of Book 3 of *The Ascent of Mount Carmel* to describe the lack of charity due to vain joy in one's works and customs. Here, however, his application is more subtle and applied to a monastic environment. Yet we have the same disorder at work.

liking. Furthermore, they hide from their confessors certain sins and present themselves in a favorable light, which reveals their fear of exposing their weaknesses and sinful patterns and the effort to maintain at all costs their idealized self-image.[19]

They also become impatient and angry with themselves when they don't measure up to the idealized image of holiness they have painted for themselves. The want to be saints in a day. Furthermore, they dislike praising anyone else, but love to receive praise, and sometimes seek it. John compares them to the foolish virgins who had to seek oil from others when their own lamps were diminishing (Matt 25:8).[20]

After exposing the prideful sins of these beginners, John describes those who are advancing in perfection and who manifest a different quality of spirit. They do not compare themselves with others but have a humble opinion of themselves; they accept themselves as they are and don't exaggerate the good that they do. Their charity and humility inspire them to serve God without the desire to be recognized by others. They have a spirit of docility and the willingness to be taught by others rather than to teach others.[21] "When they see themselves fall into imperfections, they suffer them with humility, with docility of spirit, and with loving fear of God and hope in him."[22]

---

[19] John, *CW, The Dark Night*, Book 1, chap. 2, no. 4. "Many want to be the favorites of their confessors, and thus they are consumed by a thousand envies and disquietudes. Embarrassment forbids them from relating their sins clearly, lest their reputation diminish in their confessor's eyes. They confess their sins in the most favorable light so as to appear better than they actually are, and thus they approach the confessional to excuse themselves rather than accuse themselves. Sometimes they confess the evil things they do to a different confessor so that their own confessor might think they commit no sins at all. Therefore, in their desire to appear holy, they enjoy relating their good behavior to their confessor, and in such careful terms that these good deeds appear greater than they actually are. It would be more humble of them, as we will point out later, to make light of the good they do and to wish that no one, neither their confessor nor anybody else, should consider it of any importance at all" (John, *CW, The Dark Night*, Book 1, chap. 2, no. 4).

[20] John, *CW, The Dark Night*, Book 1, chap. 2, no. 5.
[21] John, *CW, The Dark Night*, Book 1, chap. 2, no. 6.
[22] John, *CW, The Dark Night*, Book 1, chap. 2, no. 8.

John's analysis of the spiritual pride exposes the principal and gravest obstacle of all the spiritual vices, that is, the narcissistic fixation on the "I." This fixation is an appetite that is as strong as an iron cable, and until it is broken it is impossible for the spirit to fly to God.[23] Pride is ultimately a form of self-love that is the antipathy of authentic love of God, self, and others. The proud person cannot move beyond himself or herself. They fail to realize that they are radically dependent upon God, who is the Source of their being. Every characteristic of these people demonstrates their fundamental lack of love: condemning and judging others, desiring to be esteemed and first in all situations, being impatient and angry at others because they don't meet their expectations of holiness, and being angry and impatient with themselves because of their failures and imperfections. They desire to become saints in a day. By failing to accept their own weak human condition, they separate themselves from the rest of humanity and become imprisoned in a prideful stance contrary to Gospel love. John acknowledges that very few people are so perfect in the beginning to escape the sin of spiritual pride. God must purify them, which he will do, by placing them into the dark night.[24]

Spiritual Avarice

If there is one expression for those who fall into the second capital vice of avarice (greed) it is "never enough." The spiritual life of these people rests on consolations and externals. They are never satisfied with the spirit God gives them.[25] Their craving is not for riches, honors, or material things, but rather for spiritual experiences. They become discouraged and restless when they don't find the consolation they desire in prayer, in community, or in their ministry. They can never hear enough spiritual counsels, read enough spiritual books,

---

[23] Fernando Urbina, *Comentario a Noche oscura del espíritu y Subida del espíritu y Subida al Monte Carmelo de San Juan de la Cruz* (Madrid: Ediciones Marova, 1982), 50.

[24] John, *CW, The Dark Night*, Book 1, chap. 2, no. 8.

[25] John, *CW, The Dark Night*, Book 1, chap. 3, no. 1.

or collect enough pious maxims. Their piety rests on externals, what glitters and shines, rather than on a deeper relationship with God through authentic self-denial, growth in virtue, and the willingness to please and serve God and others even when they lack enthusiasm and feel spiritually dry.

John gives examples of spiritual avarice: the tendency to amass medals, rosaries, and decorated images, and to look more to the craftsmanship of religious art than to what it represents. What John criticizes is the possessiveness of heart and attachment to the external value rather than to the substance of devotion. In this sense, they lack poverty of spirit. For John, true devotion comes from the heart and seeks to please God alone and not oneself; it looks only to the truth and substance of spiritual objects.[26] We should know the difference between sacred objects and images and the Holy One they represent.[27] According to John, the avaricious base their value on craftsmanship and beauty of religious objects rather than on the Creator. Everything is on the exterior and revolves around the desire for spiritual consolations.

How do we apply the vice of spiritual avarice today? First of all, sensible consolations in prayer can be profoundly pleasurable and satisfying. Although God graces us with consolations in the early stages of the spiritual journey to ignite within us fervor and determination to let go of what obstructs us from making God the center of our lives, we can become strongly attached to the sense pleasure of consolations and go to prayer for the consolations of prayer rather than to please God and to do God's will. We see spiritual avarice in the fascination for apparitions of the Blessed Virgin Mary or other extraordinary phenomena. It is the same with apostolic activities. What motivates us in our apostolic activity—our need for sensible

---

[26] John, *CW*, *The Dark Night*, Book 1, chap. 3, no. 1.

[27] John's doctrine on spiritual avarice is similar to what he teaches in Book 3 of *The Ascent of Mount Carmel*, chaps. 34–45, where he discusses the use of spiritual goods such as statues, paintings, places of prayer, ceremonies, devotions, and sermons. Much of his emphasis on spiritual avarice reflects the baroque, ornate architecture and art of his period, when emphasis was placed on beauty and exquisite art rather than on the deeper significance, on God and our relationship with him.

consolations and recognition, or a desire to please God and those we serve?

Furthermore, we live in a secularistic society where the more we possess, the more we feel fulfilled. We are never satisfied with what we have. We may not cling to spiritual books, rosaries, or elaborate crucifixes, but to social media, cell phones, text messages, and the latest computer technology. Our attachment may be to the glitter and consolation of what we do and our work projects. Even the glitter of apostolic works can entice us, rather than the quality of our ministry and relationships. Workaholism can be a form of avarice. We may forget that there exists a hierarchy of values in our activities, work projects, and even the apostolate, such as being present to people, friendship, and prayer. The substance of good works and ministry is not the number of good things we do, but being present to God's people in a loving and healing way and doing what we can. What really satisfies our heart? This is the question regarding avarice.

John ends his description of the vice of avarice with a consoling word. It is God who must heal us of this imperfection and others. Even though we have our part to play to break free from these vices, God must intervene through the dark night. "In this cure God will heal them of what through their own efforts they were unable to remedy." No matter how much we may do through our own efforts, we cannot actively purify ourselves enough to be disposed in the least degree of divine union. God must take over and purge us in the dark fire of his purifying love.[28]

Spiritual Lust

For the most part, John's treatment of spiritual lust does not correspond to the description of a spiritual vice that produces a moral deformation and obstacle to spiritual development, as in other chapters concerning the seven capital vices. Actually, his description and the meaning of "spiritual lust" is somewhat obscure and difficult to grasp,

---

[28] John, *CW*, *The Dark Night*, Book 1, chap. 3, no. 3.

especially in light of our understanding of lust as primarily disordered sexual desire. Fundamentally, lust is disordered desire and does not always refer to sexual desire. We can lust for power, money, prestige, food, sex, and alcohol. John refers to "spiritual lust" not because lust is spiritual, but because it proceeds from spiritual practices.[29] John discusses a psychological phenomenon that is common as we grow in contemplative prayer due to a lack of psychic integration. Without any fault on their part, these beginners may experience what John defines as "impure movements" in silent prayer, or when receiving the sacraments of penance and the Eucharist. These impure movements can arise from three causes that are outside our control.

The first cause is a lack of psychic integration. As previously discussed, John understands the human person as "one suppositum," as mind-body-spirit unity. Because of the substantial unity of the human person as an incarnate spirit there exists an intercommunication between the various dimensions of our person. What is experienced on the spiritual or psychological level will have repercussions in the body and our emotional life, and vice versa. Because of this substantial unity, it is not uncommon to feel sensual, sexual stirrings in quiet prayer and other spiritual practices. What is experienced in the spirit overflows and is felt in the senses. "Since, after all, these two parts form one suppositum, each one usually shares according to the mode in what other receives."[30] The phenomenon John describes is a lack of integration of the unity of the person, whereby sexual feelings and desires may surface in prayer and cause discomfort and confusion. "It may happen that while a soul is with God in deep spiritual prayer, it will conversely passively experience sensual rebellions, movements, and acts in the senses, without its own great displeasure."[31]

---

[29] John, *CW, The Dark Night*, Book 1, chap. 4, no. 1.
[30] John, *CW, The Dark Night*, Book 1, chap. 4, no. 2.
[31] "This frequently happens at the time of Communion. Since the soul receives joy and gladness in this act of love—for the Lord grants the grace and gives himself for this reason—the sensory part also takes its share, as we said, according to its mode. Since, after all, these two parts form one suppositum, each one usually shares according to its mode in what the other receives. As the Philosopher says: Whatever is received, is received according to the mode of the receiver."

Sexual thoughts and feelings in themselves are not sinful. Sexuality is an essential and sacred part of our humanity. It is the energy we need for relationships. Integrating sexuality into the whole of our person is a lifelong process. When we are relaxed and quiet in prayer, the deeper levels of the unconscious—thoughts, feelings and emotions such as sexual desires, greed, anger, envy, or doubt—may surface because there is a whole world of thoughts, memories, and emotions lying deeper than we are conscious of.

John attributes the second cause to the devil who wants to disquiet and upset the soul through the thoughts and emotions that cause us doubt or fear to the point that we may be tempted to abandon prayer. Whether it is "objective" evil or what we would define in modern psychology as our "shadow side," John understands that unintegrated parts of our personality, sexuality being one, can surface, disquiet us, and cause scrupulosity and fear.[32] John addresses a phenomenon of

---

Because in the initial stages of the spiritual life, and even more advanced ones, the sensory part of the soul is imperfect, God's spirit is frequently received in this sensory part with this same imperfection. Once the sensory part is reformed through the purgation of the dark night, it no longer has these infirmities. Then the spiritual part of the soul, rather than the sensory part, receives God's spirit, and the soul thus receives everything according to the mode of the spirit" (John, *CW, The Dark Night*, Book 1, chap. 4, no. 2).

[32] John, *CW, The Dark Night*, Book 1, chap. 4, no. 3. "The second origin of these rebellions is the devil. To bring disquietude and disturbance on a soul when it is praying, or trying to pray, he endeavors to excite impure feelings in the sensory part. And if people pay any attention to these, the devil does them great harm. Through fear, some souls grow slack in their prayer—which is what the devil wants—in order to struggle against these movements, and others give it up entirely, for they think these feelings come while they are engaged in prayer rather than at other times. And this is true because the devil excites these feelings while souls are at prayer, instead of when they are engaged in other works, so that they might abandon prayer. And that is not all; to make them cowardly and afraid, he brings vividly to their minds foul and impure thoughts. And sometimes the thoughts will concern spiritually helpful things and persons. Those who attribute any importance to such thoughts, therefore, do not even dare look at anything or think about anything lest they thereupon stumble into them.

"These impure thoughts so affect people who are afflicted with melancholia that one should have great pity for them; indeed, these people suffer a sad life. In some who are troubled with this bad humor the trial reaches such a point that

the spiritual life and teaching that is paramount for us to grasp if we are to progress without becoming discouraged—the world of thoughts and how we relate to our thoughts that arise in quiet prayer and other activities.

Consciously or unconsciously, thinking and discursive reasoning pervade our lives. People often confess that when they pray the rosary, meditate, or attend Mass, they have various thoughts that disturb their peace and recollection. They feel responsible in some way for their thoughts and distractions. The fact is, we cannot control our thoughts or what surfaces in our mind during prayer or in daily life. What matters is how we relate to our thought process. We tend to identify with our thoughts, and this causes problems. For instance, if an angry or sexual thought arises, we may think, "I'm an angry person" or "I'm a lustful person," rather than realize that a thought is simply a thought. We are not "anger" or "lust," but we have thoughts of anger or lust and can gently let them pass as best we can. When they arise again, we can acknowledge them in a gentle way and then let them pass.

John writes that "those who attribute any importance to such thoughts, therefore, do not even dare look at anything or think about anything lest they thereupon stumble into them."[33] The key phrase is "attribute any importance to such thoughts." John realizes that there are personalities who tend toward scrupulosity, depression, or hypersensitivity and become easily disturbed by their thoughts. Thoughts, feelings, and memories of the past can "wage a war" within us and provoke fear or guilt. What is important is to disidentify with our thoughts, not to judge ourselves or become discouraged because of the nature of our thoughts. By becoming aware of our thoughts in a gentle way, refusing to identify with them, and letting them pass as

---

they clearly feel that the devil has access to them without their having the freedom to prevent it. Yet some of these melancholiacs are able through intense effort and struggle to forestall this power of the devil. If these impure thoughts and feelings arise from melancholia, individuals are not ordinarily freed from them until they are cured of that humor—unless they enter the dark night, which in time deprives them of everything" (John, *CW*, *The Dark Night*, Book 1, chap. 4, no. 3).

[33] John, *CW*, *The Dark Night*, Book 1, chap. 4, no. 3.

best we can with God's grace, we become quieter and still. We are not our thoughts; we cannot control our thoughts, but we can relate to them in a nonclinging way and realize that we are deeper than any thought that arises. In this way, we avoid falling into negative thinking and the temptation to abandon prayer. One way from the desert tradition to deal with our thoughts is to change the disturbing thought with a prayer, like the Jesus Prayer or some short verse from the Psalms: "God come to my assistance; O Lord make haste to help me."[34]

Another area of spiritual lust John addresses is our attraction and liking for other people.

> Some spiritually acquire a liking for other individuals that often arises from lust rather than the spirit. This lustful origin will be recognized if, on recalling that affection, there is remorse of conscience, not an increase in the remembrance and love of God. The affection is purely spiritual if the love of God grows when it grows, or if the love of God is remembered as often as the affection is remembered, or if the affection gives the soul a desire for God—if by growing in one the soul grows also in the other. For this is a trait of God's spirit: The good increases with the good since there is likeness and conformity between them. But when the love is born of this sensual vice it has the contrary effects. As the one love grows greater, the other lessens, and the remembrance of it lessens too.[35]

We are relational beings; we long for friendship and intimacy with other people. We can be attracted to people for various reasons: their physical appearance, natural gifts and talents, a certain charismatic personality, or just something about the person that draws us to them and remains a mystery. Why one person attracts us more than another is a mystery. Infatuation is an example of strong attraction to someone based on physical qualities and a superficial knowledge of the person.

---

[34] Regarding training our thoughts and how they relate to the capital vices, I recommend Mary Margaret Funk, OSB, *Thoughts Matter: The Practice of the Spiritual Life*.

[35] John, *CW*, *The Dark Night*, Book 1, chap. 4, no. 7.

John of the Cross was aware of this dynamic. For John, our attraction is motivated by "lust" when the relationship does not increase within us the remembrance of God and an increased desire to love God. However, the way John uses the word *lust* in this context does not necessarily mean the desire for sexual intimacy with someone but rather means "disordered desire"—that is, desire fueled more by a focus on oneself and one's affective needs.

When the friendship draws us to a deeper love for God, it is spiritual because it is rooted in God and helps each person to grow in affective maturity and closer to God. John recognizes that affective maturity is part of the spiritual path. This is why the dark night experience is necessary to purify our desires and to order them in accord with God's love. "When the soul enters the dark night, all these loves are placed in reasonable order. This night strengthens and purifies the love that is of God and takes away and destroys the other."[36]

We see an example of the purification of the desire for love and friendship in the life of St. Teresa of Jesus. She struggled for many years to resolve her affective disorder. Teresa had a great capacity for friendship, to love and be loved, but it had a dark underside. It often led her to live outside herself in other people at the expense of her own inner truth. She tells us that she was divided between "God and the world."[37] The world for St. Teresa was not the external world, but the inner world of her disordered longings to be loved through superficial friendships. Teresa learned the lesson that all of us must learn in life: Only God can ultimately satisfy our desire for love and emotional fulfillment. No human being, even those who are dearest to us and love us unconditionally, can quench our thirst for love and meaning. She explains this struggle in *The Book of Her Life*:

> I had a serious fault that did me much harm; it was that when I began to know that certain persons liked me, and I found them

---

[36] John, *CW*, *The Dark Night*, Book 1, chap. 4, no. 8.
[37] Teresa of Avila, *The Book of Her Life*, chap. 7, no. 17, in *The Collected Works of St. Teresa of Avila*, vol. 1, trans. Kieran Kavanaugh and Otilio Rodriguez (Washington, DC: ICS Publications, 1976).

attractive, I became so attached that my memory was bound strongly by the thought of them. There was no intention to offend God, but I was happy to see these persons and think about them and about the good things I saw in them. This was something so harmful it was leading my soul seriously astray. After I beheld the extraordinary beauty of the Lord, I didn't see anyone who in comparison with Him seemed to attract me or occupy my thoughts. By turning my gaze just a little inward to behold the image I have in my soul, I obtained such freedom in this respect that everything I see here below seems loathsome when compared to the excelling and beautiful qualities I beheld in this Lord.[38]

The loving gaze of the risen Lord Jesus healed Teresa's affective disorder. John tells us, once more, that only God's cure that comes through the dark night can purify our affectivity and order our love so that our relationships are rooted in evangelical love.

Anger

"Because of their strong desire for spiritual gratification, many beginners become angry when they are left without consolation in spiritual practices. When they experience dryness after a period of delightful prayer, they become easily irritated at the least thing. They can become so unbearable that it is hard to put up with them. They are like a child that becomes restless and angry when removed from its mother's breast."[39]

---

[38] Teresa of Avila, *The Book of Her Life*, chap. 37, no. 4. St. Teresa testifies to her affective conversion in 1556 when the Lord gave her the freedom to break free from superficial friendships that prevented her complete surrender to the Lord. "These words have been fulfilled, for I have never again been able to tie myself to any friendship or to find consolation in or bear particular love for any other persons than those I understand love Him and strive to serve Him; nor is it in my power to do so, nor does it matter whether they are friends or relatives. If I'm not aware that the persons seek to love and serve God or to speak about prayer, it is a painful cross for me to deal with them. To the best of my knowledge this is most certainly true" (Teresa of Avila, *The Book of Her Life*, chap. 24, no. 6). True friendships rooted in her love for Christ began at that moment.

[39] John, *CW*, *The Dark Night*, Book 1, chap. 5, no. 1.

John doesn't condemn the fact that anger and aggressivity are present. His concern is how people react to the anger that arises from the absence of consolation. "These souls are not at fault if they do not allow this dejection to influence them, for it is an imperfection that must be purged through the dryness and distress of the dark night."[40]

Among these spiritual persons are those who direct their anger toward others. Considering themselves to be lords of virtue, their indiscreet zeal pushes them to lash out in anger over the sins of others and to correct them angrily. This reveals their need to be superior, "holier than thou," and also their lack of understanding, patience, tolerance, and compassion for the faults of others. This is contrary to spiritual meekness.

The same anger and impatience toward others' faults are also directed toward their own weak human nature. "In becoming aware of their own imperfections, they grow angry with themselves in an unhumble impatience."[41] They want be saints in a day. Because they possess an exaggerated opinion of their spiritual development and are afraid to recognize and accept their imperfections, they make unrealistic resolves, only to resort to the vicious cycle of anger, impatience, and self-condemnation. "Many of these beginners make numerous plans and great resolutions, but since they are not humble and have no distrust of themselves, the more resolves they make the more they break, and the greater becomes their anger. They do not have the patience to wait until God gives them what they need, when he so desires."[42]

Spiritual Gluttony

John introduces the vice of spiritual gluttony by saying that there is hardly any beginner who does not fall into this vice. Normally, when we think of gluttony we think of a disordered appetite for food

---

[40] John, *CW*, *The Dark Night*, Book 1, chap. 5, no. 1.
[41] John, *CW*, *The Dark Night*, Book 1, chap. 5, no. 3.
[42] John, *CW*, *The Dark Night*, Book 1, chap. 5, no. 3.

or drink. John brings this vice to the spiritual world: gluttony for sensible satisfaction derived from spiritual practices, including the Eucharist.

People afflicted with spiritual gluttony, like those afflicted with avarice, are fixated on self-gratification and feelings in their spiritual exercises and forget that the essence of the spiritual life is pleasing God and not oneself. They go to the extremes and strive more for sensible satisfaction in their spiritual exercises than for spiritual purity and discretion.[43]

The examples John gives of this vice come primarily from a monastic environment. Their desire for spiritual consolations is so extreme that "they kill themselves with penances, and others weaken themselves by fasts; they overtax their weakness."[44] He describes these gluttonous people in strong terms: as beasts who "are motivated in these penances by an appetite of pleasure."[45]

Underneath spiritual gluttony lies a strong willfulness and pride, which is contrary to obedience and docility. John emphasizes obedience as the mark of an authentic spirit. These beginners find it difficult to be docile, to submit to reason, and to obey, which pleases God more than corporal penances. "Corporal penance without obedience is no more than a penance of beasts. . . . Since all extremes are vicious and since by such behavior these persons are doing their own will, they grow in vice rather than in virtue. For through this conduct they at least become spiritually gluttonous and proud since they do not tread the path of obedience."[46]

Their willful pride reveals their immaturity. They are like children who insist on following their own will and opinion. They become sad and go about like testy children, discouraged if their spiritual directors refuse them permission to follow their own will and inclinations for penances and excesses in the spiritual life.

---

[43] John, *CW*, *The Dark Night*, Book 1, chap. 6, no. 1.
[44] John, *CW*, *The Dark Night*, Book 1, chap. 6, no. 1.
[45] John, *CW*, *The Dark Night*, Book 1, chap. 6, no. 2.
[46] John, *CW*, *The Dark Night*, Book 1, chap. 6, no. 2.

For instance, if their confessors do not allow them to receive frequent Communion, they boldly insist on it. They even dare to receive Communion without their confessor's permission.[47] Their motivation for frequent Communion comes from the desire for sensible consolation rather than to receive Communion with a pure and perfect heart.

> In receiving Communion they spend all their time trying to get some feeling and satisfaction rather than humbly praising and reverencing God dwelling within them. . . . Not only in receiving Communion, but in other spiritual exercises as well, beginners desire to feel God and taste him as if he were comprehensible and accessible. This desire is a serious imperfection because it involves impurity of faith, is opposed to God's way.[48]

The example of frequent Communion is inapplicable today because frequent Communion is encouraged and many people receive the Eucharist daily. However, there are people who want to perform extra ascetical practices such as fasting or practice excessive devotions, and when their spiritual directors counsel fewer ascetical practices and more fidelity to practicing virtue in daily life, they resist and impose their own will. Even though some of John's examples are inapplicable today, what does apply—and this is his point—is the warning against willfulness and lack of docility in accepting spiritual guidance, and against the selfish motivation underlying spiritual practices and receiving the sacraments.

John's reference to "impurity of faith" is an important element of his doctrine. God is both intimate to us—that is, the ground of our being—but also transcendent and beyond what we feel, image, and understand with our intellect. John insists that we cannot evaluate our experience of God by our sensory satisfaction or even dryness;

---

[47] John's examples of permission for frequent Communion comes from the sixteenth-century practice of requesting permission to receive the Eucharist. This was a completely different sacramental theology than today's. The point John is making is the strong attachment to one's own will and opinion, and reluctance to practice obedience, which is the humble path that is pleasing to God.

[48] John, *CW, The Dark Night*, Book 1, chap. 6, no. 5.

thus faith, which is obscure to us, is the path to union with God through love.[49]

The same defect is present in these beginners' prayer. They think the whole matter of prayer consists in looking for sensory satisfaction and devotion. When they fail to receive the spiritual gratification they long for in prayer, they become disconsolate and think they have done nothing. They forget that true devotion consists in distrust of self and humble and patient perseverance so as to please God.

Spiritual Envy and Sloth

The last two vices that many beginners struggle with are envy and sloth. In regard to envy, many feel sad about the spiritual advancement of others and experience sensitive grief in noting that their neighbors are further along on the spiritual path than they. Because they are always comparing themselves with others, they are never satisfied with

---

[49] John expresses this clearly in Stanza 1 of *The Spiritual Canticle*: "It is noteworthy that, however elevated God's communications and the experiences of his presence are, and however sublime a person's knowledge of him may be, these are not God essentially, nor are they comparable to him because, indeed, he is still hidden to the soul. Hence, regardless of all these lofty experiences, a person should think of him as hidden and seek him as one who is hidden, saying: 'Where have You hidden?'

"Neither the sublime communication nor the sensible awareness of his nearness is a sure testimony of his gracious presence, nor are dryness and the lack of these a reflection of his absence. As a result, the prophet Job exclaims: If he comes to me I shall not see him, and if he goes away I shall not understand [Jb. 9:11].

"It must be understood that if a person experiences some elevated spiritual communication or feeling or knowledge, it should not be thought that the experiences are similar to the clear and essential vision or possession of God, or that the communication, no matter how remarkable it is, signifies a more notable possession of God or union with him. It should be known too that if all these sensible and spiritual communications are wanting and individuals live in dryness, darkness, and dereliction, they must not thereby think that God is any more absent than in the former case. People, actually, cannot have certain knowledge from the one state that they are in God's grace or from the other that they are not. As the Wise Man says, *We do not know if we are worthy of love or abhorrence before God* [Eccl. 9:1]" (*CW*, *The Spiritual Canticle*, Stanza 1, no. 4).

what God has given them, so they feel sad. Furthermore, they cannot spontaneously rejoice in the virtues and happiness of others, nor can they bear to hear others praised without contradicting and undoing compliments. In other words, they undermine the goodness of others. They long for preference in everything. They lack evangelical charity which rejoices in the good of others. "All of this is contrary to charity, which, as St. Paul says, rejoices in the truth (1 Cor. 13:6)."[50]

With the envious, therefore, we find a deep dissatisfaction with God, themselves, and others that is manifested in a spirit of rivalry, competition, and disparagement of others—all of which is contrary to evangelical love.

Spiritual sloth, or what we also call *acedia*, is a consequence of spiritual greed. The slothful are enslaved by their selfish desires for sensory satisfaction rather than by reason and obedience and a mature adult commitment. Consequently, they easily lose energy and commitment in the spiritual life when prayer, ministry, and daily duties become dry and difficult. "These beginners usually become weary in exercises that are more spiritual and flee from them since these exercises are contrary to sensory satisfaction."[51]

If prayer becomes dry and distasteful, they either abandon it, or they pray begrudgingly. Furthermore, they want God to fulfill their own desires. They are like children who become saddened when they have to surrender their will to God's will. They frequently believe that what is not their will, or what does not bring them satisfaction, is not God's will; on the other hand, they believe that if they are satisfied, God is too. "They measure God by themselves, and not themselves by God, which is in opposition to his teaching in the Gospel that those who lose their life for his sake, will gain it and those who gain it will lose it."[52]

Not only in prayer, but in other areas of life, the slothful have an aversion to the unpleasant and difficult realities of life. Their aversion

---

[50] John, *CW, The Dark Night*, Book 1, chap. 7, no. 1.
[51] John, *CW, The Dark Night*, Book 1, chap. 7, no. 2.
[52] John, *CW, The Dark Night*, Book 1, chap. 7, no. 3.

toward the unpleasant realities of life reveals how pervasive is their attachment to self-gratification and how much they lack fortitude and perseverance in the face of life's difficulties. They are scandalized by the cross.[53]

John's treatment of the imperfections of beginners gives us a profound psychological and moral insight into how he sees the pathology of the human person in concrete existential terms. The disorders of the soul are manifested by a childish immaturity that is fundamentally the antithesis of evangelical charity. He defines this sickness as a "base manner of loving" manifested through the seven capital vices, much of which are unconscious: judging and condemning others, undermining the goodness of others, desiring to be esteemed and preferred in everything, impatient with one's imperfections and those of others, anger, envy, seeking self-gratification in prayer and work, trying to maintain at all costs one's self-image, fearful of confronting the truth of one's own sinfulness.[54] The vices are revealed primarily in relationship to other people rather than in spiritual practices. The sickness of the soul is a wound of love, a lack of Gospel love for God and neighbor. This is a wound that only God can heal. John's purpose in analyzing the seven capital vices is to emphasize our radical dependency upon God's healing grace. Although we must strive to eradicate selfishness from our life, John assures us that, ultimately, only God

---

[53] "Beginners also become bored when told to do something unpleasant. Because they look for spiritual gratifications and delights, they are extremely lax in the fortitude and labor perfection demands. Like those who are reared in luxury, they run sadly from everything rough, and they are scandalized by the cross, in which spiritual delights are found. And in the more spiritual exercises their boredom is greater. Since they expect to go about in spiritual matters according to the whims and satisfactions of their own will, entering by the narrow way of life, about which Christ speaks, is saddening and repugnant to them [Mt. 7:14]" (John, *CW, The Dark Night*, Book 1, chap. 7, no. 4).

[54] "Since the conduct of these beginners in the way of God is lowly and not too distant from love of pleasure and of self, as we explained, God desires to withdraw them from this base manner of loving and lead them on to a higher degree of divine love" (John, *CW, The Dark Night*, Book 1, chap. 8, no. 3).

can heal this sickness through the passive purification of the "dark night of sense and spirit."[55]

Deeper Disorders

In Book Two of *The Dark Night*, John takes us to a deeper level of how he conceives the disorders of the human person in his treatment of the imperfections of those who have advanced in the spiritual life and contemplative prayer through the passive night of the senses. According to John, the passive night of senses covers a long period of purification that leads to deeper self-knowledge gained from combating the capital vices. It brings to light one's deeper motivations, attachments, sinful attitudes, weaknesses, and those undeveloped parts of one's emotional life rooted in one's past. As one of my professors remarked, "The passive night of the senses is simply human maturity, growing up to a more adult spiritual and relational life." Normally, a person passes many years in this passive phase of purification. Like a prisoner who has escaped from a cramped prison cell, they emerge from this period with greater freedom and satisfaction of spirit. Nevertheless, they need a deeper purification due to the very nature of the human person as body-sense-spirit unity. "The purgation of the principal part, that of the spirit, is not complete because of the communication existing between the two parts of the soul that form only one suppositum."[56] Due to the effects of original sin, personal sin, and historical conditioning, our disorders are rooted in

---

[55] "Yet until a soul is placed by God in the passive purgation of that dark night, which we will soon explain, it cannot purify itself completely of these imperfections or others. But people should insofar as possible strive to do their part in purifying and perfecting themselves and thereby merit God's divine cure. In this cure God will heal them of what through their own efforts they were unable to remedy. No matter how much individuals do through their own efforts, they cannot actively purify themselves enough to be disposed in the least degree for the divine union of the perfection of love. God must take over and purge them in that fire that is dark for them, as we will explain" (John, *CW*, *The Dark Night*, Book 1, chap. 3, no. 3; chap. 7, no. 5).

[56] John, *CW*, *The Dark Night*, Book 2, chap. 1, no. 1.

the spirit like an old stain on a piece of clothing, or the roots of an old tree.

> The real purgation of the senses begins with the spirit. Hence the night of the senses we explained should be called a certain reformation and bridling of the appetite rather than a purgation. The reason is that all the imperfections and disorders of the sensory part are rooted in the spirit and from it receive their strength. All good and evil habits reside in the spirit and until these habits are purged, the senses cannot be completely purified of their rebellions and vices.[57]

The sickness of the soul is more radical than psychological and moral failures. Drawing upon Pauline imagery of the "old self," John reminds us how deeply original sin has wounded human nature.[58] Even though we were created in the image and likeness of God, created out of love and for love, our disordered desires, conflicts, and egotism experienced on the sensory level have their origin in the deepest structure of our person; thus, a more profound purification is required. Due to the essential unity of the person, John maintains that the real purgation of the senses begins with the passive purification of the spirit which accommodates and disposes the person for union with God.[59]

If we reflect on our personal experience, we can understand the necessity of a deeper purification that gets to the roots of our disorders. We know from personal experience how unwholesome emotions and attitudes of impatience, jealousy, envy, bitterness, refusal to forgive, and racist attitudes can afflict us even though we struggle to break free from their influence in our lives. The roots of the capital

---

[57] John, *CW*, *The Dark Night*, Book 2, chap. 3, no. 1.
[58] Eph 4:22: "[You were taught] to put away your former way of life, your old self, corrupt and deluded by its lusts, and to be renewed in the spirit of your minds." I would refer the reader to the Pauline and Sanjuanist understanding of the "*hombre viejo*" (the old self) researched by Miguel A. Diez, *Pablo en Juan de la Cruz* (Burgos, Spain: Monte Carmelo, 1990), 180–90.
[59] John, *CW*, *The Dark Night*, Book 1, chap. 8, no. 1; Book 2, chap. 5, no. 1.

vices John analyzed in Book One of *The Dark Night* are deep within us. Furthermore, we are strongly conditioned by our parents, childhood experiences, education, culture, as well as by our unique temperament with its gifts as well as its weaknesses. Some people carry emotional wounds from their childhood, or even generational wounds or mental disorders that pass from one generation to another. Therefore, a more intense purification that reaches the depths of our person is required for union with God through love.

The Disorders of the "Old Self"

In order to explain the necessity for a more intense purification that John defines as "the passive night of the spirit," he analyzes two kinds of imperfections of those who enter into this purgative night: habitual and actual.

The habitual imperfections "are the imperfect affections and habits still remaining like roots in the spirit."[60] We could say that the habitual imperfections are those deeply ingrained and conditioned selfish attitudes, disordered desires, and attachments contrary to the degree of love to which we are called by our very creation.

John calls these habitual imperfections *hebetudo mentis*, "a natural dullness everyone contracts through sin, and a distracted and inattentive spirit."[61] *Hebetudo mentis* is a natural hardness of spirit and a narrow and limited way of understanding God and relating to him. Even though John does not give us a minute enumeration of how these habitual imperfections are manifested, he does provide some examples in *The Spiritual Canticle*: a lack of interiority and inner freedom, dispersion, fragmentation, and selfish motivation that remains rooted in the spirit even after having served God for a long time. "Ostentation, compliments, flattery, human respect, the effort

---

[60] John, *CW, The Dark Night*, Book 1, chap. 2, no. 1.
[61] John, *CW, The Dark Night*, Book 1, chap. 2, no. 2. Kieran Kavanaugh explains in a footnote in the *Collected Works of St. John of the Cross*: "An important factor in John's anthropology is that sin lies at the root of all the defects mentioned both here and in the first book" (*CW*, 397).

to impress and please others by one's actions, employing all one's care, desires and works, and energy in pleasing others" rather than God indicate an interior fragmentation, a separation from one's deepest center, and a dependency for one's emotional life in other people.[62]

John also describes some actual imperfections that have become ingrained habits or simply impulses insufficiently controlled.[63] For instance, among these actual imperfections: having an attachment to one object more than another, being finicky about food and drink, being attached to one's own ideas and perceptions, desiring and choosing the best, grasping for spiritual consolations, and having a tendency to fantasize or worry about useless things.[64] Although these are very minor attachments and preferences and seem morally harmless, John's point is not to moralize but to show how enslaved we can become by our deeply rooted attachments and the desire for sense-pleasure. These imperfections are of the same nature as those John observes in beginners of the spiritual life.[65] The difference, however, is that they are less obvious. The smallest thing prevents us from being totally directed towards God. According to John, it makes little difference whether a bird is tied by a thin thread or by a cord. Even if it

---

[62] John, *CW*, *The Spiritual Canticle*, Stanza 28, no. 7.

[63] Eulogio Pacho, *S. Juan de la Cruz, Temas fundamentales*, 2 (Burgos, Spain: Monte Carmelo, 1984), 137.

[64] "It should be known that however spiritual a soul may be there always remains, until she reaches this state of perfection, some little herd of appetites, satisfactions, and other imperfections, natural or spiritual, after which she follows in an effort to pasture and satisfy it. In the intellect there usually reside some imperfect appetites for knowing things. The will is usually allowed to be captivated by some small appetites and gratifications of its own. These may involve temporal things, such as some little possession, or the attachment to one object more than to another, or some presumptions, judgments, punctilios, and other small things having a worldly savor or tinge. These latter may concern natural things, such as eating, drinking, finding more gratification in this than in that, choosing and desiring the best. Or they may concern spiritual things, such as the desire for spiritual satisfactions or other trifles we would never finish listing that are characteristic of spiritual persons who are not yet perfect. In the memory there are usually many wanderings, cares, and useless imaginings after which she follows" (John, *CW*, *The Spiritual Canticle*, Stanza 26, no. 18).

[65] See John, *CW*, *The Ascent of Mount Carmel*, Book 1, chap. 11, no. 4.

is tied by thread, the bird will be held bound just as surely as by a cord, and thus impeded to fly.[66]

In addition to some actual imperfections for those progressing in the contemplative life, John recognizes the danger of deception, conceit, and self-aggrandizement in the spiritual life. People advancing in the spiritual life may receive an abundance of spiritual communications, even imaginative and spiritual visions. Much discernment is necessary because spiritual communications can be the result of one's own fantasy, or from the devil.[67]

Vanity and arrogance is another danger. John says that the devil can easily induce people into believing that God and the saints speak with them, and that then they begin to believe in their spiritual fantasies and fall into presumption and pride. They may desire that others see their exterior acts and their apparent holiness, such as raptures and other exhibitions. All of this is vanity, pride, conceit, and self-aggrandizement.[68]

Finally, those progressing in the spiritual life are still very lowly and natural in their communication with God and childish in their way of thinking and relating to him. The more we go on in the spiritual life, the more we realize that God is greater than anything we can grasp by our intellect, feelings, and images. "They still think of God and speak of him as little children, and their knowledge and experience of him is like little children, as St. Paul asserts (1 Cor. 13:11)."[69] Although they have grown through the passive purgation of the senses, an immaturity still lingers in their relationship with God. John says that the "old self" still lives within them. Thus, they stand in need of a radical transformation that only God can bring about because this sickness of the soul has its roots deep within the spirit. They need to be cared for like a person who suffers from an illness.[70]

---

[66] John, *CW*, *The Ascent of Mount Carmel*, chap. 11, no. 4.
[67] John, *CW*, *The Dark Night*, Book 1, chap. 2, no. 3.
[68] John, *CW*, *The Dark Night*, Book 2, chap. 2, no. 3.
[69] John, *CW*, *The Dark Night*, Book 2, chap. 3, no. 3.
[70] John, *CW*, *The Dark Night*, Book 2, chap. 16, no. 10.

As John of the Cross has stressed many times, only the divine Physician can heal the sickness of the soul. The healing of the soul must be radical and touch the deepest structure of the person. "It is clear, consequently, how God grants the soul a favor by cleansing and curing it. He cleanses it with a strong lye and a bitter purge in its sensory and spiritual parts of all imperfect affections and habits relative to temporal, natural, sensory, and spiritual things."[71]

Conclusion: The Pathology of the Soul

As previously stated in chapter 3, St. John of the Cross is a master diagnostician of the illnesses of the soul. He understands the dignity as well as the miseries and sufferings of the human heart. For the purpose of impressing upon his readers the necessity for purification, he analyzes the spiritual ills of the human person. Those texts represent his perception of the spiritual and psychological pathologies of the human person that need healing. How does John understand the spiritual illnesses of the human person?

To begin with, we need to recall once more John of the Cross's basic thesis that God created us out of love and for love, created in the image and likeness of our loving God. Woven into the very fiber of our being is a living image of our triune God, a God of loving relationship. Love, therefore, is the purpose of our existence. "After all, this love is the end for which we were created."[72] God loved us into being, and thus we are loved by God and are love at the deepest center of our being. "The soul's center is God."[73] For this reason, we have an inborn desire for God, a yearning to love and be loved. This innate desire for union with God expresses our divine vocation. It can never be erased or rejected. It is always present even though we may not be conscious of it. Therefore, love is not something we can conquer or dominate, nor is love some element added to human nature that we

---

[71] John, *CW, The Dark Night*, Book 2, chap. 13, no. 11.
[72] John, *CW, The Spiritual Canticle*, Stanza 29, no. 3.
[73] John, *CW, The Living Flame of Love*, Stanza 1, no. 2.

grow into the more we live. Rather, love is the essence of our being. Love defines who we most authentically are as human beings. It orients our lives and directs all our energies.[74]

Because love most authentically defines who we are as human beings, God's original plan in creating us is that we would be totally oriented toward him in love. All the energies and faculties of the human person, body and soul, are to be harmoniously integrated and directed toward God in love.

However, as we have seen, original sin as well as personal sin has wounded us. We experience a profound interior warfare, which gives rise to disharmony and fragmentation. Our energies and faculties are dispersed; they are not oriented toward Love. Herein lies the metaphysical sickness of the human person. We do not live from our deepest center where God dwells. Other energies and desires usurp our most fundamental desire for God and can alienate us from the divine Source of love and meaning. We attempt to satisfy our desire for God by choosing something that can never fulfill us emotionally and spiritually. The more we depend upon creatures to satisfy our longing for happiness, love, and meaning, the more we experience interior warfare, which leads to psychological and spiritual disorder. We have seen this pathology expressed through the various texts in Book One of *The Ascent of Mount Carmel* and *The Dark Night*.

In Book One of *The Ascent of Mount Carmel*, John describes people immersed in a world of dispersion and fragmentation and enslaved by their disordered appetites. Disordered appetites are best understood as a disordered relationship, the way we egotistically relate to God and creation. Fueled by our restless desires and cravings for love and meaning, we are conditioned to place our love and affection in created realities that can never satisfy the longings of our heart. Instead of centering our desire for love and meaning in God, we depend upon creatures. In relating to creation in this disordered manner, we alienate ourselves from the ground of reality. We close our heart to a

---

[74] Secundino Castro, "El amor como apertura transcendental del hombre en San Juan de la Cruz," *Revista de Espiritualidad* 35 (1979): 431–63.

loving relationship with God. The ultimate consequence of this separation is psychological and spiritual sickness.

When we are enslaved by our disordered appetites, we separate ourselves from Love. In separating ourselves from Love, we implicitly alienate ourselves from our deepest authentic nature as being created out of love and for love. We fail to respond to our divine vocation to union with God through love.

Because "the soul's center is God,"[75] John of the Cross conceives of the spiritual life as an ever-progressive movement to the center of the soul where God dwells. Love is the motivating force that moves us and unites us to the center of our being where Love dwells.[76] Therefore, the failure to grow in loving union with God is to alienate ourselves from our deepest center and authentic self. The failure to live in fidelity to our deepest nature and divine vocation is equivalent to a failure to love. This is the primary source of the maladies of the soul that lead to various psychological and spiritual disorders. John describes the symptoms of this sickness in chapters 6 through 10 of Book One of *The Ascent of Mount Carmel*, where he describes the harm caused by disordered appetites. Disordered appetites deprive us of God's grace and "weary, torment, darken, defile, and weaken us."[77] These verbs indicate a disorder in the human personality and a state of ill-being.

We also examined the imperfections of beginners as seen through the seven capital vices. Through the seven capital vices, John analyzes and diagnoses the childish immaturity and egotism hidden under a veneer of piety and search for perfection. The seven capital vices have

---

[75] John, *CW*, *The Living Flame of Love*, Stanza 1, no. 12.

[76] "It is noteworthy, then, that love is the inclination, strength, and power for the soul in making its way to God, for love unites it with God. The more degrees of love it has, the more deeply it enters into God and centers itself in him. We can say that there are as many centers in God possible to the soul, each one deeper than the other, as there are degrees of love of God possible to it. A stronger love is a more unitive love, and we can understand in this manner the many mansions the Son of God declared were in his Father's house [Jn. 14:2]" (John, *CW*, *The Living Flame of Love*, Stanza 1, no. 13).

[77] John, *CW*, *The Ascent of Mount Carmel*, Book 1, chap. 6, no. 1.

little to do with actual prayer experiences. Most of them manifest in selfish and unloving attitudes toward self and others. They exemplify a self-centered relationship with God, self, and others. Examples of these include judging and condemning others, considering oneself superior, being impatient and angry toward oneself and others, undermining the goodness of others, desiring preference in everything, desiring to be esteemed and approved of, and fearing authentic self-revelation. All these immature and narcissistic attitudes point to a fundamental lack of love.

St. John's theory is that this fundamental lack of love has its roots embedded within the spirit of the human person, on the ontological level. Even after years of the passive night of the senses, this dysfunctional manner of loving lingers deep within our heart.[78] John explains his hypothesis in Book Two of *The Dark Night* when he discusses the imperfections of the "proficient."[79] The childishness and egotism we have seen in Books One of *The Ascent of Mount Carmel* and *The Dark Night* are deeply entrenched within the human person like roots of an old tree or an old stain on clothing.[80]

For John of the Cross, therefore, the pathology of the human person is simply but profoundly the failure to love according to God's original plan in creation. He expresses his theory explicitly in *The Spiritual Canticle*:

> The reason for this is that love of God is the soul's health, and the soul does not have full health until love is complete. Sickness is nothing but the lack of health, and when the soul has not even a single degree of love she is dead. But when she possesses some degrees of love of God, no matter how few, she is then alive, yet very weak and infirm because of her little love. In the measure that love increases she will be healthier, and when love is perfect she will have full health.[81]

---

[78] John, *CW*, *The Dark Night*, Book 1, chap. 8, no. 3.
[79] John, *CW*, *The Dark Night*, Book 2, chaps. 1–2.
[80] John, *CW*, *The Dark Night*, Book 2, chap. 1, nos. 1, 2.
[81] John, *CW*, *The Spiritual Canticle*, Stanza 11, no. 11.

Considering a failure to love constitutes the sickness of the soul, we could say that for St. John of the Cross, the disordered person is dispersed, fragmented, and uncentered. He lives outside himself because he pours himself out in creatures in order to find emotional and spiritual fulfillment. By doing so, he separates himself from the divine Source of love and meaning and thus becomes more and more dispersed and alienated from his true self and call to loving communion with God. His spiritual sickness is manifested by his egotism and lack of love for others.

Because this illness is on the spiritual level, only the divine Physician can heal us and bring us to health.

> Another more basic reason the soul walks securely in darkness is that this light, or obscure wisdom, so absorbs and engulfs the soul in the dark night of contemplation and brings it so near God that it is protected and freed from all that is not God. Since the soul, as it were, is undergoing a cure to regain its health, which is God himself, His Majesty restricts it to a diet, to abstinence from all things, and causes it to lose its appetite for them all. This effect resembles the cure of sick people when esteemed by members of their household: They are kept inside so that neither air nor light may harm them; others try not to disturb them by the noise of their footsteps or even whisperings and give them a very delicate and limited amount of food, substantial rather than tasty.[82]

---

[82] John, *CW*, *The Dark Night*, Book 2, chap. 16, no. 10.

Chapter 5

The Path of Healing: Jesus the Divine Physician

IT IS CLEAR FROM our study of the texts where John of the Cross analyzes the pathologies of the soul that the sickness of which John writes is much deeper than backaches, headaches, cancer, heart disease, or depression. It is a sickness that afflicts us on a deeper level than our moral and psychological life. Ultimately, it is an ontological and existential illness. We suffer a wound that only God can heal. God is the divine Physician who must intervene and heal the infirmities of our mind, heart, and spirit. "Who can free themselves from lowly manners and limitations if you do not lift them to yourself, my God, in purity of love? How will human beings begotten and nurtured in lowliness rise up to you, Lord, if you do not raise them with your hand that made them?"[1] "Ah, who has the power to heal me," cries out the bride of *The Spiritual Canticle*, wounded in love by Christ the Beloved.[2] "Why, since you wounded this heart, don't you heal it?"[3] Healing is at the heart of the Good News of Jesus Christ.

---

[1] John, *CW*, *The Sayings of Light and Love*, no. 26.
[2] John, *CW*, *The Spiritual Canticle*, Stanza 6.
[3] John, *CW*, *The Spiritual Canticle*, Stanza 9.

In his book, *Jesus of Nazareth*, Pope Benedict XVI reminds us that Christianity is a "therapeutic religion." Healing is an essential dimension of the apostolic mission and Christian faith in general.[4] What is impressive when we read the four Gospels is the amount of healings and exorcisms that fill almost every page, particularly in the Synoptic Gospels. Jesus exercised an extensive healing ministry. People flocked to him for healing; even touching his garments could heal an afflicted person. "If I but touch his cloak, I will be made well," believed the woman in Mark's Gospel who suffered from hemorrhages for twelve years (Mark 5:28).

> That evening, at sunset, they brought to him all who were sick or possessed by demons. And the whole city was gathered around the door. And he cured many who were sick with various diseases and cast out many demons. (Mark 1:32)
>
> Jesus went throughout all Galilee, teaching in their synagogues and proclaiming the good news of the kingdom and curing every disease and every sickness among the people. (Matt 4:23)
>
> A great multitude of people from all Judea, Jerusalem, and the coast of Tyre and Sidon . . . had come to hear him and to be healed of their diseases, and those who were troubled with unclean spirits were cured. And everyone in the crowd was trying to touch him, for power came out from him and healed all of them. (Luke 6:17-19)

Not only did Jesus heal physically, but his compassionate love touched the lives of sinners and the marginalized. People experienced in him the merciful and compassionate love of the Father and came to a new understanding of themselves as God's beloved children. "Those who are well have no need of a physician, but those who are sick. Go and learn what this means, 'I desire mercy, not sacrifice.' For I have not come to call the righteous but sinners" (Matt 9:12-13).

---

[4] Pope Benedict XVI, *Jesus of Nazareth*, vol. 1 (New York: Doubleday, 2007), 176.

Blindness, leprosy, hemorrhages, fevers, and the battle to overcome demonic forces were the very means to encounter Jesus' saving power. People sought Jesus out, and their faith in him released his compassion and healing power.

The Greek noun *sōter* (savior) applied to Jesus in the New Testament comes from the verb *sōzein* (to save), which signifies not only "to deliver," or "to draw out of danger," but also "to heal." The very name of Jesus means "Yahweh saves" (Matt 1:21; Heb 4:12). The verbal root *sōzō* can mean to "rescue, save, deliver, preserve from danger." For instance, in Luke's Gospel *sōzō* is used with reference to being saved from sin (Luke 7:36-49); to being saved from demons (8:26-39); to being saved from sickness (8:43-47); to being saved from death (8:49). "Jesus is *sōter* who forgives, delivers, heals and resurrects, both temporally and eternally."[5]

The New Testament uses the Greek word *sôtèria* (salvation) to designate well-being as well as spiritual healing. In virtue of biblical anthropology that conceives of the human person as a body-soul unity, physical healing is a sign of salvation on the part of Jesus. This becomes clear in many of the miracle narratives. For example, in Mark's account of the healing of the paralytic (Mark 2:1-12), Jesus pronounces the words, "Child, your sins are forgiven" (v. 5). The paralytic's healing symbolizes the deeper healing of his heart from what alienates him from God. God offers a complete healing that begins with the human heart. Physical healing symbolizes the healing of the spirit and represents salvation which is victory over evil.[6] Salvation can only be complete if it touches the human heart. From the healing that takes place on the spiritual level is born a transformation in human relations on the personal and societal levels of life.

The Eastern patristic tradition is unanimous in considering Christ as Physician of the soul, capable of healing wounded human nature. The early Christians saw Jesus as a Physician sent by the Father to

---

[5] Michael Brown, *Israel's Divine Healer* (Grand Rapids, MI: Zondervan, 1995), 212–13.

[6] Étienne Charpentier, *Les Miracles de l'Évangile*, Cahiers Évangile 8 (Paris: Éditions du Cerf, 1974), 46.

heal humankind, sick as a consequence of original sin, and to regain their original health. For instance, St. John Climacus wrote, "Mankind needed a physician and surgeon whose skill would be commensurate with the seriousness of its illnesses and wounds. Christ alone, being God, was able to be this efficacious Physician by becoming man while remaining God. As such, the Father sent Him among men, moved by pity for the human race."[7] St. Clement of Alexandria taught, "The Word of the Father, who made man, cares for the whole nature of his creature. The all-sufficient Physician of humanity, the Savior, heals both body and soul."[8]

Fix Your Eyes on Christ

For John of the Cross, the path of healing and transformation begins by entering into a personal relationship with Jesus Christ. The first counsel John gives to beginners who are embarking on the contemplative path is to imitate Christ in all their deeds. "First, have habitual desire to imitate Christ in all your deeds by bringing your life into conformity with his. You must then study his life in order to know how to imitate him and behave in all events as he would."[9]

John does not recommend many hours of prayer, silence, and solitude; rather, he places before us the imitation of Christ in daily life. In conforming ourselves to the Gospels we journey on the road to union with Christ and grow in his image. However, the imitation of Christ to which John directs us is much deeper than mere imitation of his external actions. His approach to the imitation of Christ is primarily on the level of motivation and intentionality in daily life.

---

[7] Quoted in Jean-Claude Larchet, *Therapy of Spiritual Illnesses*, vol. 2 (Montreal: Alexander Press, 2017), 7. For a thorough study of the image of Christ as Physician and Healer of humanity according to the Eastern tradition, see Jean-Claude Larchet's three-volume work: *Therapy of Spiritual Illnesses: An Introduction to the Ascetic Tradition of the Orthodox Church* (Montreal: Alexander Press, 2017).

[8] Clement of Alexandria, *Pedagogue*, 1.2.6. Quoted in Jean-Claude Larchet, *Therapy of Spiritual Illnesses*, vol. 2 (Montreal: Alexander Press, 2012), 10.

[9] John, *CW*, *The Ascent of Mount Carmel*, Book 1, chap. 13, no. 3.

In order to be successful in this imitation, John directs us to put the love of Jesus Christ at the center of our life by striving to deny ourselves of our attachment to disordered sense-pleasure and to perform our daily actions for the honor and glory of God. Just as Jesus was always motivated by his love for the Father, we must be motivated in all we do by our love for Jesus Christ. "He had no other gratification in his life, nor desired any other, than the fulfillment of the Father's will, which he called his meat and food."[10]

As a method for imitating Christ and mortifying our attachment to the pleasure principle, John offers the following maxims:

> Endeavor to be inclined always:
> not to the easiest, but to the most difficult;
> not to the most delightful, but to the most distasteful;
> not to the most gratifying, but to the less pleasant;
> not to what means rest for you, but to hard work;
> not to the consoling, but to the unconsoling;
> not to the most, but to the least;
> not to the highest and most precious, but to the lowest and most despised;
> not to wanting something, but to wanting nothing.
> Do not go about looking for the best of temporal things, but for the worst, and, for Christ, desire to enter into complete nakedness, emptiness, and poverty in everything in the world.[11]

How do we interpret these maxims? John's councils may seem unhealthy and extreme in light of our contemporary psychology. Is he telling us that we must always be inclined to the "most difficult,"

---

[10] "For example, if you are offered the satisfaction of hearing things that have no relation to the service and glory of God, do not desire this pleasure or the hearing of these things. When you have an opportunity for the gratification of looking upon objects that will not help you love God more, do not desire this gratification or sight. And if in speaking there is a similar opportunity, act in the same way. And so on with all the senses insofar as you can duly avoid such satisfaction. If you cannot escape the experience of this satisfaction, it will be sufficient to have no desire for it" (John, *CW, The Ascent of Mount Carmel*, Book 1, chap. 13, no. 4).

[11] John, *CW, The Ascent of Mount Carmel*, Book 1, chap. 13, no. 4.

the "most distasteful," and the "unconsoling"? John is not encouraging doloristic spirituality. He teaches an active and effective therapy for the deeply rooted egotism that often motivates our behavior, work, and relationships. The purpose of these maxims is to balance our naturally conditioned tendency to always seek the pleasant and self-gratifying experiences of life and to push away the difficult and painful ones. Life is a mixture of pleasant and unpleasant experiences and of various types of relationships, some easier, others more difficult.

The key to health and equanimity is to remain open to all the various experiences and relationships that we encounter in life. Our lives are made up of delightful experiences as well as painful ones, gratifying moments as well as distasteful ones. Life can become burdensome if we are constantly avoiding the unpleasant tasks, situations, and people in our life, and seeking only the pleasant and agreeable ones. Peace, harmony, and equanimity come from accepting life under God's conditions—that is, accepting the ups and downs of daily life with an open heart, a positive attitude, and a desire to learn from every experience. Every event, task, or encounter can be the means of growing in selfless love for God and others. Taken into the laboratory of our daily life, and applying them to our particular circumstances and vocation, these maxims are a means to emptying ourselves of the ways we cling selfishly to the pleasure principle and to striving to do all for the love of Jesus Christ and for the honor and glory of God.

An Enkindling of a Greater Love

Intellectual knowledge and good intentions alone are insufficient to overcome our selfish ways of loving. A more intense enkindling of a greater love, love for Christ, is absolutely necessary to deny our disordered desires for sense pleasures. Only a personal experience of Christ's love, and our desire to respond to his love, can inspire, strengthen, and fortify us as we journey toward union with Christ. Love for Christ is the motivating force for conversion and any form of self-denial. We see this in our human relationships. It is my sincere love for my friend or spouse that motivates me to change a negative behavior pattern that prevents a deeper love for them. A greater love is necessary to overcome the lesser loves in our lives. This greater love is for Jesus Christ.

> A more intense enkindling of another, better love (love of the soul's Bridegroom) is necessary for the vanquishing of the appetites and the denial of this pleasure. By finding satisfaction and strength in this love, it will have the courage and constancy to readily deny all other appetites. The love of its Bridegroom is not the only requisite for conquering the strength of the sensitive appetites; an enkindling with urgent longings of love is also necessary. For the sensory appetites are moved and attracted toward sensory objects with such cravings that if the spiritual part of the soul is not fired with other, more urgent longings for spiritual things, the soul will be able neither to overcome the yoke of nature nor to enter the night of sense; nor will it have the courage to live in the darkness of all things by denying its appetites for them.[12]

In *The Spiritual Canticle*, John emphasizes that the spiritual journey begins with an awareness of God's personal love for us, symbolized as "a heart wounded . . . with love for God."[13] God's love "wounds" us, that is, graces us with a consciousness of God's goodness, love, and mercy. The soul, symbolized as a woman, experienced Christ's love that made her aware of God's immense love, that God created her and redeemed her solely for himself, and that she owed him the

---

[12] John, *CW*, *The Ascent of Mount Carmel*, Book 1, chap. 14, no. 2. See also John Welch, *When Gods Die* (New York: Paulist Press, 1990), 77.

[13] John, *CW*, *The Spiritual Canticle*, Stanza 1, no. 1. In the tradition of spiritual writers of the mystical tradition, John of the Cross uses the expression "wound of love" to designate certain graces that bring with them suffering: ordinary or eminent graces, ranging from pain caused by regret of past faults to the experience of transverberation, a grace reserved for souls who have reached a high degree of union with God. In this first stanza of *The Spiritual Canticle*, the wound of love designates an experience of God's love that makes the bride acutely aware of God's personal love for her, and her innate poverty and lack of fidelity to God, as well as an awareness of all that she owes God and that God created her solely for himself.

service of her life and every response of her love. God blessed her in many ways from the time of her birth, even though she had forgotten him in the midst of creatures. Moved with longing and sorrow, her wounded heart cries out and goes out in search of him:

> Where have you hidden,
> Beloved, and left me moaning?
> You fled like the stag
> after wounding me;
> I went out calling you, but you were gone.[14]

The spiritual journey begins with an experience of God's love, which comes to us through many avenues: quiet prayer, the liturgy, spiritual reading, parents and friends who love us, or the beauty of nature. Without this experience of God's love, we lack the insight, courage, and strength to respond to Christ's love and to undergo the transformation necessary for union with Christ.

Secondly, in addition to a personal relationship with Christ, John directs us to fix our eyes on him and the mysteries of his life. Over and over in his writings, John directs us to fix our eyes on Christ. "There is much to fathom in Christ, for he is like an abundant treasure mine with many recesses of treasures, so that however deep individuals may go they never reach the end or bottom, but rather in every recess find new veins with new riches everywhere. On this account St. Paul said of Christ, In Christ dwell hidden all treasures and wisdom [Col. 2:3]."[15]

In chapter 22 of the second book of *The Ascent of Mount Carmel*, John says that with the coming of Christ, God has revealed everything to us and has given us everything. "You will not take from me, my God, what you once gave me in your only Son, Jesus Christ, in whom you gave me all I desire."[16] In Christ is contained all that we need to know about God and the way that leads to him. By fixing our eyes on

---

[14] John, *CW*, *The Spiritual Canticle*, Stanza 1.
[15] John, *CW*, *The Spiritual Canticle*, Stanza 37, no. 4.
[16] John, *CW*, *The Sayings of Light and Love*, no. 26.

Christ we will understand the Father's will and how we are to live. Therefore, in all situations of life, we are to fix our eyes on Christ. "Fasten your eyes on him alone because in him I have spoken and revealed all and in him you will discover even more than you ask for and desire." Jesus is our "brother, companion, master, ransom, and reward."[17] Because he knew human afflictions, we will find consolations in times of affliction. "If you desire me to answer with a word of comfort, behold my Son subject to me and to others out of love for me, and afflicted and you will see how much he answers you."[18] In him we will find a medicine for all our ignorances and weaknesses. Therefore, we must be guided humanly and visibly in all things by the law of Christ.[19]

As we know, by our baptism we have died with Christ and have been raised up with him (Rom 6:3-4). Our life is now in Christ: "[I]t is no longer I who live, but it is Christ who lives in me" (Gal 2:20). The Christian life is living the paschal mystery of Jesus Christ that takes place in every serious Christian. It is from this perspective that John of the Cross directs us to imitate Christ. He tells us, much like St. Paul: "Let the same mind be in you that was in Christ Jesus" (Phil 2:5). What was Christ's attitude? How did he live?

Jesus was the man for God and others. In this sense, he was a man of radical love. Because he was a man of radical love, he allowed himself to become vulnerable and consequently wounded. One of the images of Christ in the works of John of the Cross is that of a wounded healer.

> A lone young shepherd lived in pain
> withdrawn from pleasure and contentment,
> his thoughts fixed on a shepherd-girl
> his heart an open wound with love.[20]

---

[17] John, *CW*, *The Ascent of Mount Carmel*, Book 2, chap. 22, no. 5.
[18] John, *CW*, *The Ascent of Mount Carmel*, Book 2, chap. 22, no. 6.
[19] John, *CW*, *The Ascent of Mount Carmel*, Book 2, chap. 22, no. 7.
[20] John, *CW*, *Poetry*, "7. Stanzas applied spiritually to Christ and the soul," no. 1.

Jesus is the Good Shepherd whose great desire is to free and ransom us completely from the hands of sensuality and the devil. He is the Good Shepherd who searches for the lost sheep along many winding paths and rejoices when he finds it—he holds it on his shoulders and rejoices (Luke 15:4-5). He is like the woman who lost the drachma and searches her whole house to find it, and then calls in her neighbors to celebrate, saying, rejoice with me—I have found the lost drachma (Luke 15:8-9).[21]

Jesus lived a life of mercy, compassion, and self-giving love that required a complete relinquishment of false securities and self-gratification, which eventually led to an agonizing death on the cross. In this sense, his life was a constant death so that others might live. "He underwent both a natural and spiritual death. During his life he died spiritually to the sensitive part, and at his death he died naturally. He proclaimed that he had no place whereupon to lay his head (Mt. 8.20)."[22] In his death he emptied himself completely and was reduced to nothing, with no consolation and in extreme abandonment. Yet it was at this moment of his deepest poverty and self-emptying love on the cross that he accomplished the most marvelous work of salvation, the reconciliation of humanity with God.[23] "[B]y his wounds we were healed" (Isa 53:5; NABRE).

Jesus, wounded and crucified, therefore becomes the model of authentic love that leads to the fullness of life, a life of reconciliation and union with God and others. Far from being an image of the exaltation of suffering, or neurotic suffering turned in on itself, the cross signifies the self-giving love and compassion of Jesus Christ. True love, in imitation of Christ, means loving God for God's sake and willing the good of others for their sake. It means dying to our disordered attachment to false securities and selfish gratification in our relationship with God and others.[24]

---

[21] John, *CW*, *The Spiritual Canticle*, Stanza 22, no. 1.
[22] John, *CW*, *The Ascent of Mount Carmel*, Book 2, chap. 7, no. 10.
[23] John, *CW*, *The Ascent of Mount Carmel*, Book 2, chap. 7, no. 11.
[24] John, *CW*, *The Ascent of Mount Carmel*, Book 2, chap. 7, no. 5.

For John, the image of Jesus crucified is one of radical self-giving love. John is clear in his teaching that the way of Christ does not consist in a multitude of considerations, consolations, experiences, and methods, although these may be a requirement for beginners, but rather in self-surrender to Christ, dying to our self-centered ways of relating to creation and other people.[25] "The ultimate reason for everything is love, whose property is to give and not to receive."[26]

---

[25] John, *CW*, *The Ascent of Mount Carmel*, Book 2, chap. 7, no. 8. "I should like to persuade spiritual persons that the road leading to God does not entail a multiplicity of considerations, methods, manners, and experiences—though in their own way these may be a requirement for beginners—but demands only the one thing necessary: true self-denial, exterior and interior, through surrender of self both to suffering for Christ and to annihilation in all things. In the exercise of this self-denial everything else, and even more, is discovered and accomplished. If one fails in this exercise, the root and sum total of all the virtues, the other methods would amount to no more than going around in circles without getting anywhere, even were one to enjoy considerations and communications as lofty as those of the angels."

[26] John, *CW*, *The Spiritual Canticle*, Stanza 38, no. 5.

Chapter 6

The Divine Therapy

OPENING OURSELVES TO THE loving gaze of Jesus Christ and striving to imitate his way of love begins the process of our healing and transformation. Yet, much more is needed. God must intervene and heal us of our deepest infirmities, brokenness, and selfish ways of relating to God, others, and creation—transforming us to a divine way of knowing, being, and loving in this world.

> No matter how earnestly beginners in all their actions and passions practice the mortification of self, they will never be able to do so entirely—far from it—until God accomplishes it in them passively by means of the purgation of this night. May God be pleased to give me his divine light that I may say something worthwhile about this subject, for in a night so dark and a matter so difficult to treat and expound, his enlightenment is very necessary.[1]

John says that trying to free ourselves from our disordered way of loving by our own efforts is like a child who cannot walk by herself, yet demands to walk when her mother wants to carry her in her arms.[2]

God is the principal agent in the healing process of purification. God must take the initiative and heal our self-centered loving. He

---

[1] John, *CW*, *The Dark Night*, Book 1, chap. 7, no. 9.
[2] John, *CW*, *The Ascent of Mount Carmel*, Book 1, Prol., no. 3.

must take us by the hand and lead us into the darkness.³ When God manifests his initiative, the challenge is to surrender and cooperate.⁴ We must adopt a receptive attitude and allow God to work.

The divine initiative is a recuring theme that appears in many forms throughout the works of St. John of the Cross. In *The Dark Night* John stresses that the entire purification process is God's action: "Souls begin to enter this dark night when God, gradually drawing them out of the state of beginners (those who practice meditation on the spiritual road), begins to place them in the state of proficients (those who entered the contemplative paths), so that by passing through this state they might reach that of the perfect, which is the divine union of the soul with God."⁵

In *The Spiritual Canticle*, the soul painfully experiences the absence of her Beloved as she moves toward union with God. She invokes the Holy Spirit to dispel her dryness and increase her love for the Beloved and to practice the virtues.⁶

The divine initiative appears several times in *The Living Flame of Love*: "The soul, then, should advert that God is the principal agent in this matter. He acts as guide of the blind, leading it by the hand to the place it knows not how to reach (to supernatural things of which neither its intellect nor will nor memory can know the nature). It should use all its principal care in watching so as not to place any obstacle in the way of God, its guide on this road ordained for it by him according to the perfection of his law and of the faith."⁷

Contemplation

If God is the principal agent in the healing process, how does God intervene and heal the sickness of our minds and hearts? John simply

---

[3] John, *CW*, *The Dark Night*, Book 2, chap. 16, no. 8.
[4] John, *CW*, *The Ascent of Mount Carmel*, Book 1, Prol., nos. 3–4.
[5] John, *CW*, *The Dark Night*, Book 1, chap. 1, no. 1.
[6] John, *CW*, *The Spiritual Canticle*, Stanza 17, no. 2.
[7] John, *CW*, *The Living Flame of Love*, Stanza 3, no. 29.

and profoundly presents his theory of healing in a text we have already encountered from the first pages of our study. It is worth reading it again:

> The reason for this is that love of God is the soul's health, and the soul does not have full health until love is complete. Sickness is nothing but the lack of health, and when the soul has not even a single degree of love she is dead. But when she possesses some degrees of love of God, no matter how few, she is then alive, yet very weak and infirm because of her little love. In the measure that love increases she will be healthier, and when love is perfect she will have full health.[8]

God's love is John's principle of healing. In other words, therapy for John of the Cross is opening ourselves more and more to God's self-communicating love, allowing God's love to penetrate ever more deeply into our psyche and spirit and responding to God's love. This healing love comes through contemplation.

John defines contemplation as "a secret and peaceful and loving inflow of God, which, if not hampered, fires the soul in the spirit of love."[9] Contemplation is God's self-communicating love that "purges us of our ignorances and imperfections, natural and spiritual, and instructs us in the perfection of love."[10] John also defines contemplation as an "inflammation of love,"[11] "a science of love."[12] In other words, contemplation is an experience of God's self-communicating love at the most profound level of our psyche and spirit that purifies us of our disordered desires, imperfections, and attachments, and instructs us in the science of love—a love free of selfish desire, possessiveness, and egotism.

---

[8] John, *CW*, *The Spiritual Canticle*, Stanza 11, no. 11.
[9] John, *CW*, *The Dark Night*, Book 1, chap. 10, no. 6.
[10] John, *CW*, *The Dark Night*, Book 2, chap. 5, no. 1.
[11] John, *CW*, *The Dark Night*, Book 1, chap. 11, no. 1.
[12] John, *CW*, *The Dark Night*, Book 2, chap. 18, no. 5.

In *The Living Flame of Love*, John poetically describes the contemplative experience as an awakening of God who dwells in the depths of our hearts:

> How gently and lovingly
> You wake in my heart,
> Where in secret you dwell alone.[13]

John explains, however, that it is not God who is asleep and suddenly awakens within us; rather, we are the ones who are asleep, God awakens us, and we become conscious of God's loving presence within us and in all of creation.[14] This is mystical consciousness that has a transforming effect in our lives.

God's self-communication "inflames us with the spirit of love."[15] In chapters 18 to 20 of Book Two of *The Dark Night*, John describes the contemplative experience as a "science of love," ascending a secret ladder of ten steps. Each step represents a quality or degree of love.[16] God instructs in "the science of love"—that is, in how to love as God loves; infusing God's love within us; expanding our capacity to love God, others, and the world as God loves, with the love we see in Jesus: selfless, compassionate, merciful, forgiving. It is a dynamic experience of being loved and learning how to love.[17]

---

[13] John, *CW*, *The Living Flame of Love*, Stanza 4.

[14] John, *CW*, *The Living Flame of Love*, Stanza 4, nos. 4–9, which in part says: "Yet, since everything in human beings comes from God, and they of themselves can do nothing good [Jas. 1:17], it is rightly asserted that our awakening is an awakening of God and our rising is God's rising. It is as though David were to say: Let us arise and be awakened twice, because we are doubly asleep and fallen. Since the soul was in a sleep from which it could never awaken itself, and only God could open its eyes and cause this awakening, it very appropriately calls this an awakening of God, saying: 'You wake in my heart.' Awaken and enlighten us, my Lord, so we might know and love the blessings that you ever propose to us, and we might understand that you have moved to bestow favors on us and have remembered us."

[15] John, *CW*, *The Dark Night*, Book 1, chap. 10, no. 6.

[16] John, *CW*, *The Dark Night*, Book 2, no. 5.

[17] "The entire doctrine of John of the Cross regarding purification of the faculties and the human senses has as its goal to expand (deepen) our capacity

The Dark Night of Sense and Spirit

If for John healing of our sick souls means opening ourselves to the inflow of God's self-communicating love and allowing that inflow to penetrate into ever deeper levels of into our psyche and spirit, then God's love will have profound repercussions within us. John's symbol for this therapeutic process is the dark night of sense and spirit.[18] The dark night of sense and spirit is contemplation.[19]

The "dark night" is a metaphor to describe the spiritual journey toward union with God. The "night" can signify many experiences. The night is a time for silence, rest, and sleep, a period of rejuvenation and quiet tranquility after a long day's labor. Night is a time when lovers meet. For some people the night evokes fear, anxiety, struggle, and temptation. Our defense mechanisms are lower at night, so the deeper levels of our unconscious may surface in our dreams and fantasies, and what surfaces can be mysterious, frightful, and unflattering to our conscious lives.

John's poem "One Dark Night" sings of urgent longings of love, fleeing at night, a quiet house, night as guiding light, secrecy, union with the Beloved, abandonment, and forgetfulness of self. All these poetic elements are rich in meaning; however, the night is more than a metaphor. The dark night is a journey of love rooted in lived experience, a journey from selfish, possessive love to love simply for the other, free from egotistic demands and possessiveness.[20]

---

to love." See Secundino Castro, "El amor como apertura transcendental del hombre," *Revista de Espiritualidad* 35 (1976): 434. See also Lucien-Marie de St. Joseph, "Dynamisme de l'amour," 170–88.

[18] Although we have already briefly defined the dark night of sense and spirit in chap. 2 in relationship to the pathologies of the soul, we need to treat of the dark night at greater length in light of how God heals us.

[19] John, *CW*, *The Dark Night*, Book 1, chap. 8, no. 1.

[20] It is important to stress that John's poems, "One Dark Night," "The Spiritual Canticle," and "The Living Flame of Love," sing of God's love for us, our longing to love God in return, and the purification of our desire to love as God has created us to love. Constance FitzGerald, OCD, has expressed the dark night journey as purification of desire. See Constance FitzGerald, "Impasse and Dark Night," in *Desire, Darkness, and Hope: Theology in a Time of Impasse*, ed. Laurie Cassidy and M. Shawn Copeland (Collegeville, MN: Liturgical Press Academic, 2021), 82–83.

When John introduces the "dark night" in the prologue to *The Ascent of Mount Carmel*, he refers to the many "darknesses, trials, spiritual and temporal that fortunate souls ordinarily undergo on their way to the high state of perfection," and he describes how, when God begins to place them in the dark night by means of these trials and darknesses, they resist, do not apply their will, and fail to abandon themselves to God's action through those very trials.[21] This gives us some idea of the dark night. With hearts enkindled in love for God, these "fortunate souls" are on a journey to union with God. On this journey, they encounter many trials. Life's journey is a dark night. John writes that there are phases of the dark night: twilight, midnight, and dawn.[22] There are many darknesses, spiritual and temporal trials, and temptations that we undergo in our journey to union with God through love. For those who seriously seek God, these experiences are the very means by which God's self-communicating love touches our lives to purify, heal, and transform us from one way of knowing, loving, and being in this world to a divine way of knowing, loving, and being.

The metaphor of the dark night must have been part of John's soul and life experience. He was born in poverty, paternally orphaned at a young age, reduced to mendicancy along with his mother and brother, and placed in a charitable organization for poor and orphaned boys (La Doctrina). He was hired as an alms-seeker and nurse's aide for patients with syphilis, worked during the day, and studied at night to complete his studies. He entered the Carmelite Order and eventually joined St. Teresa's reform. Accused as a disobedient friar, he was imprisoned for nine months in a monastery cell in Toledo, where he suffered deprivation and cruel treatment. Having

---

[21] John, *CW, The Ascent of Mount Carmel*, Book 1, Prol., nos. 1, 3.

[22] John, *CW, The Ascent of Mount Carmel*, Book 1, chap. 2, no. 5: "In actuality these three nights comprise only one night, a night divided into three parts like natural night. The first part, the night of the senses, resembles early evening, that time of twilight when things begin to fade from sight. The second part, faith, is completely dark, like midnight. The third part, representing God, is like the very early dawn just before the break of day. To provide further enlightenment about all this, we will discuss each of these causes of night separately."

escaped from the Toledo prison cell, he made his way to Andalusia, where he ministered for ten years as prior, confessor, and spiritual guide. He also served his sick brothers, served as prior and vicar provincial, and founded monasteries. He wrote his major spiritual works during the busiest time of his life. He was eventually relieved of his office as prior and suffered persecution from his confreres, and died in a monastery where the prior held a grudge against him. In all these experiences of life, John saw the hand of God. "Men do not do these things, but God, who knows what is suitable for us and arranges things for our good. Think nothing else but that God ordains all, and where there is no love, put love, and you will draw out love."[23]

We are created out of love and for love, and the dark night is a journey to reach the fullness of love for which we were created. The night is grace. "Ah, the sheer grace!"[24] It is God's merciful intervention in our life to purify, heal, and transform our way of loving of which we are incapable.[25]

The "night" is also a path of discipleship. "If any wish to come after me, let them deny themselves and take up their cross and follow me. For those who want to save their life will lose it, and those who lose their life for my sake, and for the sake of the gospel, will save it" (Mark 8:34-35). The "night" is not reserved for an elite group of pious people or professional religious. Any Christian, converted and committed to Jesus Christ, striving to imitate his life, taking up their daily cross, and dying to selfishness and whatever prevents faithful discipleship, will embark on a night journey. The dark night is entering through the narrow door (Luke 13:22-30). "A person makes progress only by imitating Christ, who is the Way, the Truth, and the Life. . . . Accordingly, I would not consider any spirituality worthwhile that wants to walk in sweetness and ease and run from the imitation of Christ."[26]

---

[23] John, *CW*, *Letters*, no. 26, July 6, 1591.

[24] John, *CW*, *The Dark Night*, Book 1.

[25] "It was a sheer grace to be placed by God in this night that occasioned so much good. The soul would not have succeeded in entering it, because souls are unable alone to empty themselves of all their appetites in order to reach God" (John, *CW*, *The Ascent of Mount Carmel*, Book 1, chap. 1, no. 5).

[26] John, *CW*, *The Ascent of Mount Carmel*, Book 2, chap. 7, no. 8.

Therefore, as a path of discipleship, the night symbolizes a lifelong journey of healing and transformation in which God purifies, heals, and transforms our disordered desires and the attachments to created things that enslave us and prevent us from living the life of Christ and placing God at the center of our lives.

We experience the Christian journey as a night because in following Jesus we must renounce our selfish desires and inordinate attachment to riches, possessions, and false securities contrary to the Gospel life.[27] Such denial and deprivation are a night because our inordinate desire for pleasure, possessions, and spiritual consolations is unsatisfied.[28] Constance FitzGerald writes, "St. John of the Cross is intent on showing what kind of affective education is carried on by the Holy Spirit over a lifetime. He delineates, therefore, the movement from a desire, love, that is possessive, entangled, complex, selfish, and unfree to a desire that is fulfilled in union with Jesus Christ."[29]

The road along which we travel to union with God is faith, which is also "night" to us. Faith is a relationship with God that does not depend upon consolations, images, and feelings. Faith is trust and surrender to God, even in dark moments.

God, too, is a night for us. God cannot be grasped by what we understand or feel. God is intimate to us, "hidden" in our depths, but also transcendent—that is, God is beyond our understanding, images, and feelings.[30] We project our own images onto God. As we move

---

[27] It is interesting to read the Gospels with the perspective of self-denial required to follow Jesus, e.g., the rich young man, the Sermon on the Mount (love your enemy, pray for your persecutors, walk the extra mile, turn the other cheek, forgive and you will be forgiven, be merciful as your heavenly Father is merciful).

[28] In chapter 2 of Book 1 of *The Ascent of Mount Carmel*, John offers three reasons why the journey to union with God is a night: (1) the denial and privation of one's disordered appetites is like a night for one's senses; (2) The road is faith, which is a night for the soul; (3) God, the goal of the journey, is a night for the soul (*The Ascent of Mount Carmel*, Book 1, chap. 2, no. 1).

[29] FitzGerald, "Impasse and Dark Night," 82.

[30] "It is noteworthy that, however elevated God's communications and the experiences of his presence are, and however sublime a person's knowledge of him may be, these are not God essentially, nor are they comparable to him because, indeed, he is still hidden to the soul. Hence, regardless of all these lofty experiences, a person should think of him as hidden and seek him as one who

through life and undergo its challenges, our image of God is progressively purified and transformed.[31] God is not who we thought. God is not a "sugar daddy" who gives me whatever I desire. Despite my prayers, I wasn't hired for the job I wanted. God did not heal me of a heart condition or prevent my mother from dying. Yet in all this, we believe in God's love despite all appearances to the contrary.

The dark night, therefore, symbolizes the spiritual journey as a process of healing and transformation at the deepest level of our being. Life is a process of growth and transformation. God wants to transform us so that we can share the fullness of God's life. God is merciful, and if we are open and receptive to him, God intervenes in our lives to free and heal us from whatever prevents us from living life in abundance. The dark night symbolizes God's love for us and our potential to share divine life. No matter how psychologically broken and messed up we may be, God knows how to bring good out of evil and sin.

Since it is our whole person in our psychosomatic unity (body-spirit) who must be purified, healed, and transformed, transformation take place in stages. Thus, John speaks of two principal nights: the night of sense and the night of spirit.[32]

There is an active and passive dimension to the nights of sense and spirit. The active element refers to what we do by our own efforts to bring about purification. In passive purification, it is God who acts,

---

is hidden, saying: 'Where have You hidden?' Neither the sublime communication nor the sensible awareness of his nearness is a sure testimony of his gracious presence, nor are dryness and the lack of these a reflection of his absence. As a result, the prophet Job exclaims: If he comes to me I shall not see him, and if he goes away I shall not understand [Jb. 9:11]" (John, *CW, The Spiritual Canticle*, Stanza 1, no. 3).

[31] FitzGerald, "Impasse and Dark Night," 86.

[32] "This night, which as we say is contemplation, causes two kinds of darkness or purgation in spiritual persons according to the two parts of the soul, the sensory and the spiritual. Hence one night of purgation is sensory, by which the senses are purged and accommodated to the spirit; and the other night or purgation is spiritual, by which the spirit is purged and denuded as well as accommodated and prepared for union with God through love" (John, *CW, The Dark Night*, Book 1, chap. 8, no. 1).

and we surrender, remaining open, passive, and receptive to God's purifying action.

Although there is a fundamental difference between the nights of sense and spirit, the nights overlap and are, practically speaking, deepening phases of a gradual process of purification and transformation that takes place through the various stages of life. Due to the essential unity of the human person as sense-spirit-body-soul, no purification of the senses is complete without a purgation of the spirit.[33]

The passage from one way of being to another is progressive through the various stages and seasons of life. Our love for God, others, and creation is refined, deepened, and matured from an imperfect self-centered love to a more selfless evangelical love of God, others, and creation. We pass from one way of being, living, and relating to God and other human beings to another new way, "a divine way."[34]

The Dark Night of the Senses

God is the protagonist of our lives who accommodates himself according to our human nature. In *The Ascent of Mount Carmel*, John presents God's pedagogy. Like a good friend and teacher, God's self-communication is developmental—that is, orderly and gentle according to our human condition.[35] God's self-communication is according to our human capacity through our five external senses (sight, smell,

---

[33] "The purgation of the principal part, that of the spirit, is lacking, and without it the sensory purgation, however strong it may have been, is incomplete because of a communication existing between the two parts of the soul that form only one suppositum" (John, *CW*, *The Dark Night*, Book 2, chap. 3, no. 1). "As we said, the purgation of the senses is only the gate to and beginning of the contemplation that leads to the purgation of spirit. This sensitive purgation, as we also explained, serves more for the accommodation of the senses to the spirit than for the union of the spirit with God. The stains of the old self still linger in the spirit, although they may not be apparent or perceptible. If these are not wiped away by the use of the soap and strong lye of this purgative night, the spirit will be unable to reach the purity of divine union" (John, *CW*, *The Dark Night*, Book 2, chap. 2, no. 1).

[34] Fernando Urbina, *La persona humana en San Juan de la Cruz* (Madrid: Ediciones, 1982), 49.

[35] John, *CW*, *The Ascent of Mount Carmel*, Book 2, chap. 17, no. 1.

hearing, taste, and touch), as well as through our discursive reflection, fantasy, and imagination.

For beginners, the first method of conversation with God is discursive meditation on the life of Christ and the mysteries of the faith. "It should be known that the practice of beginners is to meditate and make acts and discursive reflection with the imagination."[36] The purpose of discursive meditation is to bring us to a knowledge and sensible awareness of Christ's love for us. Enkindled with love for Christ, we strive with God's grace to empty ourselves of those disordered desires and attachments that prevent a more intimate relationship with him. John tells us in *The Ascent of Mount Carmel* that this enkindling of love for Christ is necessary to begin the self-emptying of the disordered appetites required for union with Christ. If there were no satisfaction in the beginning stages of our relationship with Christ, we wouldn't begin the journey.[37] However, intellectual knowledge and good intentions alone are insufficient to overcome our selfish ways of loving. "A more intense enkindling of a greater of love," love for Christ, is necessary.[38] A greater love, even urgent love, for Christ is necessary to overcome "the lesser loves," that is, our attachments and selfish desires.[39]

---

[36] John, CW, *The Living Flame of Love*, Stanza 3, no. 32.

[37] John, CW, *The Ascent of Mount Carmel*, Book 1, chap. 14, no. 2.

[38] "A more intense enkindling of another, better love (love of the soul's Bridegroom) is necessary for the vanquishing of the appetites and the denial of this pleasure. By finding satisfaction and strength in this love, it will have the courage and constancy to readily deny all other appetites. The love of its Bridegroom is not the only requisite for conquering the strength of the sensitive appetites; an enkindling with urgent longings of love is also necessary. For the sensory appetites are moved and attracted toward sensory objects with such cravings that if the spiritual part of the soul is not fired with other, more urgent longings for spiritual things, the soul will be able neither to overcome the yoke of nature nor to enter the night of sense; nor will it have the courage to live in the darkness of all things by denying its appetites for them" (John, CW, *The Ascent of Mount Carmel*, Book 1, chap. 14, no. 2).

[39] John insists on the same principle in *The Spiritual Canticle* when he describes the soul symbolized as a woman who has been wounded by the Beloved. The "wound" is a metaphor of an experience of Christ's love for the bride that initiates a conversion process, a search for the Beloved. She leaves all things she sets out to seek the Beloved (*The Spiritual Canticle*, Stanza 1, no. 1).

In the initial phase of discursive meditation, God often graces us with special graces, spiritual consolations, insights, and beautiful ideas about God, which are necessary to begin the journey, just as falling in love begins with romantic feelings. Meister Eckhart believed that we treat God as a cow, wanting milk at our whim, so we need to be purified of our selfish desire. If we remain faithful to prayer and dependent upon God's grace, God's communication changes and becomes more interior, communicating on the transcendent spiritual level, which is beyond what we can feel or understand. Our prayer changes. This is disconcerting, mysterious, and obscure; we wonder where we went wrong. John explains God's new manner of communicating with the image of a loving mother weaning her child from her breast. God is like a loving mother who warms her child with the heat of her breast, feeds the child with good milk and tender food, and caresses him in her arms. But there comes a moment when she withholds her caresses and rubs bitter aloes on her sweet breast and makes the child walk on his own feet.[40] God's grace is like a loving mother who in the beginning engenders in us new enthusiasm and fervor in God's service, and this grace causes us to experience intense satisfaction in spiritual exercises. The moment comes when God, as a loving mother, deprives us of the early satisfaction and pleasures so that we will mature and grow into deeper self-knowledge and love God for God's sake instead of for the consolations of God.

For instance, when prayer becomes dry as ashes and I find it impossible to reflect discursively, I am tempted to abandon prayer. It has become boring. I no longer feel inspired by spiritual reading and devotions. I even find the liturgy unsatisfying.

This dryness in prayer extends to other parts of our lives. "Souls do not get satisfaction or consolation from the things of God; they do not get any from creatures either. Since God puts a soul in this

---

[40] John, *CW*, *The Dark Night*, Book 1, chap. 1, no. 2.

dark night in order to dry up and purge its sensory appetite, he does not allow it to find sweetness or delight in anything."[41]

The enthusiasm and consolation I once felt in my ministry has dried up, and I find it arid and unappealing. My first months in the community were life-giving, and I related well with everyone. Everyone seemed wholesome. Now I feel antipathy toward some members because of their personality traits. It is a challenge for me to be accepting of them, patient, and generous.

In the early days of my prayer life, I felt spiritually consoled, inspired, and eager to serve others. Being kind and generous came easy. Now I combat impatience, anger, jealousy, and the tendency to criticize others who are different than I. Past sins haunt me, and I struggle with my oversensitivity to people's reactions. Painful childhood memories surface and I realize that I am more wounded by past childhood experiences than I imagined. Even though I strive to be more charitable, generous, and patient, I am aware of how radically dependent I am on God's grace to heal and transform me. Through the experience of dryness, and my brokenness and inner poverty, God invites me to open to God's healing and transforming. We tend to think of contemplative prayer as a level of prayer beyond discursive meditation, a prayer of consolation and spiritual insights, but this is an incomplete perception. The very experience of our brokenness, poverty, and helplessness is a contemplative experience because it is the fruit of God's inflowing love purging us of selfish desire, piercing the illusions we have of ourselves, and igniting within us, through darkness, the fire of a more authentic, mature love of God and neighbor.

In this new phase of God's self-communication, God is placing us in the night of the senses. A new level of spiritual development begins by withdrawing the sensible satisfaction once enjoyed in prayer, relationships, and ministry, and bringing us to a mature spiritual love, free from the self-centered desire for pleasure and consolations—a more deeply committed love and fidelity. Much of the night of the

---

[41] John, *CW*, *The Dark Night*, Book 1, chap. 9, no. 2. See also *The Ascent of Mount Carmel*, Book 1, chap. 9, no. 2.

senses is growth in human maturity: self-knowledge, affective maturity, and purification of the pleasure principle and of our immature and inadequate images of God.

The Dark Night of the Spirit

The night of the spirit transforms us on the most profound level of our being. As we have noted, the disorders, conflicts, and egotism experienced on the sensory level have their origin in the spirit, a more profound purification is required.[42] This purification takes place in the passive night of the spirit when God's purifying grace acts as "a strong lye" that cleanses the deepest disorders of our being.[43] We become, as John states, "gods through participation."[44] St. Paul might express it this way: "[I]t is no longer I who live, but it is Christ who lives in me" (Gal 2:20). God's self-communication fully transforms our human faculties of knowing and loving into God's own way of knowing and loving. Our natural way of knowing, loving, and being in this world is transformed into a divine way of knowing, loving, and being. We are drawn into the trinitarian life and radiate God's love in our world.

The night of the spirit reveals our finitude, poverty, and mortality as the soul is purified "like gold in the crucible" and brought to this awareness, but "God humbles the soul greatly in order to exalt it greatly afterwards."[45]

> It remains to be said, then, that even though this happy night darkens the spirit, it does so only to impart light concerning all things; and even though it humbles individuals and reveals their miseries, it does so only to exalt them; and even though it impoverishes and empties them of all possessions and natural affection, it does so only that they may reach out divinely to the enjoyment

---

[42] John, *CW, The Dark Night*, Book 2, chap. 3, no.1.
[43] John, *CW, The Dark Night*, Book 2, chap. 2, no. 1.
[44] John, *CW, The Living Flame of Love*, Stanza 2, no. 34.
[45] John, *CW, The Dark Night*, Book 2, chap. 6, no. 6.

of all earthly and heavenly things, with a general freedom of spirit in them all.[46]

We see an example of the passive night of the spirit in the life of St. Thérèse of Lisieux. From her early childhood, St. Thérèse's spirituality was imbued with the thought of eternal life. On Easter Sunday of 1896, she entered a trial against faith that lasted for eighteen months, till her death on September 30, 1897. The trial consisted of doubts about the existence of eternal life. After nine years of faithful religious life, she was severely oppressed with doubts about the existence of eternal life. "Advance, advance; rejoice in death which will give you not what you hope for but a night still more profound, the night of nothingness."[47] God's love for her was called into question. Thérèse entered Carmel at fifteen years of age. After nine years of striving to be "love in the Heart of the Church," would God be there for her after her last breath, on the other side of the grave? This trial was so intense that it tried and purified Thérèse's trust in God's merciful love to such an extreme that she literally wrote the Creed in her own blood. In this dark night of faith, Thérèse experienced her extreme "littleness" and helplessness before God and abandoned herself completely to God. She learned that she was made from the same clay as all human beings. Before this trial, Thérèse could not understand how atheists and unbelievers could doubt God's existence and eternal life. Through this trial she became a sister to agnostics, atheists, and sinners. It placed her at the same table with atheists and unbelievers to share the same bitter bread and united her to all those who doubt the existence of God or eternal life.[48] She offered her trial for all those who struggle with their faith. In this sense, her trial had an apostolic

---

[46] John, *CW*, *The Dark Night*, Book 2, chap. 9, no. 1.

[47] St. Thérèse writes about this trial in manuscript "C" of her autobiography: St. Thérèse of Lisieux, *Story of a Soul*, 3rd ed., trans. John Clarke, OCD (Washington, DC: ICS Publications, 1996), 210–17.

[48] For a profound study of St. Thérèse's trial of faith, see Emanuel Renault, *L'Épreuve de la Foi: Le Combat de Thérèse de Lisieux* (Paris: Éditions du Cerf, 1991).

value because it united her to others who battle with their faith and doubt God's love.

Another way to understand the passive night of the spirit is that through this purifying experience, God recreates us and enlarges our capacity to receive God. God created us with an infinite capacity for God, which makes it possible for God to communicate to us his loving knowledge.[49] However, our infinite capacity has shrunk due to sin; therefore, God must enlarge our capacity to its original dimensions. Think of a woolen glove that has been washed in hot water. No doubt, the glove will have shrunk from the temperature. To fit the hands again, the glove must be stretched to its original size. In an analogous way, our infinite capacity for God, which has shrunk due to sin, must be stretched back to its original size to receive all that God wishes to give us. In the night of the spirit, God re-creates us and reestablishes our original capacity for God. We learn to love in a way diametrically opposed to our habitual way of acting and loving. Our human way is changed to a divine way of being, knowing, and loving.[50]

The Dark Night Incarnated in Daily Life

Reading John's description of the dark night, we can easily think that the dark night is solely a prayer experience. To think that the dark night is limited to the realm of prayer is to confuse John's understanding of contemplation.[51] The dark night is not a surgical procedure or supernatural intervention in a clinic or laboratory, after which one returns home purified and whole. The purifying night involves

---

[49] John, *CW*, *The Living Flame of Love*, Stanza 3, no. 22.

[50] Wilfred Stinissen, *La nuit comme le jour* (Louvain-la-Neuve, Belgium: Éditions du Moustier, 1990), 19–20. For a thorough study of the ontological dimension of the night of the spirit, I would refer the reader to the following study: Lucien-Marie de St. Joseph, "À la recherche d'une structure essentielle de la nuit de l'esprit," *Études Carmélitaines* 23 (1938): II, 254–81.

[51] Federico Ruiz, *Místico y maestro San Juan de la Cruz*, 2nd ed. (Madrid: Editorial de Espiritualidad, 2006), 241–42.

a combat in daily life; it is in the events and encounters in daily life that God's purifying grace touches our lives.[52]

God does not work in a vacuum. As we have seen in John's life, the dark night is conditioned by a variety of factors and exterior circumstances.[53] John uses the symbol of the dark night in a variety of ways throughout his writings. He uses it profusely in the book *The Dark Night* but less frequently in *The Ascent of Mount Carmel*. It is completely absent in *The Living Flame of Love*, although *The Living Flame* speaks abundantly of purification and transformation. In his letters, the dark night appears through references to trials, struggles with scrupulosity, complications in founding a monastery, and the discomfort that comes from the scorching heat of Andalusia.[54]

John provides a good example of how God purifies us through the concrete life experiences in *The Precautions* and *Counsels to a Religious*. The purifying hand of God touches us primarily through human relationships.

> The first precaution is to understand that you have come to the monastery so that all may fashion you and try you. Thus, to free yourself from the imperfections and disturbances that can be engendered by the mannerisms and attitudes of the religious and draw profit from every occurrence, you should think that all in

---

[52] Fr. Marie-Eugene, OCD, *Je veux voir Dieu* (Venasque, France: Éditions du Carmel, 1998; 1st ed., 1947), 818. The English edition: P. Marie Eugene, *I Am a Daughter of the Church*, vol. 2 (Westminster, MD: Christian Classics, 1989), 371–72.

[53] Ruiz, *Místico y maestro San Juan de la Cruz*, 240. Ruiz has emphasized the existential variety of the passive night of the spirit. See also the enlightening study of the existential experience of the dark night, P. Bruno de J-M., "Témoignages de l'expérience mystique nocturne," *Études Carmélitaines* 22 (1937): 237–301. Also, Augusto Guerra, "Para la intégración existencial de la noche oscura," in *Experiencia y pensamiento en San Juan de la Cruz* (Madrid: Editorial de Espiritualidad, 1990), 225–50.

[54] Ruiz, *Místico y Maestro San Juan de la Cruz*, 240. Here is an example from a letter to Madre Maria de Jesús, prioress of Córdoba. "It was ordained by God that you enter such poor houses and in such heat so that you could give some edification and let them know what you profess, which is the naked Christ, so that those who are inclined to join you may know with what spirit they ought to come" (John, *CW*, Letters, no. 16).

the community are artisans—as indeed they are—present there in order to prove you; that some will fashion you with words, others by deeds, and others with thoughts against you; and that in all this you must be submissive as is the statue to the craftsman who molds it, to the artist who paints it, and to the gilder who embellishes it.[55]

In our daily interactions with others whose temperament grates against us; when we struggle to be patient, compassionate, forgiving, and merciful; when we suffer misunderstanding or rejection patiently without reacting in a vengeful or passive-aggressive manner; when we are challenged to accept people whose ideas about the faith or politics are opposed to ours; when we have to forgo our own projects to respond generously to another's urgent needs; and when we deny our need to be praised and instead praise another's gifts—this is when we are chiseled and learn to love as Christ loves. Of course, we have to submit patiently to the artisans who chisel us with their words, attitudes, and different personalities and see them as vessels of God's grace and means of growth.

In *The Living Flame of Love*, John enumerates the trials through which one must pass in order to arrive at union with God through love: "The trials that those who are to reach this state suffer are threefold: trials, discomforts, fears, and temptations from the world; and these in many ways: temptations, aridities, and afflictions in the senses; and tribulations, darknesses, distress, abandonment, temptations, and other trials in the spirit. In this way a soul is purified in its sensory and spiritual parts."[56]

From this text we can discern the multiple ways in which God's purifying grace may be active in our lives: through temptations, failures, conflictual relationships, physical illnesses, humiliations, and loneliness. Even psychological states such as sadness, discouragement, and depression are an invitation to open more profoundly to God's transforming grace.

---

[55] John, *CW*, *The Precautions*, no. 15.
[56] John, *CW*, *The Living Flame of Love*, Stanza 2, no. 25.

Our psychological constitution, temperament, limitations, and personal history also influence our path of purification.[57] There are as many dark nights as there are people seeking union with God through love. We each have our particular dark night depending upon our personal past history, temperament, gifts, talents, and weaknesses. For instance, we may have a sensitive temperament and an intense longing for affection and affirmation due to low self-esteem or fear of rejection born from childhood experiences. One day, we find ourselves in a community situation where we are not given the affection or attention for which we long; we may feel overlooked, forgotten, or unappreciated for our gifts. We can either close in on ourselves and feel angry and withdrawn, or we can open to the situation, seeing it as a means of greater self-knowledge and surrender to God, and as an invitation to find our true security and sense of worth in God's love.

Perhaps we are perfectionistic, driven to succeed in everything out of an unconscious fear or need to control others and situations. We may fail an exam, lose our job, or be excluded for an office or position which we have worked hard to acquire. The failure can become the means to purify our drive for perfection, and make us more humble, less controlling, and accepting of our limited humanity.

Ministry can be a place where God's purifying hand purifies us of our disordered desires and attachments to self. A demanding parish ministry or community leadership role can reveal those areas in our life where we are deficient and need to grow in patience, mercy, forgiveness, and generosity. The demands of the ministry, conflictual and difficult relationships, and stressful decisions constellate within us our strengths and limitations. These very situations can be a "dark night," enlightening us to those areas of our life where we need conversion and growth. The key is to remain open and receptive to learning from them, and to see them with the eyes of faith.

The experience of temptation is one area where God's purifying grace works to bring us to the truth of who we are, and our radical need for God's merciful and transforming grace. The Desert Fathers

---

[57] Ruiz, *Místico y maestro San Juan de la Cruz*, 251.

and Mothers believed that temptations are places and moments of transformation because they reveal the deeper regions of our heart where we need God's purifying and redemptive grace. Abba Anthony said, "Whoever has not experienced temptation cannot enter the kingdom of heaven. Without temptation no one can be saved."[58] Like St. Paul, we each have some sort of "thorn" in our side that brings us to our knees: some vulnerable and emotional wound, some defect of character, or tendency toward some particular sin such as greed, gluttony, anger, jealousy, envy, impatience, lust, or sloth that reminds us that we are radically dependent upon God's grace. John writes about certain temptations that may afflict people who will pass into the passive night of the spirit.

Some people are buffeted by an "angel of Satan," a spirit of fornication. Powerful sexual temptations, foul thoughts, and vivid images assail them.[59] Sexuality is a powerful force within human nature, and the integration of sexual energy into our spiritual life is a lifelong process. Some people struggle more than others with their sexual energy and issues. When we consider the pornographic dark side of social media, how accessible and addictive it is, we can understand how the spirit of fornication can afflict a person.

A blasphemous spirit is another temptation. Blasphemous, angry, and hateful thoughts against God, the faith, creation, and life in general can become a grave torment.[60] The terrifying and horrendous wars and violence in our world can lead to blasphemous thoughts and doubts about God's existence and his concern for humankind. Why doesn't God intervene in this inhuman war? A painful childhood can become the seedbed for anger and blasphemous thoughts against God.

Another loathsome spirit, the *spiritus vertiginis*, is one of the most burdensome goads and horrors of the night—very similar to what a

---

[58] Benedicta Ward, trans., *The Sayings of the Desert Fathers: The Alphabetical Collection*, Cistercian Studies 59 (Collegeville, MN: Cistercian Publications, 1975), 5.

[59] John, *CW*, *The Dark Night*, Book 1, chap. 14, no. 1.

[60] John, *CW*, *The Dark Night*, Book 2, chap. 14, no. 2.

person suffers in the dark night of the spirit. "The spirit so darkens the senses that souls are filled with thousands of scruples and perplexities, so intricate that such persons can never be content with anything, nor can their judgment receive support of any counsel or idea."[61] Scrupulosity, fears, anxiety, and rumination and remorse over one's sins, past and present, can be an oppressive trial for some people passing through the dark night. It is not uncommon for people coming to the end of their life to recall their past sins, ruminate over them, and doubt God's forgiveness. This is a trial that purifies their faith in God's merciful love and calls for confident surrender to God in the midst of darkness.

These temptations are a foreshadow of the night of the spirit and reveal the deeper regions of our psyche and spirit. They shed light on our inner desires, fears, and weaknesses. We must confront and accept them and offer them to the purifying grace of God. They bring us to our inner truth, our "littleness" and poverty, to be surrendered into the furnace of God's purifying love.

Every experience of life, therefore, may become a sacrament of God's transforming grace; even the experience of having sinned, if repented of and used as a learning experience, can become a vessel of reconciliation and purification. John expresses this idea in a passage in *The Living Flame of Love* where he explains the different experiences of a "cautery of love" and "wounds of love." A "wound of love" is a mystical experience of God's love that inflames the soul with the fire of God's love. However, John tells us that there are "wounds" not caused by the mystical wound of love. These are our sins and miseries, and they can become "wounds of love" if offered to God.[62]

Recall St. Thérèse's letter of September 17, 1896, to her sister Marie of the Sacred Heart, who felt discouraged by aridity, the absence of desire, and her interior poverty. Thérèse reminded her sister that our poverty, dryness, and misery have a magnetic force that draws the

---

[61] John, *CW*, *The Dark Night*, Book 2, chap. 14, no. 3.
[62] John, *CW*, *The Living Flame of Love*, Stanza 2, no. 7.

flames of God's merciful love to heal and transform us and unite us to God.

> The weaker one is, without desires or virtues, the more suited one is for the workings of this consuming and transforming Love. . . . "The truly poor in spirit, where do we find him? You must look for him from afar," said the psalmist, that is to say in *lowliness*, in nothingness . . . Ah! let us remain then *very far* from all that sparkles, let us love our littleness, let us love to feel nothing, then we shall be poor in spirit, and Jesus will come to look for us, and however far we may be, He will transform us in flames of love. It is confidence and confidence alone that must lead us to Love.[63]

Suffering or Dark Night?

However, it is important to clarify that trials, temptations, and sufferings alone do not mean a person is passing through a "dark night." For suffering to become a vessel of the purifying night, we must walk the path of personal conversion, seriously committed to the spiritual life and open to what life brings us as a means of purification, health, and transformation. Just because a person is having a bad day, suffers a sudden heart attack, or struggles with depression, this does not mean they are in a dark night. Discernment is necessary. As we know, life is full of good days and bad days, joys and sorrows, trials, and sufferings of all kinds. None of us can escape the trials, stresses, and sufferings of life. John does not believe in suffering for suffering's sake. He believes in the end of suffering that comes from God's love that purifies and transforms us so that our whole life is directed toward loving God with our whole heart, mind, and strength, and our neighbor as ourselves. He believes that suffering, which is part of human life, can be the means of purification and transformation if we sincerely seek union with God and are open to life's joys and sorrows with the eyes of faith, and surrender to God in faith,

---

[63] St. Thérèse of Lisieux, Letter 197, *The Letters of St. Thérèse of Lisieux*, vol. 2, trans. John Clarke, OCD (Washington, DC: ICS Publications, 1988), 999.

hope, and love. We must cooperate and apply our will to what God asks of us.

John believes that life has everything we need for transformation if we are open and cooperate with God. Many people desire loving union with God, and ask God for the grace, but when God begins to prepare them with trials and sufferings, they resist God's invitation and flee as from death to seek their ease and comfort. "They resemble children who kick and cry and struggle to walk by themselves when their mothers want to carry them; in walking by themselves they make no headway, or if they do, it is at a child's pace."[64]

---

[64] John, *CW*, *The Ascent of Mount Carmel*, Book 1, Prol.

Chapter 7

Sitting in the Fire

Modern Psychology and Healing

CONTEMPORARY PSYCHOLOGY HAS greatly influenced mystical theology. Sigmund Freud and Carl Jung recognized that the Western psyche was sick and desperately needed healing and transformation.[1] Jung was convinced that the root of much of the personal and collective sickness of society, as well as personal neurosis, was a disconnection with the deeper levels of the spirit. He believed in the healing dimension of religion and that healing and wholeness come from connecting with one's spiritual nature. Jung's theory of the personality, specifically his concept of the unconscious, is helpful in understanding the process by which we come to spiritual and psychological healing.[2]

---

[1] William Johnston, *Mystical Theology: The Science of Love* (Maryknoll, NY: Orbis Books, 1995), 214.

[2] I refer the reader to the following studies that have related the insights of modern psychology, in particular the unconscious, to contemplative purification and healing: Kevin Culligan, "St. John of the Cross and Modern Psychology: A Brief Journey in the Unconscious," in *A Fresh Approach to St. John of the Cross*, ed. John McGowan (Middlegreen, England: St Pauls, 1993), 83–102; William Johnston, *Silent Music* (London: HarperCollins, 1974); John Welch, *When Gods Die* (New York: Paulist Press, 1990); Mary Wolff-Salin, *No Other Light: Points of Convergence in Psychology and Spirituality* (New York: Crossroad, 1986); and

Jung's Theory of the Development of Consciousness

Jung divided the personality into three levels of consciousness: conscious ego, personal unconsciousness, and collective unconscious.[3] The conscious ego is that part of the psyche that calls itself "I" and is self-conscious, aware of itself. As Jack Welch explains in his work *Spiritual Pilgrims: Carl Jung and Teresa of Avila*, the ego "is the gatekeeper to consciousness since experiences of the outer and inner worlds must pass through the ego to be conscious. It is an island of identity and continuity for the personality. A healthy ego consciousness is an important goal in human development."[4] A healthy ego is necessary to get up in the morning, dress, go to work, fulfill one's obligations, cope with the stresses of daily life, and relate well to people.

The conscious mind includes thoughts, feelings, and memories of which we are aware. Jung compared the conscious mind to the tip of an iceberg that rises above the surface of the water. Ninety-five percent of an iceberg is hidden beneath the dark, icy waters. The unconscious is like that submerged portion of the iceberg. It is that part of our mental life, the psyche, that lies outside the boundaries of the conscious mind and has a dynamic influence on much of our thoughts, feelings, and behavior, even though we may be unaware of it.

Jung divided the unconscious into two levels: the personal and the collective. Within the personal unconscious lies a realm of memories and experiences, both positive and negative, that date even before birth. We find in the personal unconscious emotions, images, forgot-

---

Gerald G. May, MD, *Care of Mind, Care of Spirit: A Psychiatrist Explores Spiritual Direction* (San Francisco: Harper & Row, 1982).

[3] The conscious mind includes perceptions, thoughts, feelings, and memories of which we are aware. I have relied on the following sources for my discussion of Jung and the levels of consciousness: C. G. Jung, *Psychological Reflections*, ed. Jolande Jacobi and R. F. C. Hill (Princeton: Princeton University Press, 1978); Robert E. Johnson, *Inner Work* (San Francisco: HarperCollins, 1986); and Easter Harding, *The I and the Not I: A Study in the Development of Consciousness* (Princeton: Bolligen, 1975).

[4] John Welch, OCarm, *Spiritual Pilgrims: Carl Jung and Teresa of Avila* (New York: Paulist Press, 1982), 66.

ten ideas, half-forgotten memories of which we are unaware and which remain unintegrated. Jung refers to this unintegrated and repressed psychic material as the "shadow." The "shadow" stands for everything within us that we do not want to see—that is, that we try to ignore, repress, or push out of consciousness so that we can avoid confronting it to protect our conscious ego. This includes positive contents as well as negative. The positive shadow may be the gifts, talents, and positive desires of which we are unaware, or that we may find hard to face and accept. The negative may be repressed sexual impulses, unresolved anger, bitterness, narcissism, and the tendency to present an idealized image of ourselves.

This dark side also includes the repression of painful memories from childhood or past relationships that become the fuel for fear, anger, and feelings of unworthiness that disturb the personality. As depth psychology has discovered, most neuroses and emotional disturbances are associated with the memory. The brain is like a taperecorder that retains every experience we have had since birth, perhaps even in the womb.[5]

Deeper than the personal unconscious is what Jung referred to as the "collective unconscious." It is that layer of psychic life where we connect with all that is part of the cultural, psychological, and spiritual background of the human race. It can be compared to a "deep underground stream" that feeds the wells of individual lives.[6] Jung understood the psyche as more ancient and larger than our personal lives; therefore, the collective unconscious connects us with the human race and years of psychic development.

Jung believed that human development is a lifelong process of growth that he defined as individuation. Individuation is the process of becoming the person God created us to be, calls for an awareness and integration of the unconscious elements of the personality, and relates us to our spiritual nature.

---

[5] Johnston, *Silent Music*, 124.
[6] Welch, *When Gods Die*, 58.

Jung conceived of psychotherapy as a path of healing and transformation of the personality. Healing takes place when the unconscious becomes conscious and the ego consciousness becomes more and more related to one's deeper spiritual depths. Jung pictured the unconscious as a rich source of energy for the personality. The psyche is like a deep ocean full of beautiful jewels and treasures as well as ugly and dark creatures. Healing requires a purification process whereby we must recognize our capacity for sin and evil. This requires a descent into the dark depths of the personality where we must face the truth of who we are and where we must confront our illusions, addictions, selfish desires, repressed memories, and impulses. This transformation process engages us in a battle with our passions, such as pride, lust, anger, envy, and jealousy. We must allow the repressed memories of past wounding experiences to emerge into the light so that they can be recognized, accepted, integrated, and healed. All this psychic material must become conscious and integrated for healing to take place. Only in this way do we become whole human beings related to our spiritual nature.

The implications of Jung's theory of the unconscious are helpful for the spiritual journey. In his work *The Varieties of Religious Experience*, William James considered "the discovery of the unconscious states as the most important step forward in psychology."[7] Even though we generally attribute the discovery of the unconscious to Freud and Jung, Lancelot White demonstrates in his book *The Unconscious Before Freud* that people long before Freud recognized that human beings are motivated in their behavior by unconscious factors.[8] St. Paul acknowledged that there was another law at work in his personality that prompted him to do things he would have preferred not to do (Rom 7:22-23). The Desert Fathers and Mothers, like St. Anthony of the Desert, spoke of their desert life as an interior battle with the

---

[7] Quoted in Kevin Culligan's article "John of the Cross and Modern Psychology: A Brief Journey into the Unconscious," 90.

[8] See Lancelot L. White, *The Unconscious Before Freud* (New York: Basic Books, 1960).

demons of anger, lust, and sloth. These "demons" symbolized their shadow side that called for recognition and integration.[9]

John of the Cross and the Unconscious

As we have seen in the previous chapters, John of the Cross recognizes that the human person is like a sick person in need of God's healing.[10] We do not find the word *unconscious* in John's vocabulary, but it is evident that he recognizes that there exists a whole realm of the human psyche and spirit that is unconscious. John used the psychological categories of his day to describe the transformation process. He understood that human behavior is influenced by desires, impulses, attachments, and memories of which we are unaware and that need to come into the light of consciousness if we desire healing and liberation and to arrive at union with God through love.

For instance, in *The Dark Night* he discerns the selfish motivations of those entering into the night of senses: "Although spiritual persons do practice these exercises with great profit and persistence, and are very careful about them, spiritually speaking, they conduct themselves in a very weak and imperfect manner. Since their motivation in their spiritual works and exercises is the consolation and satisfaction they experience in them, and since they have not been conditioned by the arduous struggle of practicing virtue, they possess many faults and imperfections in the discharge of their spiritual activities."[11]

Furthermore, John does not use the symbol of shadow to describe the dark side of human nature, yet the reality of the personal "shadow" is evident when he demonstrates the need for purification. The shadow, or inferior and sinful side of human nature, comprises the disordered desires that enslave the heart and compel us to live outside ourselves in creatures, the deeply rooted selfishness manifested

---

[9] Culligan, "St. John of the Cross and Modern Psychology: A Brief Journey into the Unconscious," 90. See also Anselm Gruen, *Heaven Begins Within You: Wisdom from the Desert Fathers* (New York: Crossroad, 1994), 36–44.
[10] John, *CW*, *The Dark Night*, Book 2, chap. 16, no. 10.
[11] John, *CW*, *The Dark Night*, Book 1, chap. 1, no. 3.

through the seven capital vices, and the tendency to close our hearts to God's love. We see the dark side of beginners in those who fall into spiritual pride. Their "shadow side" is their pharisaical attitude that leads them to condemn and disparage others. Unconscious of their own sinfulness and misery, they project their evil on others; they exalt themselves and judge their neighbor.[12]

John is aware that there are depths of brokenness, sinful attitudes, and character defects of which we are unaware until God's light shines in the dark corners of our minds and hearts. "This divine purge stirs up all the foul and vicious humors of which the soul was never before aware; never did it realize there was so much evil in itself, since these humors were so deeply rooted."[13]

John's doctrine on the memory reveals his psychological insight into the human mind. All our experiences, positive and negative, are recorded in our memory and influence our behavior without our conscious awareness. Painful childhood memories, traumatic or even slight, can cause much suffering, unhappiness, and serious psychological disturbances if unrecognized or if we obsessively ruminate on them. This inner world needs to become conscious for healing, integration, and transformation.

As we will see, John believes that the healing process requires becoming conscious of the unconscious contents of our psyche and spirit and a deepening union with God who dwells in the center of our being.

The Divine Physician

According to John of the Cross, trying to heal ourselves from our disordered way of loving by our own efforts is like being a child who struggles to walk by himself when his mother wants to carry him in her arms. God is the divine Physician who must intervene and heal the sicknesses of our mind and heart.

---

[12] John, *CW*, *The Dark Night*, Book 1, chap. 2, no. 2.
[13] John, *CW*, *The Dark Night*, Book 2, chap. 10, no. 2. See also *The Living Flame of Love*, Stanza 1, no. 22.

For John, therapy is allowing the inflow God's self-communicating love to penetrate at ever deeper levels of our mind and heart. "The love of God is the soul's health."[14] This love comes through contemplation, which is a personal encounter with God's Spirit of love dwelling within our depths; it is the experience of being loved by God and of loving at the most profound level of our being. In light of these affirmations, it is clear that John of the Cross understands the dark night of contemplation as a healing of the sicknesses of the mind and heart. The challenge is to open and surrender to God's purifying and transforming action.

> Yet until a soul is placed by God in the passive purgation of that dark night, which we will soon explain, it cannot purify itself completely of these imperfections or others. But people should insofar as possible strive to do their part in purifying and perfecting themselves and thereby merit God's divine cure. In this cure God will heal them of what through their own efforts they were unable to remedy. No matter how much individuals do through their own efforts, they cannot actively purify themselves enough to be disposed in the least degree for the divine union of the perfection of love. God must take over and purge them in that fire that is dark for them.[15]

In *The Living Flame of Love*, the healing quality of contemplation comes into clear focus.[16] There, John describes contemplation as the experience of God's self-communicating love symbolized by "a living flame of love" that penetrates and burns deep within us when we open and surrender to it. "This flame of love is the spirit of its Bridegroom, who is the Holy Spirit."[17] The flame of love is the gentle, selfless, tender

---

[14] John, *CW*, *The Spiritual Canticle*, Stanza 11, no. 11.

[15] John, *CW*, *The Dark Night*, Book 1, chap. 3, no. 3. Other texts from *The Dark Night* in which John refers to the night as a cure: Book 2, chap. 12, no. 4; chap. 16, no. 10. John also speaks of the night as a process of maturity in *The Dark Night*, Book 1, chap. 8, no. 3.

[16] Stanzas 18 through 26 of *The Living Flame of Love* are a synthesis of the passive night treated in *The Ascent of Mount Carmel* and *The Dark Night*. In these paragraphs, John describes the Holy Spirit's healing grace through contemplation.

[17] John, *CW*, *The Living Flame of Love*, Stanza 1, no. 3.

spirit of Christ, whose love wells up within the human person.[18] "Since this flame is a flame of divine life, it wounds the soul with the tenderness of God's life, and it wounds and stirs it so deeply as to make it dissolve in love."[19]

It is important to emphasize the primacy of God's love. In mystical literature, fire is an archetypal symbol that represents concretely God's love for humankind and, specifically, infused contemplation.[20] Therefore this "flame of love" is not our love for God, but rather, God's love that sets us on fire with God's love.[21]

Referring to God's love, John writes, "Love is never idle. It is always in continual movement."[22] God's love is like a fire that is in continual movement in our lives. God's presence is never static or idle. We can interpret this statement in a personal way. Our love can never be contained. When we love, our love is like a fire that gives warmth to all. It is always in movement like a flickering flame.

---

[18] Although John speaks of contemplation as an experience of the Holy Spirit in *The Living Flame of Love*, he recognizes that the contemplative experience is a trinitarian experience. "Since this soul is so close to God that it is transformed into a flame of love in which the Father, the Son, and the Holy Spirit are communicated to it . . ." *The Living Flame of Love*, Stanza 1, no. 6.

[19] John, *CW*, *The Living Flame of Love*, Stanza 1, no. 7.

[20] María J. Mancho Duque, *El símbolo de la noche en San Juan de la Cruz* (Salamanca, Spain: Ediciones Universidad de Salamanca, 1982), 186. Fire also represents the purifying and transforming action of God. "Fire in the Bible symbolizes God's action that purifies and purges; it is the agent of destruction of all that is infectious, reducing to ashes idols and annihilating enemy forces." See also Olegario González de Cardenal, *La entraña del cristianismo* (Salamanca, Spain: Secretario Trinitario, 1997), 839.

[21] "It should be known that this touch of a spark is a very subtle touch that the Beloved sometimes produces in the soul, even when least expected, and which inflames her in the fire of love, as if a hot spark were to leap from the fire and set her ablaze. Then with remarkable speed, as when one suddenly remembers, the will is enkindled in loving, desiring, praising, and thanking God, and reverencing, esteeming, and praying to him in the savor of love. She calls these acts 'flowing from the balsam of God.' These flowings result from the touch of the sparks shot forth by the divine love that enkindles the fire. This divine love is the balsam of God that with its fragrance and substance comforts and cures the soul" (John, *CW*, *The Spiritual Canticle*, Stanza 25, no. 5).

[22] John, *CW*, *The Living Flame of Love*, Stanza 1, no. 8.

In *The Living Flame of Love*, fire is the unifying theme of the work. It is repeated in all four stanzas and unites the poem. Fire has five distinct functions: it purifies, delights, heals, transforms, and consumes. If we take this image and apply it to God's action in our lives, we can say that the Holy Spirit is like a fire that purifies us, delights us, heals us, transforms us, and consumes us.[23] God's love is always in movement in our lives, purifying us at times, delighting us at other times, healing and transforming us in different periods of our lives, and, finally, consuming us.

The Holy Spirit, the "living flame of love," heals the disorders and sicknesses of our heart and mind. In *The Living Flame of Love*, John comments on the verse, "*Pues ya no eres esquiva*" ("Now you are no longer oppressive"):

> O Living Flame of love
> that tenderly wounds my soul
> in its deepest center! Since
> now you are no longer oppressive,
> now consummate! if it be your will:
> tear through the veil of this sweet encounter.[24]

Paragraphs 18 through 28 of Stanza 1 of *The Living Flame of Love* synthesize the passive dark night treated in *The Ascent of Mount Carmel* and *The Dark Night*.[25] The Holy Spirit penetrates into the caverns of our mind and heart, into those deep recesses of our memory, and draws out all the hidden disorders and wounded memories and heals them in the fire of love.

---

[23] See Gabriel Castro, "Llama de amor viva," in *Introdución a la lectura de San Juan de la Cruz*, ed. Salvador Ros et al. (Avila: Junta de Castilla y León, 1991), 524.

[24] John, *CW, The Living Flame of Love*, Stanza 1, no. 19. Kieran Kavanaugh's translation of "*esquiva*" as "oppressive" fails to express the richness of the term. *Esquivar* means that which frightens easily. One way to understand *esquiva* is to think of how we can frighten a bird when we suddenly draw close to its cage. It draws back out of fright. This is *esquiva*. Therefore, this flame is experienced at first as frightening and we draw back.

[25] See John, *CW, The Living Flame of Love*, Stanza 1, no. 25.

> Since in this fashion God mediates and heals the soul of its many infirmities, bringing it health, it must necessarily suffer from this purge according to its sickness. For here Tobias is placing the heart on the coals to release and drive out every kind of demon [Tb. 6:8]. All the souls' infirmities are brought to light; they are set before its eyes to be felt and healed.[26]

Contemplation as Enlightenment and Being Loved

If God's love is the medicine and cure for the infirmities of our psyche, then how does this healing take place? This question touches upon the passive dimension of transformation.

As we have discussed, we find a whole world in our psyche: light and darkness, good and bad. There is an enormous part of our psychic life that is unconscious: fears, anxieties, forgotten memories, repressed sexuality and anger, and hidden gifts and talents. This inner world fuels our behavior. Wholeness and healing are a matter of becoming more and more aware of our unconscious life. Healing involves a deepening awareness and integration of this inner world.

John understands the process of healing as a deepening awareness, an illumination, that purifies, heals, and disposes us for union with God.

> Before this divine fire is introduced into the substance of the soul and united with it through perfect and complete purgation and purity, its flame, which is the Holy Spirit, wounds the soul by destroying and consuming the imperfections of its bad habits. And this work is the Holy Spirit, in which he disposes it for divine union and transformation in God through love.[27]

---

[26] John, *CW*, *The Living Flame of Love*, Stanza 1, no. 21.

[27] John, *CW*, *The Living Flame of Love*, Stanza 1, no. 19. See also *The Dark Night*, Book 2, chap. 5, no. 2: "Insofar as infused contemplation is loving wisdom of God, it produces two principal effects in the soul: by both purging and illumining, this contemplation prepares the soul for union with God through love. Hence the same loving wisdom that purges and illumines the blessed spirits purges and illumines the soul here on earth."

The Holy Spirit begins the healing process by "wounding" us. The symbol of the "wound" is frequent in *The Spiritual Canticle* and *The Living Flame of Love* and can have several meanings.[28] In *The Spiritual Canticle*, the soul begins the spiritual journey as a result of a love-wound.

> Where have you hidden,
> Beloved, and left me moaning?
> You fled like the stag
> after wounding me;
> I went out calling you, but you were gone.[29]

The wound of God's love makes the soul aware of all that she owes to God, that God has created her solely for himself and that she has forgotten the Beloved in midst of creatures.

In *The Living Flame of Love*, the wound produces an acute awareness of our deep poverty and misery. The fire of God's love wounds us by driving its flames into the deepest recesses of our memory and revealing all the pathology of our heart and mind, both personally and collectively, that we have been unaware of or that we have successfully

---

[28] Spiritual writers give the expression "wound of love" a broad or strict meaning. In the broad sense, it designates various graces that bring with them suffering, ordinary, or eminent graces, ranging from pain caused by regret of past faults to transverberation, a mystical grace reserved for souls who have reached a high degree of transforming union with God. In the strict sense, the "wound of love" refers to a special grace, clearly determined, having special distinctive characteristics and its own effects. It belongs to the purification of the spirit. All of a sudden the person is seized with an intense awareness of God's love that impresses itself in the intelligence and ignites an ardent, impetuous desire and movement toward the Beloved, and then, paradoxically, a sense of the Beloved's absence. The absence of the Beloved pierces the soul like an arrow that causes both pain and delight. See A. Cabassut, OSB, "Blessures d'amour," *Dictionnaire de spiritualité*, vol. 1 (Paris: Editions du Cerf, 1973), 1724–25. St. John of the Cross insists on the purifying role of love wounds. "He bestows these to wound more than heal, and afflict more than satisfy, since they serve to quicken the knowledge and increase the appetite (consequently the sorrow and longing) to see God" (*The Spiritual Canticle*, Stanza 1, no. 19).

[29] John, *CW*, *The Spiritual Canticle*, Stanza 1.

repressed through our defense mechanisms. It manifests all our sinfulness and weaknesses that are contrary to God's love.

> Now with the light and heat of the divine fire, it sees and feels those weaknesses and miseries that previously resided with it hidden and unfelt, just as the dampness of the log of wood was unknown until the fire applied to it made it sweat and smoke and sputter. And this is what the flame does to the imperfect soul.
> When this flame shines on the soul, since its light is excessively brilliant, it shines within the darknesses of the soul, which are also excessive. Persons then feel their natural and vicious darknesses contrary to the supernatural light because they do not have it within themselves as they do their darknesses—and the darknesses do not comprehend the light [Jn 1:5]. They feel these darknesses inasmuch as the light shines on them, for it is impossible to perceive one's darknesses without the divine light focusing on them.[30]

In *The Dark Night*, John explains the process of healing and transformation with the symbol of fire that penetrates a log of wood.[31] When fire is applied to wood, the fire first dehumidifies the wood by dispelling all moisture from it. Then it turns the wood black and ugly and causes it to emit a bad odor. The fire expels from the wood all those elements that are contrary to fire. Eventually, the fire transforms the wood into fire itself and makes it share in the properties and actions of fire. Although the wood remains, it is a transformed log of wood that shares the properties of fire and gives off warmth and light.

John's metaphor describes well the healing of the unconscious as a gradual progressive enlightenment of the hidden disorders of the mind and heart. This illumination purifies, heals, and disposes us for union with God. He writes:

> Similarly, we should philosophize about this divine, loving fire of contemplation. Before transforming the soul, it purges it of all contrary qualities. It produces blackness and darkness and bring

---

[30] John, *CW*, *The Living Flame of Love*, Stanza 1, no. 22.
[31] John, *CW*, *The Dark Night*, Book 2, chap. 10, no. 1.

to the fore the soul's ugliness; thus one seems worse than before and unsightly and abominable. This divine purge stirs up all the foul and vicious humors of which the soul was never before aware; never did it realize there was so much evil in itself, since these humors were so deeply rooted. And now that they may be expelled and annihilated they are brought to light and seen clearly through the illumination of the dark light of divine contemplation. Although the soul is no worse than before, either in itself or in its relationship with God, it feels clearly that it is so bad as to be not only unworthy that God see it but deserving his abhorrence.[32]

The image of the fire consuming a log of wood describes the healing of our unconscious through contemplative experience. When the fire of God's love begins to flare up within us, it penetrates the darkest corners of our minds and opens up the deeper levels of our unconscious. It reveals all that is sinful and wounded within us, all that is contrary to love, and impedes us from receiving the fullness of life and love. It reveals the "shadow" part of our lives, our selfishness, pride, jealousy, greed, childhood traumas, fears, and obsessions. As Jesus in his healing ministry associated with the sick, the tax collectors, prostitutes, and outcasts in order to bring healing and salvation, we similarly have to descend into the depths of our unconscious and see and feel all those painful and unacceptable parts of our personality that have remained unconscious.

As one author noted, "God is a master in the art of recyclage."[33] God takes all the debris of our lives and recycles them. Nothing is wasted. What seems wasted, worthless, garbage, unwanted, and cast aside becomes the very fuel for growth and love.

As we noted before, our miseries and sins become "wounds of love" if they are accepted and offered to God.

> To understand the nature of this wound, which is addressed by the soul, it should be known that the cautery of material fire always

---

[32] John, *CW*, *The Dark Night*, Book 2, chap. 10, no. 2.
[33] Wilfred Stinissen, OCD, *La nuit comme le jour illuminé: La nuit obscure chez Jean de la Croix* (Toulouse: Éditions du Carmel, 2010), 35.

leaves a wound where it is applied. And it possesses this property: If applied to a wound not made by fire, it converts it into a wound caused by fire. Whether a soul is wounded by other wounds of miseries and sins, or whether it is healthy, this cautery of love immediately effects a wound of love in the one it touches, and those wounds deriving from other causes become wounds of love.[34]

God uses everything within us to bring us to wholeness and union with God. God uses all of what we think of as waste or debris for healing and transformation and union with him.

John accentuates the illumination of unconscious material hidden within us. It is as though we are sicker than we realized. This is the situation of those who enter into the purification process. In the beginning we consider ourselves rather healthy, but as we progress further into the purifying process, we realize that there exist layers of pathology and brokenness of which were unaware. Purgative contemplation must reach the deepest recesses of our being where sin has sunk its roots, that is, in the spirit.

Isn't this the way it is in our lives? The more we live, the more layers of our being are disclosed. Our psyche is like an onion whose skin is gradually peeled away. We can never be surprised by what might surface. As we encounter different circumstances and enter into new relationships, all kinds of interior issues emerge.

It is interesting to note that the healing process is not only a matter of seeing the misery within us; it also involves feeling the misery. We feel our poverty and brokenness. "All the soul's infirmities are brought to light; they are set before its eyes to be felt and healed."[35] This is similar to psychotherapy; the healing of inner conflicts only takes place when the person sees and feels their pathology.[36]

---

[34] John, *CW, The Living Flame of Love*, Stanza 1, no. 7.
[35] John, *CW, The Living Flame of Love*, Stanza 1, no. 21.
[36] Culligan, "John of the Cross and Modern Psychology: A Brief Journey into the Unconscious," 95. See also John E. Perito, MD, "God, Psychoanalysis and Contemplative Prayer," *Human Development* 18 (1997): 22–25.

Therefore purgative contemplation heals the deepest disorders of the unconscious by enlightening them. This illumination is itself a sign of growing health. "This illumination is for the soul a sign of the health the purgation is producing within it and a foretaste of the abundance for which it hopes."[37] As healing in psychotherapy comes through making the unconscious conscious, so contemplation brings to light the disorders of the personality so that they may be clearly seen, felt, expelled, and healed.[38] The more conscious we become of our inner world, even though it may be painful and disorienting, the healthier we become.

We often have an erroneous grasp of the contemplative experience. It is easy for us to think that contemplation is a peaceful prayer experience beyond discursive meditation. As we know, there are periods of contemplative experience in which we feel our poverty, brokenness, and sinfulness to an intense degree. This, too, is a contemplative experience. It is an experience of the power of grace at work in human weakness. When God gets close to us, we see and feel our weakness.

However, it is important to clarify that entering into deeper levels of consciousness alone will not heal the mind and spirit.[39] Although the psychotherapeutic process taught by great psychologists such as Jung can help capture the psychological ramifications of the dark night, the healing process we find in the works of John of the Cross is more than a psychological insight wherein a person becomes aware of their past, their neuroses, and their sinfulness. John described the dark night experience in categories of his day. He attempts to present the impact of God on the personality and to describe the transformation of the psyche and spirit. Healing is primarily God's action, not a spontaneous psychological transformation of the psyche.[40]

---

[37] John, *CW, The Dark Night*, Book 2, chap. 7, no. 4.
[38] Culligan, "John of the Cross and Modern Psychology: A Brief Journey into the Unconscious," 94.
[39] Johnston, *Silent Music*, 125.
[40] Welch, *When Gods Die*, 103–4.

Healing involves more than entering into deeper levels of consciousness. Healing is a matter of grace. It is God's self-communicating love that is therapeutic in the contemplative experience. Love is the most therapeutic energy in the cosmos, the most effective source of healing we know.

William Thompson has defined the mystical dark night as a plunge into the ocean of the radically selfless love of God.[41] Mystical love is a devouring fire that consumes everything that might oppose it. Suffering, therefore, is felt when our selfish, narrow, and hard will encounters the selfless, tender, and compassionate love of God. In the presence of the selfless and gentle love of God, all within us that is contrary to God's love is seen for what it is—self-centeredness and misery.

> This flame of itself is extremely loving, and the will of itself is excessively dry and hard. When the flame tenderly and lovingly assails the will, the hardness is felt beside the tenderness, and dryness beside the love. The will does not feel the love and tenderness of the flame since, because of its contrary hardness and dryness, it is unprepared for this until the love and tenderness of God expel the dryness and hardness and reign within it. Accordingly, this flame was oppressive to the will, making it feel and suffer its own hardness and dryness.[42]

This text speaks of an experience that is more than just an enlightenment of one's selfishness and misery. The encounter with the Holy Spirit is an experience of God's self-communicating love. In being loved by the gentle and tender Spirit of Christ who draws out all our infirmities and miseries, our capacity to love is enlarged and expanded so we can love more and more as God loves and, in doing so, become authentically who God created us to be.

The healing and transforming energy of love is essential to the doctrine of John of the Cross. "This flame of love is the Spirit of its

---

[41] William Thompson, "The Dark Night: A Theological Consultation," in *Fire and Light: The Saints and Theology* (New York: Paulist Press, 1987), 92.
[42] John, *CW*, *The Living Flame of Love*, Stanza 1, no. 23.

Bridegroom, who is the Holy Spirit."⁴³ The "Spouse" is Jesus Christ, the Spirit of the risen Lord.

The Spiritual Canticle presents the spiritual life as an inner journey in which we come to know and experience the healing love of Christ the Beloved. "Ah! who can heal me?" asks the Bride in the *Canticle*.⁴⁴ Only the love of the Beloved who wounded her with love can heal her. "The reason lovesickness has no other remedy than the presence and the image of the Beloved is that, since this sickness differs from others, its medicine also differs. In other sicknesses, following sound philosophy, contraries are cured by contraries, but love is incurable except by things in accord with love."⁴⁵

Jesus Christ is the great healer. Just as in his earthly life Jesus cured those with an inability to walk, those with leprosy, and those with blindness, to symbolize the deeper healing on the spiritual level, so he continues his ministry of healing through the power of the Holy Spirit who has been poured into our hearts.

John of the Cross sees Jesus as the divine Physician. This is expressed beautifully in *The Spiritual Canticle*. Original sin wounded human nature but a healing process began on the cross.

> Beneath the apple tree:
> there I took you for my own,
> there I offered you my hand,
> and restored you,
> where your mother was corrupted.⁴⁶

John reflects on the effects of original sin on human nature and how God has healed and espoused us to Christ through his redeeming work. Human nature, our mother, was wounded by means of the forbidden fruit of the tree of Paradise, but a process of healing began through the passion and death of Jesus on the cross. On the cross

---

⁴³ John, *CW*, *The Living Flame of Love*, Stanza 1, no. 3.
⁴⁴ John, *CW*, *The Spiritual Canticle*, Stanza 6.
⁴⁵ John, *CW*, *The Spiritual Canticle*, Stanza 11, no. 11.
⁴⁶ John, *CW*, *Poetry*, "15. The Spiritual Canticle," no. 23.

God pledged God's self to us and raised us to be God's companion and spouse. This was an espousal offered to all of humanity. The crucifixion of Jesus, therefore, is nothing less than an expression of Christ's spousal love for humanity, for the church, and for each one of us. John goes on to explain that the espousal begun on the cross and bestowed upon each of us at our baptism deepens in our lives and takes place little by little.[47]

He makes his own allegorical reflection on chapter 16 of the book of Ezekiel to advance his thought.

> This espousal we are dealing with is what God makes known through Ezekiel by saying to the soul: You were cast out upon the earth in contempt of your soul on the day you were born. And by passing by you I saw you trodden under foot in your blood. And I said to you as you were in your blood: Love and be as multiplied as the grass of the field. Increase and grow great and enter and reach the stature of womanhood. And your breasts grew and your hair increased, and you were naked and full of confusion. And I passed by you and looked at you and saw your time was the time of lovers, and I held my mantle over you and covered your ignominy. And I swore to you and entered into a pact with you and made you mine. And I washed you with water and cleansed the blood from you and anointed you with oil; and I clothed you in color and shod you with violet shoes, girded you with fine linen and clothed you with fine woven garments. And I adorned you with ornaments, put bracelets on your hands and a chain on your neck. And above your mouth I placed a ring, and I put earrings in your ears and a beautiful crown on your head. And you were adorned with gold and silver and clothed with fine linen and embroidered silk and many colors. You ate very choice bread and honey and oil, and you became exceedingly beautiful, and advanced to rule and be a queen. And your name was spread among the people because of your beauty [Ezek. 16:5-14]. And so it happens with the soul of which we are speaking.[48]

---

[47] John, *CW, The Spiritual Canticle*, Stanza 23, no. 6.
[48] John, *CW, The Spiritual Canticle*, Stanza 23, no. 6.

Ezekiel's text offers John an evocative image of the process of healing and transformation: a prepubescent girl cast on the ground, abandoned, wounded, and vulnerable. The text illustrates God's merciful, loving, and healing gaze. God covers our shame and nakedness. From the day of her birth, she was cast upon the ground in blood. She was trodden on in her blood. It is the image of a newly born baby cast out on the ground. The Beloved passed by and looked at her in her blood, poverty, and abandonment. Moved with compassionate love, he calls her to love and to grow into womanhood. He recognizes her innate and potential beauty. He looks at her and sees that it is time for her to experience love. He washes and cleanses her wounds and anoints her with medicinal oil. He heals her. He clothes and adorns her with jewels, imparting dignity to her. He nourishes her which choice food. His love brings out her beauty, dignity, and worth. She becomes a queen and rules with the one who has loved her.

The Spiritual Canticle sings similarly of the loving and healing gaze of Christ:

> When you looked at me
> your eyes imprinted your grace in me;
> for this you loved me ardently;
> and thus my eyes deserved
> to adore what they beheld in you.[49]

When John comments on this stanza, he tells us that the "the look of God is love."[50] The merciful loving gaze of Christ makes us beautiful and enables us to share in divine life. God gazes at us with love, loves us as we are in all our poverty and brokenness and sinfulness. We don't merit God's love; we don't have to be good or perfect for God to love us. God loves us because God is love.[51] The unconditional and

---

[49] John, *CW*, *Poetry*, "15. The Spiritual Canticle," no. 32.
[50] John, *CW*, *The Spiritual Canticle*, Stanza 32, no. 3.
[51] "It should be noted for an understanding of this that just as God loves nothing outside himself, he bears no love for anything lower than the love he has for himself. He loves all things for himself; thus love becomes the purpose for

pure love of Christ who loves us as we are and makes us sharers in divine life is what heals the infirmities and miseries of our hearts and minds. Herein lies the health of the person, to know ourselves as loved and thus to love more and more with the selfless and unconditional love of God.

---

which he loves. He therefore does not love things because of what they are in themselves. With God, to love the soul is to put her somehow in himself and make her his equal. Thus he loves the soul within himself, with himself, that is, with the very love by which he loves himself" (John, *CW*, *The Spiritual Canticle*, Stanza 32, no. 6).

Chapter 8

The Theological Life: A Path of Healing

AS WE HAVE SEEN in the previous chapter, contemplation is the experience of God's self-communicating love that heals the deepest disorders of the psyche and spirit. However, contemplation is a collaborative work between God and the human person. John insists on collaborating with God's grace. This collaboration may take the form of surrender to God's action like a child who surrenders into the arms of her mother.[1] Collaboration also takes the form of actively doing what we can to purify our minds and hearts from what prevents us from deeper union with Christ.

In Stanza 1 of *The Spiritual Canticle*, the bride, wounded by the Beloved's love, embarks on a journey to seek the Beloved who has fled like a stag in the woods. She longs for union with him. She understands that it is not those who say "Lord, Lord" who enter the kingdom

---

[1] "Although God does lead them—since he can do so without their cooperation—they do not accept his guidance. In resisting God who is conducting them, they make little progress and fail in merit because they do not apply their wills; as a result they must endure greater suffering. Some souls, instead of abandoning themselves to God and cooperating with him, hamper him by their indiscreet activity or their resistance. They resemble children who kick and cry and struggle to walk by themselves when their mothers want to carry them; in walking by themselves they make no headway, or if they do, it is at a child's pace" (John, *CW*, *The Ascent of Mount Carmel*, Prol., 3).

of God, but only those who do the will of the Father (Matt 7:21). As John says, "the soul that truly loves God is not slothful in doing all she can to find the Son of God her Beloved."[2]

John teaches us an important gospel truth we learn from Jesus—discipleship costs. "If any wish to come after me, let them deny themselves and take up their cross and follow me" (Matt 16:24). Seeking the Beloved requires more than feelings, longings, and wishful thinking; to seek the Beloved requires an active search through the practice of the virtues and the exercise of the active and contemplative life.

> She points out here that for the attainment of God it is not enough to pray with the heart and tongue or receive favors from others, but that together with this a soul must through its own efforts do everything possible. God usually esteems the work persons do by themselves more than many works done for them. And mindful of the words of the Beloved, Seek and you shall find [Lk. 11:9], the soul decides to go out searching for him in the way we mentioned, to seek him through works that she may not be left without finding him. Many desire that God cost them no more than words and even these they say badly. They desire to do for him scarcely anything that might cost them something. Some would not even rise from a place of their own liking if they were not to receive thereby some delight from God in their mouth and heart. They will not even take one step to mortify themselves and lose some of their satisfactions, comforts, and useless desires. . . . Those who seek God and yet want their own satisfaction and rest seek him at night and thus will not find him. Those who look for him through the practice and works of the virtues get up from the bed of their own satisfaction and delight and seek him by day and thus will find him.[3]

Contemplation is also a response to God's love. The bride must get up from her bed of satisfaction and go in search for the Beloved. Furthermore, contemplation as an experience of God's self-communicating love is not limited to formal prayer periods; rather,

---

[2] John, *CW, The Spiritual Canticle*, Stanza 3, no. 1.
[3] John, *CW, The Spiritual Canticle*, Stanza 3, nos. 2–3.

contemplation is a way of being and living, a transparency to life that extends to all dimensions of our activities and relationships. It includes our human response in seeking God through a life of virtue and good works. Many people misconceive Sanjuanist contemplation. They think it is a level of prayer higher than discursive meditation. Although some of John's practical analysis of contemplation can lead us in this direction, this is not his fundamental teaching. Contemplation is not primarily a form of prayer, but a quality of living the virtues of faith, hope, and love.[4]

One of the richest and most original contributions of John of the Cross to spiritual theology is his doctrine on the theological virtues of faith, hope, and love. The theological virtues are central to John's understanding of mysticism, asceticism, and our relationship with God and others. They are the beginning, the middle, and the end of the spiritual journey through the night of faith to union with God through love. They are the means by which we are transformed and arrive at union with God through love. They are all gifts of God, that is, divine life communicated to us that capacitates us to enter into communion with God, as well as the way we welcome and freely respond to God's life within us.[5]

> You have been told, O soul, of the conduct you should observe if you want to find the Bridegroom in your hiding place. Still if you want to hear this again, listen to a word abounding in substance and inaccessible truth: Seek him in faith and love, without desiring to find satisfaction in anything, or delight, or desiring to understand anything other than what you ought to know. Faith and love are the blind person's guides. They will lead you along a path unknown to you, to the place where God is hidden. Faith, the secret we mentioned, is comparable to the feet by which one journeys to God, and love one's guide.[6]

---

[4] Federico Ruiz, *Místico y maestro San Juan de la Cruz*, 2nd ed. (Madrid: Editorial de Espiritualidad, 2006), 327.

[5] Federico Ruiz, "Estructuras de la vida teologal," *Monte Carmelo* 88 (1980): 367. See also Federico Ruiz, *Caminos del espíritu* (Madrid: Editorial de Espiritualidad, 1998), 67–109.

[6] John, *CW*, *The Spiritual Canticle*, Stanza 1, no. 11.

Faith, hope, and love have a transforming effect on the psychology of the human person, that is, on our intellect, memory, and will. They purify us and unite us to God.[7]

For John, self-love is the greatest obstacle to growth in the Christian life. Therefore, the virtues of faith, hope, and love provide the means for emptying self-love in order to be filled with God's love. They encompass a whole way of life and form the nucleus of an entire spiritual foundation. Each of the virtues transforms the totality of the human person and makes us believers, lovers of God and others, and hopeful. In this sense, the virtues of faith, hope, and love become a path of healing.

We must ask ourselves: How must we conduct ourselves under God's purifying action that comes through prayer and life? What must we do to collaborate with God's healing love through purgative contemplation? What are the attitudes of heart that we must adopt and try to live if we are to respond to God's healing love? John gives us an answer in chapter 21 of the second book of *The Dark Night*.

In this chapter, John passes a retrospective glance over the dark and purifying journey that that soul has made toward union with the Beloved. The soul becomes conscious of her interior dispositions during the entire obscure journey. By God's sheer grace she has gradually climbed the secret ladder of love.[8] Having passed through the purifying flames of God's love, she is freed and healed from selfish desire, and burns gently with love for the Beloved.[9]

---

[7] "As a result it will be seen how necessary it is for the soul, if it is to walk securely, to journey through this dark night with the support of these three virtues. They darken and empty it of all things. As we said, the soul is not united with God in this life through understanding, or enjoyment, or through imagination, or through any other sense; but only faith, hope, and charity (according to the intellect, memory, and will) can unite the soul with God in this life" (John, *CW, The Ascent of Mount Carmel*, Book 2, chap. 6, no. 1).

[8] John, *CW, The Dark Night*, Book 2, chaps. 18–20.

[9] "The ninth step of love causes the soul to burn gently. It is the step of the perfect who burn gently in God. The Holy Spirit produces this gentle and delightful ardor by reason of the perfect soul's union with God. St. Gregory accordingly says of the Apostles that when the Holy Spirit came upon them visibly, they burned interiorly and gently with love" (John, *CW, The Dark Night*, Book 2, chap. 20, no. 4).

What were her dispositions and attitudes as she surrendered to the Spirit's purifying action? How did she collaborate with God's purifying love? She says she made the journey "disguised."[10] In order to protect herself from the harm that can come from the devil, the world, and herself, she wore a disguise of three colors—white, green, and red:

> These three colors stand for the three theological virtues: faith, hope, and charity, by which she not only gains the favor and good will of her Beloved but also advances very safely, fortified against her three enemies.[11]

The "disguise" image signifies a garment that one adopts in order to dissemble one's identity from enemies and to manifest the dispositions and aspirations of one's heart.[12] The theological virtues determine the conduct and attitude of our relationship with God throughout the entire spiritual journey.[13]

The White Tunic of Faith

A pure white tunic is the first garment that disguises the soul. This white tunic is faith.[14] Faith protects us against the devil who is the

---

[10] John, *CW*, *The Dark Night*, Book 2, chap. 21, no. 1.
[11] John, *CW*, *The Dark Night*, Book 2, chap. 21, no. 3.
[12] John, *CW*, *The Dark Night*, Book 2, chap. 21, no. 2.
[13] Federico Ruiz, "Vida teologal durante la purificación interior en los escritos de San Juan de la Cruz," *Revista de Espiritualidad* 18 (1959): 371. See also the following articles that discuss how the soul is guided by faith, hope, and love during the dark night: P. Juan de Jesús María, OCD, "Le amará tanto como es amada," *Ephemerides Carmelitanae* 6 (1955): 55–61; and P. Emeterio del S. Corazón, OCD, "La noche pasiva del espíritu de San Juan de la Cruz," *Revista de Espiritualidad* 18 (1958): 54–56.
[14] "Faith is an inner tunic of such pure whiteness that it blinds the sight of every intellect. When the soul is clothed in faith the devil is ignorant of how to hinder her, neither is he successful in his efforts, for faith gives her strong protection—more than do all the other virtues—against the devil, who is the mightiest and most astute enemy" (John, *CW*, *The Dark Night*, Book 2, chap. 21, no. 4).

most astute and strong enemy.[15] Faith is not only a safeguard against the devil, but a way to obtain the favor of the Beloved and union with him.

> As a result, St. Peter found no greater safeguard than faith in freeing himself from the devil, when he advised: *Cui resistite fortes in fide* [1 Pt. 5:9]. To obtain the favor of the Beloved and union with him, the soul can have no better inner tunic than this white garment of faith, the foundation and beginning of the other garments or virtues. *Without faith, as the Apostle says, it is impossible to please God* [Heb. 11:6]; and with faith it is impossible not to please him, since he himself declares through the prophet Hosea, *Desponsabo te mihi in fide* [Hos. 2:20], which is similar to saying: If you desire, soul, union and espousal with me, you must come interiorly clothed in faith.[16]

This text is rich and content concerning the theological virtue of faith. John has a biblical understanding of faith as a form of personal communion with Christ.[17] In Scripture, in both the Old and New Testaments, faith is understood in terms of a personal relationship, as surrender to God in humility and trust. The essence of biblical faith is our encounter with a God who reveals God's self to us and to whom we respond.

Faith is above all a relationship with God because "faith gives and communicates God himself to us but covered with the silver of

---

[15] John of the Cross makes reference to the three traditional enemies of the soul: the devil, the world, and the flesh. We must be careful and how we interpret these traditional "enemies." The world is best understood as empty, passing values that are indifferent to God and opposed to the Gospel. The "flesh" is best understood as the human condition in its fallen nature. St. Paul often uses the Greek term *sarx*, which is translated as "flesh." We can understand flesh as disordered passions that lead to vices such as gluttony, sexual immorality, and selfishness. We can understand the "devil" as a force of evil in our world, an objective evil force at work contrary to divine life.

[16] John, *CW*, *The Dark Night*, Book 2, chap. 21, no. 4.

[17] Ruiz, "Estructuras de la vida teologal," 367–87. See also Eulogio Pacho, *San Juan de la Cruz, Temas fundamentales*, 2 (Burgos, Spain: Editorial Monte Carmelo), 104.

faith."[18] To explain faith, John draws upon the image of a gold plate covered with silver. The propositions and articles of faith are like silver that covers gold, gold being God, who is the essence of faith. The content of faith is God himself, Christ, the Beloved. "O faith of Christ, my Bridegroom," professes the bride of *The Spiritual Canticle*.[19] "Faith is like crystal because it concerns Christ, her Bridegroom, and has the characteristics of crystal, being pure in its truths, strong, clear, and cleansed of errors and natural forms."[20] Faith, therefore, comes from Christ and is founded on Christ. Not only is faith an adherence to the divine message enclosed in human words (propositions and articles of revealed truth), but, above all, faith is a personal commitment and surrender to Jesus Christ and becoming one with Christ.

John tells us that faith is obscure and a dark night for the soul. "Faith is a certain and obscure habit of soul."[21] If faith is obscure for us, it is because the object of faith, God, is obscure for us. John tells us that God is hidden. "Where have you hidden, Beloved, and left me moaning?"[22] God cannot be understood or grasped by the intellect, nor by the will, nor by the imagination, nor by any of the senses. God transcends all that we can image, think, or feel.[23] "Faith does not fall into the province of the senses," that is, God cannot be grasped by the senses.[24] Because God communicates Godself as God is, that is, as transcendent Being, we experience obscurity because of the excessive light of his Being.

This brings us to an important theme in John's doctrine: God's transcendence. John has a profound respect for God's transcendence. God is intimate to us, closer to us than our very breath (God lives in

---

[18] John, *CW*, *The Spiritual Canticle*, Stanza 12, no. 4.

[19] John, *CW*, *The Spiritual Canticle*, Stanza 12, no. 2.

[20] John, *CW*, *The Spiritual Canticle*, Stanza 12, no. 3.

[21] John, *CW*, *The Ascent of Mount Carmel*, Book 2, chap. 3, no. 1.

[22] John, *CW*, *The Spiritual Canticle*, Stanza 1.

[23] John, *CW*, *The Dark Night*, Book 2, chap. 8, no. 1.

[24] John, *CW*, *The Ascent of Mount Carmel*, Book 1, chap. 2, no. 3. The original Spanish reads: "*La fe es cosa que no cae en sentido.*" We need faith because God cannot be grasped by the senses.

the depths of our being), but God is also totally other. However elevated God's communications and the experiences of his presence are, and however sublime our knowledge of him may be, these are not essentially God.[25] Because God is *hidden*, we must also hide ourselves. Why does God remain hidden and invisible? If God would manifest himself plainly, we wouldn't need faith.

God's transcendence is a transcendence of love, not an indifferent transcendence, but rather one that is dynamic and operative. If God didn't make his presence known in us, he wouldn't preoccupy us. God's transcendent presence is dynamic. God acts as God, and this disconcerts us. God's ways are not our ways; God doesn't meet our limited expectations and manner of reasoning.

The transcendence of God leads us to say that all our words about God betray who God really is. The more we grow closer to God, the more obscure is our knowledge of him. For this reason, the mystics tells us that we journey to God by unknowing rather than knowing. The mystics suffer from the ineffability of their experience. Words are inadequate to speak of God and his way of communicating to us. "What God communicates to the soul in this intimate union is totally beyond words. One can say nothing about it, just as one can say nothing about God himself that resembles him."[26] The closer we come to know God, the more we enter into "a cloud of unknowing."

Ronald Rolheiser offers three analogies that might help us understand why we experience God as hidden, or absent.[27] The first is a baby in its mother's womb:

> In the womb, the baby is so totally enveloped and surrounded by the mother that, paradoxically, it cannot see the mother and cannot have any concept of the mother. Its inability to see or picture its mother is caused by the mother's omnipresence, not by her absence. The mother is too present, too all enveloping, to be seen

---

[25] John, *CW*, *The Spiritual Canticle*, Stanza 1, no. 3.
[26] John, *CW*, *The Spiritual Canticle*, Stanza 26, no. 4.
[27] Ronald Rolheiser, *Wrestling with God: Finding Hope and Meaning in Our Daily Struggles to Be Human* (New York: Image, 2018), 99–102.

or conceptualized. The same holds true for us with God. The scriptures tell us that we live, and move, and breathe in God, and have our being in God. We are in God's womb, enveloped by God, and like a baby, we must first be born (death as our second birth) to see God face to face. This is faith's darkness.[28]

Excessive light is another analogy. John of the Cross speaks of faith and God in terms of an excessive light. Excessive light causes us darkness. When we look at the sun without sunglasses, we see nothing. The very excessive light causes blindness as if we were in darkness. And this is the reason we have difficulty in seeing God. The more we journey into God, the more we enter into darkness; he seems to disappear. We are being blinded, not by his absence, but by the light of his presence.

Deep intimacy also offers an analogy. The deeper our intimacy with a person, the more the person becomes a mystery to us. We can live with someone for years, and grow in deep friendship, but the more our intimacy grows the more we realize the mystery of our friend. We can never know another person fully. He or she will always remain a mystery. When we begin our journey with God, we have strong feelings and ideas about God. But the deeper we journey, the more those ideas and feelings begin to feel false and empty. We are not so sure because our intimacy with God opens us more fully to the mystery of God.[29]

Because of God's hiddenness, we seek him in faith. We must seek satisfaction never in what we understand about God, but in what we do not understand about him. We must never pause to love and delight in our understanding and experience of God, but to love and delight in what we cannot understand or experience of him. Such is the way we seek God in faith.

> However surely it may seem that you find, experience, and understand God, because he is inaccessible and concealed you must

---

[28] Rolheiser, *Wrestling with God*, 101.
[29] Rolheiser, *Wrestling with God*, 102.

> always regard him as hidden, and serve him who is hidden in a secret way. Do not be like the many foolish ones who, in their lowly understanding of God, think that when they do not understand, taste, or experience him, he is far away and utterly concealed. The contrary belief would be truer. The less distinct is their understanding of him, the closer they approach him, since in the words of the prophet David, *he made darkness his hiding place* [Ps. 18:11 {Ps. 17:12}]. Thus in drawing near him you will experience darkness because of the weakness of your eye.[30]

As Rolheiser incisively observes, "one of the reasons why we struggle with faith is that God's presence within us and in our world is rarely dramatic, overwhelming, sensational, something impossible to ignore."[31] The prophet Elijah experienced the presence of God not in the earthquake, but in the gentle breeze. Jesus was born in poverty, a helpless baby, not in a royal palace surrounded by honorary guards. Jesus did not perform his miracles to draw attention to himself; rather, they were acts of compassion. Jesus withdrew from the crowds after feeding the five thousand for fear that people wanted to make him a king (John 6:15). In the temptations in the desert, Jesus renounced the temptation to change stones into bread and to throw himself down from the temple to prove his divinity. He taught us the kingdom of God is like a tiny mustard seed, or leaven in dough. It is hidden and secret but has potential for growth. God's presence within us is mostly quiet, "a plant growing silently as we sleep, yeast leavening dough in a manner hidden from our eyes, . . . an insignificant mustard plant eventually surprising us with its growth." It seems that the God of Jesus Christ is not dramatic but quiet, working in hidden ways.[32] God's transcendence and hidden presence within us and in our world disconcert us. We are inclined to ground our faith on something extraordinary.

---

[30] John, *CW*, *The Spiritual Canticle*, Stanza 1, no. 12.
[31] Rolheiser, *Wrestling with God*, 103.
[32] Rolheiser, *Wrestling with God*, 103–4.

In *The Ascent of Mount Carmel*, John tells us that we are foolish to seek some vision of revelation, or some extraordinary experience of God, because God has revealed everything in his Word, Jesus Christ. In him we will discover all we desire and long for. Jesus is the Father's sole locution and revelation. "Fasten your eyes on him alone because in him I have spoken and revealed all and in him you will discover even more than you ask for and desire."[33] If we wish some word of comfort or revelation, behold the life of Jesus, how he was subject to the Father and others, how he lived and died. In him lie all the treasures of wisdom and knowledge.

> Thus we must be guided humanly and visibly in all by the law of Christ, who is human, and that of his Church and of his ministers. This is the way to remedy our spiritual ignorances and weaknesses. Here we shall find abundant medicine for them all. Any departure from this road is not only curiosity but extraordinary boldness. One should not believe anything coming in a supernatural way but believe only the teaching of Christ who is human, as I say, and of his ministers who are human.[34]

In our healing journey toward union with God we must clothe ourselves with the white garment of faith, which is a personal relationship with Jesus Christ. One of the reasons why we journey by faith is because life has its trials and sufferings, its moments of joy and sorrow. John recognizes that our communion with Christ is lived out in history through the concrete experiences of life. Our faith is tested, purified, and deepened through the internal and external trials and temptations of life.

> The soul wore her white tunic of faith when she departed on this dark night and walked, as we said, in the midst of interior darknesses and straits, without the comfort of any intellectual light—neither from above, because heaven seemed closed and God

---

[33] John, *CW*, *The Ascent of Mount Carmel*, Book 2, chap. 22, no. 5.
[34] John, *CW*, *The Ascent of Mount Carmel*, Book 2, chap. 22, no. 7.

hidden, nor from below, because she derived no satisfaction from her spiritual teachers, and suffered with constancy and perseverance, passing through these trials without growing discouraged or failing the Beloved. The Beloved so proves the faith of his bride in tribulations that she can afterward truthfully declare what David says: *Because of the words of your lips I have kept hard ways* [Ps. 17:4 {Ps. 16:4}].[35]

John tells us that Christ exercises our faith through life's trials and tribulations. Another way to express this is that Christ communicates his love to us not only in delightful and pleasing experiences, not only in consoling moments, but also in life's difficult experiences. John's words leads us into an important, and often misunderstood, theme of his writings: the role of suffering in the purification process. John firmly believes that we grow and mature more through what we suffer in life than through pleasure.

> There is another reason the soul walks securely in these darknesses: It advances by suffering. Suffering is a surer and even more advantageous road than that of joy and action. First, in suffering, strength is given to the soul by God. In its doing and enjoying, the soul exercises its own weakness and imperfections. Second, in suffering, virtues are practiced and acquired, and the soul is purified and made wiser and more cautious.[36]

The curative and maturing role of suffering appears more than once in John's treatment of the dark night. For instance, when he discusses the spiritual gluttony in *The Dark Night*, he says that the Lord cures these imperfections "through temptations, aridities, and other trials that are all a part of the dark night."[37] It is through "pure dryness and interior darkness" that God weans the soul from childish attachment to spiritual consolations.[38]

---

[35] John, *CW*, *The Dark Night*, Book 2, chap. 21, no. 5.
[36] John, *CW*, *The Dark Night*, Book 2, chap. 16, no. 9.
[37] John, *CW*, *The Dark Night*, Book 1, chap. 6, no. 8.
[38] John, *CW*, *The Dark Night*, Book 1, chap. 7, no. 5.

Suffering and Purification

In a dense and profound text in *The Living Flame of Love*, John comments on the verse, "pays every debt."[39] He insists on the necessity of suffering of all kinds to grow toward union with God through love.[40] The dark night, as we explained, is incarnated in daily life and comes through many channels: temptations, dryness in prayer, illnesses, humiliations, interpersonal conflicts, and differences.[41] John explains the necessity of suffering as a means of healing by comparing the human person to a sturdy flask that needs to be prepared and purified in order to contain precious liquor.

Through these trials our attachment to sense pleasure is purified and we are strengthened for a deeper love. Our capacity to love is refined and purged from self-love. Through these trials we acquire virtues because virtue is strengthened in weakness. Trials and temptations reveal the deeper layers of our heart and motivations and become the fuel for spiritual and psychological growth. Wisdom is wrought by the hard knocks of life.

John maintains that the reason why many fail to grow in freedom, healing, and union with God is because they shun and flee from the small as well as the great trials of life. They flee from the royal way of the cross.

> There are many who desire to advance and persistently beseech God to bring them to this state of perfection. Yet when God wills to conduct them through the initial trials and mortifications, as is necessary, they are unwilling to suffer them and they shun them, flee from the narrow road of life [Mt. 7:14] and seek the broad

---

[39] John, *CW*, *The Living Flame of Love*, Stanza 2, no. 23.

[40] "To know the nature of these debts for which the soul feels compensated here, it should be noted that ordinarily no one can reach this high state and kingdom of espousal without first undergoing many tribulations and trials. As is said in the Acts of the Apostles, *It is necessary to undergo many tribulations to enter the kingdom of heaven* [Acts 14:22 {Acts 14:21}]. In this state these tribulations are ended; the soul being purified suffers no more" (John, *CW*, *The Living Flame of Love*, Stanza 2, no. 24).

[41] John, *CW*, *The Living Flame of Love*, Stanza 2, no. 25.

> road of their own consolation, which is that of their own perdition [Mt. 7:13]; thus they do not allow God to begin to grant their petition. They are like useless containers, for although they desire to reach the state of the perfect they do not want to be guided by the path of trials that leads to it. They hardly even begin to walk along this road by submitting to what is least, that is, to ordinary sufferings.[42]

John believes that suffering can be a path of transformation when accepted in faith, hope, and love. He does not believe in suffering for suffering's sake; his doctrine is not doloristic or masochistic. John desires the end of suffering and the healing of the human person. He is rooted in the Gospel teaching that through the cross we come to the fullness of life in Christ.[43] The cross becomes the path of healing because we participate in the paschal mystery of Jesus Christ, a life of self-giving love in imitation of Jesus Christ.[44]

The imitation of Christ calls for dying to self-centered love. Communion with God does not come through external sacrifices or other religious practices; it comes rather through dying to selfishness in conformity to the life of Christ and an attitude of openness and acceptance of small and great sufferings of life, which are inevitable in this life.

It is here where John presents the challenge of the life of faith. Faith calls for an attitude of openness, patience, and perseverance in the midst of life's innumerable and various struggles and sufferings. Suffering rejected only crushes a person. Suffering embraced and borne patiently leads to inner peace and healing.

> People, then, should live with great patience and constancy in all the tribulations and trials God places on them, whether they be exterior or interior, spiritual or bodily, great or small, and they

---

[42] John, *CW*, *The Living Flame of Love*, Stanza 2, no. 27.
[43] John, *CW*, *The Spiritual Canticle*, Stanza 23, no. 5.
[44] John, *CW*, *The Ascent of Mount Carmel*, Book 2, chap. 7, no. 8. I have quoted this text in chap. 5. It is a fundamental text for understanding the dark night as a path of discipleship.

should accept them all as from God's hand as a good remedy and not flee from them, for they bring health. In this matter let them take the counsel of the Wise Man: *If the spirit of him who has power descends upon you, do not abandon your place* (the place and site of your probation, which is the trial he sends you), *for the cure will make great sins cease* [Eccl. 10:4]; that is, it will cut of the roots of your sins and imperfections—your evil habits. The combat of trials, distress, and temptations deadens the evil and imperfect habits of the soul and purifies and strengthens it. People should hold in esteem the interior and exterior trials God sends them, realizing that there are few who merit to be brought to perfection through suffering and to undergo trials for the sake of so high a state.[45]

John encourages us to find meaning in the inevitable sufferings of life. Trials and tribulations can become the means of and insight into wisdom, compassion, and deeper healing if we are open to learn their lessons. It all depends upon our attitude toward what happens to us.[46] Healing is God's work, but we can resist it by a negative attitude that fights and rebels against God's transforming grace that is offered through the difficulties and sufferings of life. We have to surrender to God's action, allow God to carry us.

Meister Eckhart often speaks of *"Gelassenheit."* It is a significant word because it includes the verb *lassen* (to allow to happen). *Gelassenheit* means an attitude of openness, to allow to happen what may happen. It means to remain open and to accept life under God's conditions with confidence. It is the exact opposite of tightening up in the face of suffering.[47]

---

[45] John, *CW, The Living Flame of Love*, Stanza 2, no. 30.

[46] John's teaching on the role of suffering for purification has much in common with Viktor Frankl's logotherapy. Frankl insists on the importance of an open attitude toward the inevitable trials and sufferings of life. See Viktor Frankl, *Man's Search for Meaning* (Boston: Beacon Press, 2006). Carl Jung wrote, "Man needs difficulties; they are necessary for health. See C. G. Jung, *Psychological Reflections*, ed. Jolande Jacobi and R. F. C. Hull (Princeton: Princeton University Press, 1978), 304.

[47] Wilfred Stinissen, OCD, *La nuit comme le jour illuminé: La nuit obscure chez Jean de la Croix* (Toulouse: Éditions du Carmel, 2010), 38.

This open attitude to allowing healing and transformation in through whatever happens is seen in a concrete way in *Four Counsels to a Religious On How to Reach Perfection*. In this short text John sees the give-and-take and frictions of interpersonal community relationships as a means of growth in evangelical love if accepted and embraced with patience and love.[48]

In conclusion, the first "disguise" John asks us to wear during the purifying night of contemplation is an inner white tunic of faith. Faith is a personal commitment and surrender to Jesus Christ even in the midst of uncertainty, dryness, and obscurity. Our faith in Jesus Christ is expressed and purified concretely through the joys, sorrows, and trials that life presents. Faith calls for an attitude of constancy, perseverance, patience, and confidence in and through life's challenges. For John, "faith is confident, loving, and courageous."[49]

---

[48] John, *CW*, *Counsels to a Religious On How to Reach Perfection*, nos. 3–4.
[49] Ruiz, *Místico y maestro San Juan de la Cruz*, 171.

Chapter 9

Hope: A Green Coat of Mail

THE SECOND DISGUISE THAT the soul wears during her purifying journey toward union with God is a "green coat of mail" that signifies the virtue of hope.[1] The virtue of hope protects us against the world, our second enemy.[2] Hope imparts courage and valor and elevates us to things of eternal life. John draws upon Pauline imagery to explain hope. He notes that "St. Paul calls hope the helmet of salvation [1 Thes. 5:8]." John describes the helmet of salvation in terms of medieval armor used for battle to protect the head from injuries and to keep one's vision focused ahead.[3]

As a helmet of salvation, hope has this characteristic: it covers all the senses of a person's head so they do not become absorbed in any worldly thing, nor is there any way some arrow from the world might wound them. Hope allows the soul only a visor, that it may look

---

[1] John, *CW*, *The Dark Night*, Book 2, chap. 21, no. 6.
[2] John, *CW*, *The Dark Night*, Book 2, chap. 21, no. 7. The created "world" is not an enemy to us. God created our world and he saw that it was good (Gen 1). The world as an enemy signifies the empty and passing material and cultural values of life that are indifferent to God. Hope keeps us fixed on eternal values, the values of God's kingdom.
[3] "A helmet is a piece of armor that protects the entire head and covers it so there is no opening except a visor through which to see" (John, *CW*, *The Dark Night*, Book 2, chap. 21, no. 7).

toward heavenly things and no more. This is the ordinary task of hope in the soul; it raises our eyes to look at God alone.[4] Supernatural hope, therefore, looks to God alone who loves us and has created us to share in divine life. Hope purifies the memory and unites it with God. Because hope looks to God alone, it is an attitude of poverty; it empties the heart and mind of all that is not God.[5]

As a helmet of armor, hope protects the head, the seat of our memory, fantasy, imagination, and thoughts. The world and the "head" are closely related. André Bord makes an important observation. If the world is exterior to us, it is also within us, especially through the memory.[6] It is through the memory that we risk becoming attached to the world. Purifying and healing the memory is the path toward freedom from the interior world.

John gives us an idea in *The Spiritual Canticle* of this interior "world" to which we can be attached. As we have seen in a previous chapter, in her search for Christ the bride must rise from the bed of her satisfaction and seek Christ through the mountains and watersides. The mountains represent the exercise of the contemplative life by means of the virtues. The watersides are the mortifications, penances, and spiritual exercises by which she practices the active life. As she journeys up the mountains and along the watersides, she is not "to gather flowers," that is, she must empty her heart of anything that hinders her search for Christ.[7]

---

[4] John, *CW*, *The Dark Night*, Book 2, chap. 21, no. 7.

[5] John, *CW*, *The Dark Night*, Book 2, chap. 21, no. 6.

[6] André Bord, *Mémoire et espérance chez Jean de la Croix* (Paris: Beauchesne, 1971), 208.

[7] "Since seeking God demands a heart naked, strong, and free from all evils and goods that are not purely God, the soul speaks in this and the following verses of the freedom and fortitude one should possess in looking for him. She declares she will not gather the flowers she sees along the way. The flowers are all the gratifications, satisfactions, and delights that may be offered to her in this life and will hinder her should she desire to gather and accept them. They are of three kinds: temporal, sensory, and spiritual. All three occupy the heart and hinder the spiritual nakedness required for the direct way of Christ, if the soul pays attention to them or becomes attached. Consequently she says that in order to seek him she will not gather these things" (John, *CW*, *The Spiritual Canticle*, Stanza 3, no. 5).

Furthermore, she must "not fear wild beasts."[8] The wild beasts represent the world. A close examination of this "world" reveals that it is not so much the outside world of people and material reality but rather the world that lives in our imagination, fantasy, and memory.

> She calls the world "wild beasts" because in the imagination of the soul that begins to tread the path leading to God the world is pictured as wild animals threatening and scaring her. The world frightens her principally in three ways:
> First, it makes her think she must live without its favor, and lose her friends, reputation, importance, and even wealth.
> Second, through another beast, no less ferocious, it makes her wonder how she will ever endure the permanent lack of the consolations and delights of the world and all its comforts.
> Third, which is still worse, it makes her think that tongues will rise up against her and mock her, there will be many remarks and jeers, and she will be considered almost worthless.
> These fears are brought before some souls in such a way that not only does persevering against these wild beasts become most difficult, but so does being able to get started on the journey.[9]

The "world" is made up of the fears, worries, obsessions, ruminations, and self-preoccupations that live within the imagination and to which the memory attaches itself. These "beasts" war against us and make our journey difficult. This inner world needs to be purified and healed. It is here where we need to briefly discuss the memory, for it is hope that purifies the memory and unites it to God.

Memory is central to our Judeo-Christian identity. The Hebrew Scriptures celebrate over and over the Israelites' liberation from slavery in Egypt and God's providential care during their forty-year journey through the desert to the Promised Land. At every eucharistic liturgy we remember and celebrate the life, death, and resurrection of Jesus Christ.

---

[8] "Seeking my Love / I will head for the mountains and for watersides, / I will not gather flowers, / nor fear wild beasts; / I will go beyond strong men and frontiers" (John, *CW*, *The Spiritual Canticle*, Stanza 3).

[9] John, *CW*, *The Spiritual Canticle*, Stanza 3, no. 7.

Our memory shapes who we are. Without our memory we would have no identity. We realize the importance of memory with victims of Alzheimer's. When a person loses their memory, it is as though the person we knew is no longer there. We know how frustrating it can be when we forget names of significant people in our lives.

John takes up the purification of the memory in Book Three of *The Ascent of Mount Carmel*, chapters 2 to 15, and in the second book of *The Dark Night*. His doctrine on the purification of the memory is one of the most essential teachings of his doctrine; unfortunately, it is often overlooked or dismissed due to the vocabulary and the depth of his treatment of the memory.[10]

For John, the memory is not a pure repository of past events as we usually understand it. Coming from a scholastic psychological perspective, our memories, experiences, and images are stored in what he calls the "fantasy." The function of the memory, which is a spiritual faculty, is to recall memories from the fantasy. It goes to the fantasy and imagination looking for material to feed upon. It has an immensely active role and can have grave repercussions for the spiritual life because it goes to the fantasy looking for past memories, experiences, and images that can become the fuel for anger, pride, bitterness, and depression.[11] John recognizes the powerful influence of the memory when he writes:

> I should like spiritual persons to have full realization of how many evils the devils cause in souls that make much use of their memories; of how much sadness, affliction, vain and evil joy from both spiritual and worldly thoughts these devils occasion; and of the number of impurities they leave rooted in the spirit. They also seriously distract these souls from the highest recollection, a recollection that consists in concentrating all the faculties on the incomprehensible Good and withdrawing them from all appre-

---

[10] For a penetrating explanation of the memory see Constance FitzGerald, OCD, "From Impasse to Prophetic Hope: Crisis of Memory," in *Desire, Darkness, and Hope: Theology in a Time of Impasse*, ed. Laurie Cassidy and M. Shawn Copeland (Collegeville, MN: Liturgical Press Academic, 2021), 425–53.

[11] Federico Ruiz, *Místico y maestro San Juan de la Cruz*, 2nd ed. (Madrid: Editorial de Espiritualidad, 2006), 186.

hensible things, for these apprehensible things are not a good that is beyond comprehension.[12]

The problem lies not in the memories or images within the fantasy, but in what the memory does with this material. The sickness of the memory is its tendency to possessively cling to memories, experiences, and images and to relive and ruminate on them. This clinging becomes a form of self-preoccupation. For John, a lot of wasted energy is spent in harboring and reliving memories of past or present experiences. This keeps us from living in the present moment.

For instance, there are people who possessively cling to memories of past hurts and relive them. They become enslaved by their past experiences, which become fuel for bitterness, an inability to forgive oneself or others. There are also those who tend toward scrupulosity and compulsively obsess over their past sins, imperfections, and character flaws; this robs them of their interior peace and leads them to discouragement or depression. The letters of John of the Cross provide some examples of his therapy of the memory. I will limit myself to two examples.

The first letter was written just before the feast of Pentecost to a Carmelite nun suffering from scruples. John begins by advising the sister to keep herself interiorly occupied with a desire for the Holy Spirit. Preserving herself peacefully in the presence of the Holy Spirit should be her only care without concern over disturbing memories.

> In these days try to keep interiorly occupied with a desire for the coming of the Holy Spirit and on the feast and afterward with his continual presence. Let your care and esteem for this be so great that nothing else will matter to you or receive your attention, whether it may concern some affliction or some other disturbing memories. And if there be faults in the house during these days, pass over them for love of the Holy Spirit and of what you owe to the peace and quietude of the soul in which he is pleased to dwell.[13]

---

[12] John, *CW*, *The Ascent of Mount Carmel*, Book 3, chap. 4, no. 2.
[13] John, *CW*, *Letters*, no. 20.

Then John addresses her struggles with scruples. He advises her when to confess, what matters to confess, and how to confess them. She is not to confess thoughts and imaginings that she does not deliberately desire or advert to, nor should she pay attention to them or worry about them. It is best to strive to forget them no matter how they afflict her.

When something distasteful or unpleasant comes her way, she is to refocus her attention and remember Christ crucified. John encourages her to live in faith and hope and to trust that God is present and protects her in moments of darkness. She is to cast her care on God who watches over her and will not abandon her. To think that God would abandon her would be an affront to God. She is to read, pray, and rejoice in God.[14] This is hope: keeping her gaze and trust in God's loving care.

John's direction reveals keen psychological insight into obsessive scrupulosity. He advises her throughout the letter to strive to preserve interior peace and not to worry about thoughts, imaginings, and emotional states over which she has no control and to which she has not willingly consented. In other words, she must try to let go of obsessive rumination over unpleasant and troubling thoughts that enter her consciousness by refocusing her attention to the positive: God's loving care. Her only care must be to remember the presence of the Holy Spirit and avoid focusing on her defects as well as on the faults that take place within the community. John's words are full of encouragement, confidence, and hope for a scrupulous person. They reveal the importance of living in faith, hope, and love and propose a method of positive thinking.

The second letter provides an example of how some people tend to obsess over past experiences and relationships. The letter is addressed to M. Leonor de San Gabriel, the prioress of Cordoba.[15] Evidently, M. Leonor had displeased Fr. Doria, the present superior general. The fear of having fallen into disgrace with Fr. Doria eroded

---

[14] John, *CW*, *Letters*, no. 20.
[15] John, *CW*, *Letters*, no. 22.

her interior peace. Recognizing her tendency to obsessively ruminate over what she imagined as a strained relationship, John is concerned for her health. He invites her to live in freedom and peace.[16]

> In reading your letter I felt sorry for you in your affliction, and I grieve over it because of the harm it can do your spirit and even your health. But you ought to know that I don't think you should be as afflicted as you are. For I do not see in Our Father any kind of dissatisfaction with you or even any recollection of such a thing. And even if he may have had some, now with your repentance it would be lessened. And if he should still show some displeasure, I will take care to speak well of the matter. Do not be troubled or pay any attention to this, for you have no reason to. I certainly believe it is a temptation the devil brings to your mind so that what should be employed in God is taken up with this.
>
> Be courageous, my daughter, and give yourself greatly to prayer, forgetting this thing and that, for after all we have no other good or security or comfort than this, for after having left all for God, it is right that we not long for support or comfort in anything but him, and it is still a great mercy.[17]

In these letters we see John's therapy for the memory. It consists in trying to "forget" troubling and unpleasant memories that come into our consciousness.

> I will treat here only of the manner in which, through the spiritual person's own efforts, the memory must be brought into this night and purgation. In short, the spiritual person should ordinarily take this precaution: Do not store objects of hearing, sight, smell, taste, or touch in the memory, but leave them immediately and forget them, and endeavor, if necessary, to be as successful in forgetting them as others are in remembering them.[18]

---

[16] Ruiz, *Místico y maestro San Juan de la Cruz*, 187. Ruiz also uses this example in his treatment of hope and the memory.
[17] John, *CW, Letters*, no. 22.
[18] John, *CW, The Ascent of Mount Carmel*, Book 3, chap. 2, no. 14.

The word *forget* appears many times in John's counsel for purifying the memory. However, it is impossible to forget the past. We cannot make our minds into a tabula rasa. From the context of the ways in which John expresses forgetting, he seems to signify doing what we can to change our thought pattern by gently letting go of excessive thinking, worry, and preoccupation about some event, person, or experience and focusing on God or something positive.[19] It requires a discipline of our thinking process by gently letting go of our attachment to negative or troublesome thoughts that disturb our peace. This requires an awareness of our tendency to cling to troublesome thoughts; we must discipline our minds by gently surrendering them and drawing our attention to the present moment or God's presence. We can say that this is John's "asceticism" of the mind and our thinking process.

Forgetfulness also applies to excessive curiosity and thinking about other people that leads to criticism and gossip. In his *Precautions*, John warns us against the danger of thinking about other people and their behavior and complaining about them. Such behavior robs us of inner peace and leads to many sins and evils.

> The third precaution is that you very carefully guard yourself against thinking about what happens in the community, and even more against speaking of it, of anything in the past or present concerning a particular religious: nothing about his or her character or conduct or deeds no matter how serious any of this seems. Do not say anything under the color of zeal or of correcting a wrong, unless at the proper time to whomever by right you ought to tell. Never be scandalized or astonished at anything you happen to see or learn of, endeavoring to preserve your soul in forgetfulness of all that.[20]

However, it is important to note that it is not only painful past memories and our attachment to them that concern John, but also positive spiritual experiences, human achievements, and natural gifts.

---

[19] Bord, *Memoire et esperance chez Jean de la Croix*, 124.
[20] John, *CW, Precautions*, no. 8.

We can become attached to spiritual experiences and consolations, as well as past human achievements such as positions of honor, leadership, or academic or professional success.[21]

We may go through a period of prayer with consoling spiritual experiences and insights. Then all of a sudden we enter into a period of aridity and darkness. We struggle to remain faithful to prayer. The temptation is to make efforts to relive the previous experiences of consoling and insightful prayer. Our effort to regain the previous spiritual experiences is an attachment, which prevents us from encountering God in the present moment and allowing God to purify our faith, hope, and love and to meet us in a deeper way beyond what we feel or understand.

Therefore, it is not only unpleasant memories and experiences that we must surrender, but even consoling spiritual experiences, memories, graces, and human achievements. We cannot hold onto anything, but must persevere in faith, hope, and love, allowing God to be God without clinging to past memories or spiritual consolations.

John's teaching on hope and the memory is particularly important for cooperating with God's healing action in the dark night. As we have seen in a previous chapter, the fire of divine love penetrates deep into the unconscious and draws out the pathologies of the psyche and spirit. The discomfort of seeing and feeling painful memories, our woundedness and past sins, can lead to an unhealthy self-preoccupation and discouragement. John invites us to change our vision. Instead of concentrating on self, we are to look to God. Like the prophet Jeremiah, we are to put our mouth to the dust and remain in silence and hope, patiently suffering God's healing grace.[22] What God asks of us is trust, patience, silence, and perseverance in prayer.[23]

The effort to let go of thoughts, memories, worries, and self-preoccupation and to remain peacefully and quietly in God's presence

---

[21] FitzGerald, "From Impasse to Prophetic Hope," 436.
[22] John, *CW*, *The Dark Night*, Book 2, chap. 8, no. 1.
[23] John, *CW*, *The Dark Night*, Book 1, chap. 10, nos. 3–4.

may be a challenge, but John assures us that if we persevere we will create space for the healing peace of Christ.

> The soul should remain closed, then, without cares or afflictions, for he who entered the room of his disciples bodily while the doors were closed and gave them peace, without their knowing how this was possible [Jn. 20:19-20], will enter the soul spiritually without its knowing how or using any effort of its own, once it has closed the doors of its intellect, memory, and will to all apprehensions. And he will fill them with peace, *descending on them*, as the prophet says, *like a river of peace* [Is. 66:12]. In this peace he will remove all the misgivings, suspicions, disturbances, and darknesses that made the soul fear it had gone astray. The soul should persevere in prayer and should hope in the midst of nakedness and emptiness, for its blessings will not be long in coming.[24]

Of course, it can be a difficult challenge let go of troubling thoughts and memories that surface from childhood memories or deeply seated fears. Therefore, psychological intervention and spiritual direction may be necessary to resolve the inner conflicts and reach the source of the memories and troubling thoughts so a person can know inner freedom.[25]

Supernatural hope, therefore, expresses the attitude we must adopt as we journey through the process of healing and transformation. Hope is the "green coat of mail," the "helmet of salvation" we wear on our journey. Hope expresses our attitude before the infirmities of our psyche and spirit. This attitude is one of interior poverty, keeping our gaze on God with confidence, patience, and perseverance. Hope is an act of confidence and peaceful surrender to the fire of God's love that penetrates ever more deeply into the deepest recesses of our psyche and spirit.

---

[24] John, *CW*, *The Ascent of Mount Carmel*, Book 3, chap. 3, no. 6.
[25] Kevin Culligan, "St. John of the Cross and Modern Psychology: A Brief Journey into the Unconscious," in *A Fresh Approach to St. John of the Cross*, ed. John McGowen (Middlegreen, England: St. Pauls, 1993), 97.

Chapter 10

Red Toga of Charity

OVER THE WHITE AND green disguise, the soul puts on a precious red toga. "Red denotes charity, the third virtue, which not only adds elegance to the other two colors but so elevates the soul as to place her near God. Charity makes her beautiful and pleasing to God."[1] John tells us three important truths about the virtue of charity.

First of all, as in the other two virtues, charity provides a protection for us. It protects and conceals us from the third enemy, which is the flesh, "because where there is true love of God, love of self and of one's own things finds no entry."[2] As John indicates, the flesh refers to self-love. True charity seeks to love God for God's sake. "Accordingly, the soul can know clearly whether or not she loves God purely. If she loves him her heart or love will not be set on herself or her own satisfaction and gain, but on pleasing God and giving him honor and glory. In the measure she loves herself, that much less she loves God."[3]

Secondly, not only does charity protect us from self-love, but it makes the other virtues genuine, strengthens and invigorates them in order to fortify us, and bestows on us loveliness and charm so as to please Christ. "Without charity no virtue is pleasing to God."[4]

---

[1] John, *CW*, *The Dark Night*, Book 2, chap. 21, no. 10.
[2] John, *CW*, *The Dark Night*, Book 2, chap. 21, no. 10.
[3] John, *CW*, *The Spiritual Canticle*, Stanza 9, no. 5.
[4] John, *CW*, *The Dark Night*, Book 2, chap. 21, no. 10.

Finally, like the virtues of faith and hope, the theological virtue of charity has an emptying and purifying effect on us. Charity empties us of our disordered desires and attachments that prevent us from placing God's love at the center of our lives.[5] This last element directs us to the purification of the will for a clearer understanding of how the soul wears the red toga in daily life. Just as active faith purifies the intellect, and active hope purifies the memory, so active charity purifies the will and unites us to God. Let us direct our attention briefly to John's treatment of the purification of the will in *The Ascent of Mount Carmel*.[6]

Purification of the Will

Love is the source of life; it is the health of the soul. We were created out of love and for love—created for an intimate communion of life with God, others, and creation. "After all, this love is the end for which we were created."[7] God's original plan in creating us was that we would direct all our faculties, energies, affections, and desires completely toward God. But as we have discussed in chapter 3, original sin has wounded human nature. Consequently, we are dispersed and scattered; we are separated from our deepest center. Each component of the human person tends to direct itself toward designs and plans centered on itself, rather than on God. In other words, we fail to respond to our vocation to love.

Human experience proves that love is not a simple energy that conforms to the Gospel with the decision of the will.[8] There is a dispersion and disorder in our affective energies. Therefore, growing in love requires an ongoing and deepening formation and strengthening of the will, for the will is the affective arbiter that governs the whole person. The will is the organ of love; it governs our natural emotions

---

[5] John, *CW*, *The Dark Night*, Book 2, chap. 21, no. 11.

[6] Due to the complexity of John's treatment on the purification of the will, I will synthesize the main elements of John's teaching.

[7] John, *CW*, *The Spiritual Canticle*, Stanza 29, no. 3.

[8] Federico Ruiz, *Místico y maestro San Juan de la Cruz*, 2nd ed. (Madrid: Editorial de Espiritualidad, 2006), 195.

and appetites and directs them to their proper end willed by God.⁹ The will establishes harmony and unity within the person by directing our faculties toward God. John realizes that it takes much grace and effort to establish unity within the person. John teaches an energetic formation and purification of the will in chapters 16 to 45 of Book Three of *The Ascent of Mount Carmel*.¹⁰

These chapters dedicated to the purification of the will are a treatise on the emotions—joy, hope, sorrow, and fear—what John refers to as "affections and passions."¹¹ John begins his treatise by stressing the importance of the virtue of charity for the purification of the will.

> We would have achieved nothing by purging the intellect and memory in order to ground them in the virtues of faith and hope had we neglected the purification of the will through charity, the third virtue. Through charity works done in faith are living works and have high value; without it they are worth nothing, as St. James affirms: *Without works of charity, faith is dead* [Jas. 2:20].¹²

This text tells us that although faith and hope are important purifying and healing virtues, ultimately, it is the virtue of love that purifies and heals us. Love must inform the virtues of faith and hope, for love is the source of the entire purifying and transforming process.

---

⁹ E. W. Trueman Dicken, *The Crucible of Love* (New York: Sheed and Ward, 1963), 334.

¹⁰ Ruiz refers to chaps. 15–45 of Book 3 of *The Ascent of Mount Carmel* as "formation in love." He writes: "An authentic theological life implies much freedom and strength of will. Spiritual people generally cultivate little the development of the will, leaving it in the hands of sentiments and arbitrariness." Thus, we see the need for a "formation in love." See Ruiz, *Mistico y maestro San Juan de la Cruz*, 204. I would refer the reader to the study already cited in chap. 2 by Kevin Culligan, "St. John of the Cross and Modern Psychology," *Studies in Formative Spirituality* 13 (1992): 29–48. Culligan studies the purification of the will from a psychological perspective. These two authors have helped me in my discussion of the purification of the will.

¹¹ John, *CW*, *The Ascent of Mount Carmel*, Book 3, chap. 16, no. 2. John does not refer to joy, hope, sorrow, and fear as "emotions." Rather, he calls them "affections and passions." "Emotions," however, correspond with contemporary psychology's understanding of this phenomena. See Culligan, "St. John of the Cross and Modern Psychology," 47.

¹² John, *CW*, *Ascent of Mount Carmel*, Book 3, chap. 16, no. 1.

John bases his teaching on the great commandment of love, which contains all one needs to do to live an integrated and harmonious life with God.

> *You shall love the Lord, your God, with all your heart, and with all your soul, and with all your strength* [Dt. 6:5]. This passage contains all that spiritual persons must do and all I must teach them here if they are to reach God by union of the will through charity. In it human beings receive the command to employ all the faculties, appetites, operations, and emotions of their soul in God so that they will use all this ability and strength for nothing else, in accord with David's words: *Fortitudinem meam ad te custodiam* (I will keep my strength for you) [Ps. 59:10 {Ps. 58:10}].[13]

John's fundamental theory is that selfish love leads to disintegration and dispersion, whereas love for God unifies and harmonizes all the energies, affectivities, passions, and appetites of the person.[14] John believes that our spiritual life and emotional health depend upon where we center the soul's strength, whether in God or objects other than God.[15] The key to spiritual and emotional health lies in loving God above all things. Centering our energy in God brings about harmony to our emotions and preserves them from conflicts that result from attempting to satisfy our emotional needs on diverse objects. On the other hand, disorder and interior warfare arise when we depend upon creatures rather than on God for emotional and spiritual fulfillment. From this interior warfare are born all kinds of vices and imperfections that eventually lead to a breakdown of the well-being of the personality.[16]

---

[13] John, *CW, Ascent of Mount Carmel*, Book 3, chap. 16, no. 1.

[14] "The strength of the soul comprises the faculties, passions, and appetites. All this strength is ruled by the will. When the will directs these faculties, passions, and appetites toward God, turning away from all that is not God, the soul preserves its strength for God, and comes to love him with all its might" (John, *CW, Ascent of Mount Carmel*, Book 3, chap. 16, no. 2).

[15] John, *CW, The Ascent of Mount Carmel*, Book 3, chap. 19, no. 1.

[16] Culligan, "St. John of the Cross and Modern Psychology," 31.

In chapter 17 of Book Three of *The Ascent of Mount Carmel*, John begins to demonstrate his thesis that depending upon creatures for emotional and spiritual fulfillment leads to psychic and spiritual disintegration. Originally, he intended to treat all four emotions; however, he ends his discussion of joy at chapter 45 without treating the other emotions. Nevertheless, the interrelated character of emotions and John's extensive treatment of joy enables us to make the same applications to all the emotions and to see the essential role they have for human well-being.[17]

Much like John's treatment of the disordered appetites in Book One of *The Ascent of Mount Carmel*, he describes the harm that comes to a person when the will directs the emotion of joy to objects other than God. Then he explains the benefits which a person experiences from not rejoicing in objects other than God.[18]

John provides six categories of objects or goods in which a person can actively rejoice: temporal, natural, sensory, moral, supernatural, and spiritual. We can divide these six categories into two major groups of goods: goods of the earth and spiritual goods. Under goods of the earth are the following:

Temporal goods: riches, status, positions, and other things claiming prestige; and children, relatives, marriages. All these are possible objects of joy for the will.[19]

Natural goods: beauty, grace, elegance, bodily constitution, and all other corporeal endowments; also, in the soul, good intelligence, discretion, and other talents belonging to the rational part of humans.[20]

---

[17] Culligan, "St. John of the Cross and Modern Psychology," 32.
[18] John explains the harm in chaps. 19, 22, 25, 28, 31, and 41. He explains the benefits in chaps. 20, 23, 26, 29, and 32.
[19] John, *CW*, *The Ascent of Mount Carmel*, Book 3, chap. 18, no. 1. Temporal goods are discussed in chaps. 18–20.
[20] John, *CW*, *The Ascent of Mount Carmel*, Book 3, chap. 21, no. 1. Natural goods are discussed in chaps. 21–23.

> **Sensory goods:** all goods apprehensible to the senses of sight, hearing, smell, taste, and touch, and to the interior faculty of discursive imagination; all goods pertinent to the exterior and interior senses.[21]

Under spiritual goods we can place:

> **Moral goods:** virtues and their habits insofar as they are moral, the exercise of virtues, the practice of the works of mercy, the observance of God's law, political prudence, and the practice of manners.[22]
>
> **Supernatural goods:** all the gifts and graces of God that exceed our natural faculties and powers. Examples include the gifts of wisdom and knowledge given by God to Solomon; the graces St. Paul enumerates: healing, working of miracles, prophecy, knowledge, discernment of spirits, interpretation of words, the gift of tongues.[23]
>
> **Spiritual goods:** all those goods that are an aid and motivating force in turning the soul to divine things and communion with God, as well as a help in God's communications to the soul.[24]

We see from the foregoing list of categories that John establishes a wide range of goods that cover every dimension of human existence where we place our affectivity, from earthly goods to spiritual goods. The reason for this is that John is concerned about the totality of the person and human existence. He excludes nothing from the field of

---

[21] John, *CW, The Ascent of Mount Carmel*, Book 3, chap. 24, no. 1. Sensory goods are discussed in chaps. 24–26.

[22] John, *CW, The Ascent of Mount Carmel*, Book 3, chap. 27, no. 1. Moral goods are discussed in chaps. 27–29.

[23] John, *CW, The Ascent of Mount Carmel*, Book 3, chap. 30, no. 1. Supernatural goods are discussed in chaps. 30–32.

[24] John, *CW, The Ascent of Mount Carmel*, Book 3, chap. 33, no. 2. Spiritual goods are discussed in chaps. 33–45.

human existence. All of our being is to be ordered toward God. No human activity or object of affection is excluded from the love of God. We are called to love God and everything else in God, not to love anything outside of God—that is, taking it out of its being and natural horizon which is God. When we say "outside of God," this does not refer to objects of our love. Everything exists in God. Every person or reality deserves our love when seen in the light of God. We are to love all things in the light of God. John excludes nothing from the horizon of God's love. John's concern is not with goods, the objects of our love, but rather with the quality of our love.

Federico Ruiz makes a distinction between love and joy. Love and joy are two orientations of our affectivity. Love is gift; joy is possession. Love seeks union; joy seeks satisfaction. These four dimensions (gift, possession, union, and satisfaction) can be lived fully in the experience of love. There is nothing wrong with joy. It stimulates love. The problem lies when joy becomes the sole motivating factor for love—when we cling to the satisfaction we receive rather than loving for the sake of the one we love regardless of the sensible satisfaction we receive. Loving is at a deeper level, independent of sensible satisfaction. To love is to give and receive gratuitously, to share, whereas to be selfish is to possess, hoard, and appropriate to oneself.[25]

Isn't this the love Jesus teaches in the Sermon on the Mount? Do not resist evil (take revenge); walk the extra mile; give to those who beg from you; do not refuse anyone who wants to borrow from you. Love your enemies; pray for your persecutors; love and greet those who reject or ignore you (Matt 5:38-48).

Matthew 25 is definitely an example of selfless love: "I was hungry and you gave me food, I was thirsty and you gave me something to drink, I was a stranger and you welcomed me, I was naked and you gave me clothing, I was sick and you took care of me, I was in prison and you visited me" (vv. 35-36).

John makes this distinction between and love and sensible joy and satisfaction in a letter to a Carmelite friar:

---

[25] Ruiz, *Místico y maestro San Juan de la Cruz*, 294.

> The feelings only serve as stimulants to love, if the will desires to pass beyond them; and they serve for no more. Thus the delightful feelings do not of themselves lead the soul to God, but rather cause it to become attached to delightful feelings. But the operation of the will, which is the love of God, concentrates the affection, joy, pleasure, satisfaction, and love of the soul only on God, leaving aside all things and loving him above them all.
>
> Hence if persons are moved to the love of God without dependence on the sweetness they feel, they leave aside this sweetness and center their love on God whom they cannot feel. Were they to love the sweetness and satisfaction, pausing and being detained in it, making an end and goal of the means, the work of the will would consequently be faulty. Since God is incomprehensible and inaccessible, the will, if it is to center its activity of love on him, must not set itself on what it can touch and apprehend with the appetite, but on what is incomprehensible and inaccessible to the appetite. Loving in this way, a soul loves truly and certainly according to the demands of faith.[26]

John recognizes that selfish and possessive love leads to dispersion, fragmentation, and a breakdown in the well-being of the person. On the other hand, centering all our energy in God, doing all for the honor and glory of God, loving people and creation in God—all these bring unity and harmony in us and are thus the key to spiritual and psychological health. For this reason, John advises us to consciously lift our joy to God as soon as we become aware of seeking vain joy in objects alone. For example, he gives the following advice concerning temporal goods such as money, status, or positions:

> At the first movement of joy toward things, the spiritual person ought to curb it, remembering the principle we are here following: There is nothing worthy of a person's joy save the service of God and the procurement of his honor and glory in all things. One should seek this alone in the use of things, turning away from vanity and concern for one's own delight and consolation.[27]

---

[26] John, *CW*, *Letters*, no. 13.
[27] John, *CW*, *The Ascent of Mount Carmel*, Book 3, chap. 20, no. 3.

He gives similar advice regarding natural goods such as physical beauty, bodily constitution, and good intelligence. He recommends that spiritual persons remember the following:

> Spiritual persons, then, must purge and darken their will of this vain joy, and bear in mind the following: Beauty and all other natural endowments are but earth, arising from the earth and returning to it; grace and elegance are but the smoke and air of this earth, and should be considered and valued as such for the sake of avoiding a lapse into vanity. Regarding these goods, spiritual people must direct their heart to God in joy and gladness that God is himself all this beauty and grace—eminently and infinitely so, above all creatures. As David affirms, all these things will grow old and pass away like a garment, while God alone will remain immutable forever [Ps. 102:26-27 {Ps. 101:27}].[28]

John also recommends the following advice concerning vanity in natural goods:

> As soon as the heart feels drawn by vain joy in natural goods, it should recall how dangerous and pernicious it is to rejoice in anything other than the service of God. One should consider how harmful it was for the angels to have rejoiced and grown complacent in their natural beauty and goods, since they thereby fell into the ugly abyss; and how many evils come on humans every day because of this very vanity.[29]

John's therapy for the will, therefore, is a process of formation and strengthening of the will so it may put order and harmony in the emotions and appetites and direct them toward their proper end willed by God—that is, the honor, glory, and love of God. This is how we wear the red toga of charity in daily life: when we patiently surrender to God's healing love in contemplation. We try to do all we can by actively purifying our love. With the help of God's grace we

---

[28] John, *CW*, *The Ascent of Mount Carmel*, Book 3, chap. 21, no. 2.
[29] John, *CW*, *The Ascent of Mount Carmel*, Book 3, chap. 22, no. 6.

try to become more and more conscious of where we place our emotions and affectivity—in God or in goods apart from God. In this way we become increasingly centered in God. Indeed, this requires a lifelong process of prayer, discernment, and deepening consciousness of our motivations.

John gives us another example of how we can wear the red toga of charity in daily life. In *The Spiritual Canticle*, he tells us:

> It is worthy of note that God does not place his grace and love in the soul except according to its desire and love. Those who truly love God must strive not to fail in this love, for they will thereby induce God, if we may so express it, to further love them and find delight in them. And to acquire this charity, one ought to practice what St. Paul taught: *Charity is patient, is kind, is not envious, does no evil, does not become proud, is not ambitious, seeks not its own, does not become disturbed, thinks no evil, rejoices not in iniquity, but rejoices in the truth, suffers all things* (that are to be suffered), *believes all things* (that must be believed), *hopes all things, and endures all things* (that are in accord with charity) [1 Cor. 13:4-7].[30]

In this text, we see another way to wear the red toga of charity. St. Paul shows us the way: the great hymn of charity. "Love is patient; love is kind; love is not envious or boastful or arrogant or rude. It does not insist on its own way; it is not irritable; . . . it does not rejoice in wrongdoing but rejoices in the truth. It bears all things, believes all things, hopes all things, endures all things. Love never ends" (1 Cor 13:4-8).

---

[30] John, *CW*, *The Spiritual Canticle*, Stanza 13, no. 12.

Chapter 11

Healed by Love

AS I STATED EARLY in our study of St. John of the Cross, the perfection of love constitutes the full health of the human person. John of the Cross has a broad understanding of health. Health includes not only religious aspiration but also psychological and spiritual integration. Essentially, health is a matter of love. The more we grow in love, the healthier we become.

Contemplation is the experience of God's self-communicating love that heals the deepest disorders of our psyche and spirit and sets us on fire with God's love. Through the contemplative experience of the dark night of sense and spirit, the Holy Spirit heals and transforms us so that we can reach our divine vocation to love God, creation, and others with God's love.

John believes that "the love of God is the soul's health. In the measure that love increases the healthier she will be, and when love is perfect, she will have full health."[1] These words from *The Spiritual Canticle* express the essence of health for John of the Cross. Perfect love constitutes the full health of the human person. This perfect love is realized in union with God, the beginning, the way, and the end of

---

[1] John, *CW*, *The Spiritual Canticle*, Stanza 11, no. 11. Of course, only in eternal life will love be complete and perfect. Only in heaven will we know complete union with God through love.

the spiritual journey, according to John of the Cross. We possess an insatiable longing to love and be loved, a natural and supernatural desire to love as God loves.[2] This is the union of likeness to which we are called. Union with God means transformation at the deepest level of our being, transforming us into a new way of knowing, being, and loving in this world. We participate in God's way of knowing, loving and being. It means to love God, others, and creation with the very love of God. It is worth reading this important text from *The Spiritual Canticle*:

> It should be noted that the soul does not say that there he will give her his love—although he really does—because she would thereby manifest only that God loves her. She states rather that there he will show her how to love him as perfectly as she desires. It is precisely by giving her his love there that he shows her how to love as she is loved by him. Besides teaching her to love purely, freely, and disinterestedly, as he loves us, God makes her love him with the very strength with which he loves her. Transforming her into his love, as we said, he gives her his own strength by which she can love him. As if he were to put an instrument in her hands and show her how it works by operating it jointly with her, he shows her how to love and gives her the ability to do so.[3]

John of the Cross describes union with God as a relationship of love that reaches its maximum expression in spiritual marriage.[4] This loving relationship is a mutual surrender on both parts that heals the disorders and sickness of the soul. Therefore, ultimate healing comes

---

[2] "The soul's aim is a love equal to God's. She always desired this equality, naturally and supernaturally, for lovers cannot be satisfied without feeling that they love as much as they are loved" (John, *CW*, *The Spiritual Canticle*, Stanza 38, no. 3).

[3] John, *CW*, *The Spiritual Canticle*, Stanza 38, no. 4.

[4] "This spiritual marriage is incomparably greater than the spiritual betrothal, for it is a total transformation in the Beloved, in which each surrenders the entire possession of self to the other with a certain consummation of the union of love. The soul thereby becomes divine, God through participation, insofar as is possible in this life" (John, *CW*, *The Spiritual Canticle*, Stanza 22, no. 3).

through union with Jesus Christ. As we read in a previous chapter, John speaks of the espousal as a gradual healing of the human person.[5]

Since the perfection of love constitutes the full health of the human person, and this perfection of love is realized in intimate union with Christ, what are the effects on us? What are the fruits of this union and what does the health that comes from union with Christ look like?

Centered in God

Because "God is the soul's center,"[6] John of the Cross sees human development as an ever-progressive movement toward the center of the personality where God dwells. As we noted in chapter 2, our fundamental sickness, which is a failure to love, comes from being separated from our deepest center, from God, the divine Source of love, and thus from our most authentic self.

The divine therapy that comes from the dark night of sense and spirit rejoins us to our center.[7] Since contemplation is a "science of love,"[8] and it is love that unites us to God, then growing in love rejoins us to our center where God dwells. When we say "our center," we mean this in a dynamic sense rather than a material point of locality. Our center is the point to which all the energies of the person tend.[9] The contemplative experience is becoming more and more centered in God through love. It is love that centers us. John expresses this well in *The Living Flame of Love*:

> It is noteworthy, then, that love is the inclination, strength, and power for the soul in making its way to God, for love unites it with God. The more degrees of love it has, the more deeply it enters

---

[5] John, *CW*, *The Spiritual Canticle*, Stanza 23, no. 6.
[6] John, *CW*, *The Living Flame of Love*, Stanza 1, no. 12.
[7] Wilfred Stinissen, OCD, *La nuit comme le jour illuminé: La nuit obscure chez Jean de la Croix* (Toulouse: Éditions du Carmel, 2010), 94.
[8] John, *CW*, *The Dark Night*, Book 2, chap. 18, no. 5.
[9] Fernando Urbina, *La persona humana en San Juan de la Cruz* (Madrid: Ediciones Marova, 1956), 210.

into God and centers itself in him. We can say that there are as many centers in God possible to the soul, each one deeper than the other, as there are degrees of love of God possible to it. A stronger love is a more unitive love, and we can understand in this manner the many mansions the Son of God declared were in his Father's house [Jn. 14:2].

Hence, for the soul to be in its center—which is God, as we have said—it is sufficient for it to possess one degree of love, for by one degree alone it is united with him through grace. Should it have two degrees, it becomes united and concentrated in God in another, deeper center. Should it reach three, it centers itself in a third. But once it has attained the final degree, God's love has arrived at wounding the soul in its ultimate and deepest center, which is to illuminate and transform it in its whole being, power, and strength, and according to its capacity, until it appears to be God.[10]

Rejoining our center is a fruit of a journey of love. Paradoxically, being centered in God means that we become uprooted from selfish preoccupation and egotism. John expresses this well in the last stanza of the poem *The Dark Night*.[11] Because the center is God, arriving there means opening ourselves to God, others, and creation.

In the seventh dwelling places of *The Interior Castle*, St. Teresa of Jesus explains concretely what it means to have arrived at the center of the personality. All the graces of contemplative prayer are meant to free us to live a life in imitation of Jesus crucified, to be branded with the cross—that is, a life of self-giving service—to be a slave of everyone as Jesus was.[12]

For John of the Cross, as for St. Teresa, arriving at the center of the soul is not a dead end or a place of isolation; rather, it means opening

---

[10] John, *CW*, *The Living Flame of Love*, Stanza 1, no. 13.

[11] "I abandoned and forgot myself, / laying my face on my Beloved; / all things ceased; I went out from myself, / leaving my cares / forgotten among the lilies" (John, *CW*, *Poetry*, *The Dark Night*).

[12] Teresa of Avila, *The Interior Castle*, Dwelling Places 7, chap. 7, nos. 4 and 8, in *The Collected Works of St. Teresa of Avila*, vol. 2, trans. Kieran Kavanaugh and Otilio Rodriguez (Washington, DC: ICS Publications, 1980).

up to God and to all that God created. Being centered in God means being rooted in love and aware of others and their needs.

Peace

Having joined our center brings about interior peace and harmony. The word *peace* appears many times in the texts where John speaks of the fruits of the healing journey to union with God.

As we discussed in chapter 3, original sin as well as personal sin have created a state of inner conflict with us. This conflict gives rise to inner warfare. We attempt to satisfy our desire for God by choosing something that can never satisfy us emotionally and spiritually. The more we depend upon creatures to satisfy our longing for love, happiness, and meaning, the more we experience interior warfare, dispersion, and fragmentation. Being centered in God, however, brings profound inner peace and harmony, peace with God, with ourselves, and others. "For when the appetites and concupiscences are quenched, the soul dwells in spiritual peace and tranquility. Where neither the appetites nor concupiscence reign, there is no disturbance but only God's peace and consolation."[13]

In *The Dark Night*, John writes that the dark night stirs up an inner war in order to remove all false peace and establish true peace and tranquility.[14] Peace is a sign of spiritual and psychological health and John often encourages those he guides to strive to maintain their inner peace.

---

[13] John, *CW*, *The Dark Night*, Book 1, chap. 13, no. 3.

[14] "Moreover, the soul should leave aside all its former peace, because it is prepared by means of this contemplative night to attain inner peace, which is of such a quality and so delightful that, as the Church says, it surpasses all understanding [Phil. 4:7]. That peace was not truly peace, because it was clothed with many imperfections, although to the soul walking in delight it seemed to be peace. It seemed to be a twofold peace, sensory and spiritual, since the soul beheld within itself a spiritual abundance. This sensory and spiritual peace, since it is still imperfect, must first be purged; the soul's peace must be disturbed and taken away. In the passage we quoted to demonstrate the distress of this night, Jeremiah felt disturbed and wept over his loss of peace: My soul is withdrawn and removed from peace [Lam. 3:17]" (John, *CW*, *The Dark Night*, Book 2, chap. 9, no. 6).

> It is very important and fitting for Your Reverence, if you desire to possess profound peace in your soul and attain perfection, that you surrender your whole will to God so that it may thus be united with him and that you do not let it be occupied with the vile and base things of earth.[15]
>
> Strive to preserve your heart in peace; let no event of this world disturb it; reflect that all must come to an end.[16]

Humility

The deep and authentic peace which is a fruit of union with God, and a sign of psychological and spiritual health, is experienced only after having passed through the inner war of the dark night of sense and spirit.[17] Under the movement of the Holy Spirit, we must descend into the dark depths of the unconscious and see, feel, examine, and integrate the "shadow" parts of our personality: our gifts and talents as well as our half-forgotten memories, childhood wounds, fears, obsessions, compulsions, addictions, and personality or character defects. We must become conscious of, confront, and struggle patiently and perseveringly with this inner world in order to discover true peace of heart. As John explains so well in the book *The Dark Night*, this interior descent is absolutely necessary to regain true health and authentic peace of mind and heart.

> The first and chief benefit this dry and dark night of contemplation causes is the knowledge of self and of one's own misery. Besides the fact that all the favors God imparts to the soul are ordinarily wrapped in this knowledge, the aridities and voids of the faculties in relation to the abundance previously experienced and the difficulty encountered in the practice of virtue make the soul recognize its own lowliness and misery, which was not apparent in the time of its prosperity.[18]

---

[15] John, *CW, Letters*, no. 13.
[16] John, *CW, The Sayings of Light and Love*, no. 154.
[17] John, *CW, The Dark Night*, Book 2, chap. 9, no. 6.
[18] John, *CW, The Dark Night*, Book 1, chap. 12, no. 2.

The dark night pierces the illusions we have of ourselves and makes us stand in the truth. This brings us face to face with the reality of our lives and challenges us to embrace all we are before God, our goodness as well as our sinfulness. There can be no healing or spiritual growth unless we face our inner poverty and dependency upon God and stand in the truth. Jesus said, "the truth will make you free" (John 8:32).

The self-knowledge born from the dark night has many benefits. The first is that we begin "to commune with God more respectfully and courteously, the way one should always converse with the Most High."[19] Meister Eckhart believed that we tend to treat God like a cow who must give us milk as much as we desire.[20] Through the dark night we realize that God cannot be manipulated or milked like a cow. The dryness and aridity of the purgative contemplation purifies our desires for deeper commitment to God and makes us aware of God's transcendence and greatness, and that we must approach God respectfully.[21] We have a deeper and more authentic knowledge of God. "We conclude that self-knowledge flows first from this dry night, and that from this knowledge as from its source proceeds the other knowledge of God. Hence St. Augustine said to God: Let me know myself, Lord, and I will know you. For as the philosophers say, one extreme is clearly known by the other."[22] In other words, we cannot know God if we do not know ourselves, and we cannot know ourselves unless we know God. It is only in our relationship with God that our authentic humanity is revealed.

Love of Neighbor

Having faced the truth of our sinfulness and misery in the purifying flames of God's tender and compassionate love has profound implications for our relationship with other people. The fruit of

---

[19] John, *CW*, *The Dark Night*, Book 1, chap. 12, no. 2.
[20] Cited by Stinissen, *La nuit comme le jour illuminé*, 12.
[21] John, *CW*, *The Dark Night*, Book 1, chap. 12, no. 4.
[22] John, *CW*, *The Dark Night*, Book 1, chap. 12, no. 5.

humble self-knowledge is love of neighbor. "A soul enkindled in love is a gentle, meek, humble, and patient soul."[23]

One of the major benefits of the dark night of sense and spirit is freedom from the seven capital vices.[24] As we examined in chapter 4, the seven capital vices manifest the childish immaturity and egotism hidden under the veneer of piety and search for perfection. The vices have little to do with actual prayer experiences. Most of them manifest selfish and unloving attitudes towards self and others, for instance, by judging and condemning others, undermining the goodness of others, and having a desire for preference in everything, as well as through anger, impatience, envy, and the desire to be esteemed and approved by others and confessors. John tells us that to have seen and felt one's misery brings about a different attitude toward other people.

> Aware of their own dryness and wretchedness, the thought of their being more advanced than others does not even occur in its first movements, as it did before; on the contrary, they realize that others are better. From this humility stems love of neighbor, for they esteem them and do not judge them as they did before when they were aware that they enjoyed an intense fervor while others did not. These persons know only their own misery and keep it so much in sight that they have no opportunity to watch anyone else's conduct.[25]

Therefore, the egotism manifested through judging and condemning others and considering oneself better is uprooted and replaced by a nonjudgmental and compassionate spirit born from an awareness of one's own dark tendencies. The trials, temptations, and sufferings of the night cure the soul of the prideful and narcissistic attitudes manifested through the capital vices. Softened and humbled by aridities and hardships and by other temptations and trials in which God exercises the soul in the course of this night, individuals become meek

---

[23] John, *CW*, *The Sayings of Light and Love*, no. 29.
[24] John, *CW*, *The Dark Night*, Book 1, chap. 12, no. 7.
[25] John, *CW*, *The Dark Night*, Book 1, chap. 12, nos. 7–8.

toward God and themselves and toward their neighbor, and they do not lose patience and become angry because they don't achieve perfection quickly.[26]

God's divine therapy humbles the person and makes her gentle and meek toward her neighbor and others. No longer does she need preference in all things or to be the center of attention. Rather, she sees the goodness in others and places their needs before hers. Furthermore, she is no longer envious or distressed because others may seem more advanced than she. If she is envious, it is a holy envy.[27]

Memory and Solicitude for God

Another benefit is that the person bears a habitual remembrance of God.[28] Living from one's center leads to a deeper sensitivity to God's presence and a desire to remain faithful to the relationship with God. There is a mistrust of self and more dependency upon God's faithful love. One desires to truly serve God.[29]

The memory of God and solicitude to please God are fruits of freedom. One is free to place God at the center of life. John often writes about the freedom from egotism in one's relationship with God as a fruit of the purification of selfish desire.[30] One becomes free to love God and others without selfish motivations. A deeper love and commitment to God and others is born.

> These aridities, then, make people walk with purity in the love of God. No longer are they moved to act by the delight and satisfaction they find in a work, as perhaps they were when they derived this from their deeds, but by the desire of pleasing God.[31]

---

[26] John, *CW, The Dark Night*, Book 1, chap. 13, no. 7.
[27] John, *CW, The Dark Night*, Book 1, chap. 13, no. 8.
[28] John, *CW, The Dark Night*, Book 1, chap. 13, no. 4.
[29] John, *CW, The Dark Night*, Book 1, chap. 13, no. 13.
[30] John, *CW, The Dark Night*, Book 1, chap. 13, no. 14.
[31] John, *CW, The Dark Night*, Book 1, chap. 13, no. 12.

Integral Healing: A Loving Humanity

As I presented in chapter 2, God's original plan in creating us is that we would direct all our energies and faculties of our body and soul—that is, our whole person—toward God in loving service. This intimate friendship with God for which we were created is to be the source of interior harmony and peace reflected in our relationship with ourselves, others, and creation. However, original sin and personal sin have disrupted this harmony and integration. Like St. Paul, we do not do what we would like to do (Rom 7:15). Despite our best intentions and efforts, we are not directed completely toward God. We find ourselves divided, dispersed, and fragmented. There is another law at work in our hearts. According to John, God's healing love that comes through purgative contemplation gathers the dispersed and divided energies and faculties of the person and integrates the whole person. Contemplation brings about unity and harmony with God, self, and others.

> One might, then, in a certain way ponder how remarkable and how strong this enkindling of love in the spirit can be. God gathers together all the strength, faculties, and appetites of the soul, spiritual and sensory alike, so the energy and power of this whole harmonious composite may be employed in this love. The soul consequently arrives at the true fulfillment of the first commandment which, neither disdaining anything human nor excluding it from this love, states: *You shall love your God with your whole heart, and with your whole mind, and with your whole soul, and with all your strength* [Dt. 6:5].[32]

John describes this integration in *The Spiritual Canticle*:

> Now I occupy my soul
> and all my energy in his service;
> I no longer tend the herd,
> nor have I any other work
> now that my every act is love.[33]

---

[32] John, *CW*, *The Dark Night*, Book 2, chap. 11, no. 4.
[33] John, *CW*, *Poetry*, "15. The Spiritual Canticle," no. 28.

In this stanza we find a portrait of the fullness of health to which we are called by our creation. The individuals who have reached this fullness of health, that is, who have reached loving union with Christ, are totally given over to the love and service of Christ, the Beloved. Love becomes the foundation of their life: "All my energy in his service." The energy of the soul comprises the entire person in their natural being, composed of soul and body.[34] Nothing is excluded from the love and service of God: body, soul, energies, intellect, memory, and will. The whole person is directed toward the love and service of the Beloved.[35] We have a portrait of a unified personality that has reached the simplicity of a life of love. The supreme ideal of life has become a reality: the surrender of all one's being to God's love, the fulfillment of the great commandment of love of God and neighbor.

There are several qualities of this loving person we need to examine. To begin with, this person is no longer a slave to other "works." She is no longer dependent upon created reality and other people to satisfy her emotionally and spiritually. Love is now the source of her life, not the world of selfish desire, honors, prestige, and pleasing other people. She centers all her emotions, desires, and energies in God, the source of true happiness and meaning. Because she lives from her center, from the Source of love, she no longer suffers from the type of fragmentation that leads to emotional and spiritual dysfunction.[36]

Before reaching this state of loving union, the person had many other "works" and unprofitable occupations by which she endeavored to satisfy her own desires and those of others, such as speaking about useless things and thinking about them; desiring to please others through ostentation, compliments, flattery, and human respect; the

---

[34] Eulogio Pacho, "La antropologia sanjuanistica," in *Estudios sanjuanistas* II (Burgos, Spain: Monte Carmelo, 1997), 49.

[35] John, *CW*, *The Spiritual Canticle*, Stanza 28, no. 4.

[36] We see in the description of the person in this state of union of love the opposite of the harms explained in *The Ascent of Mount Carmel*, chaps. 16–45, where John analyzes the purification of the will. In those chapters John explains how selfish and possessive love leads to dispersion and fragmentation, and thus to a breakdown in the well-being of the person, whereas centering all one's energy in loving God brings about unity and harmony to the personality.

effort to please people by her actions; and employing all her care, desires, and energy in pleasing other people. It is obvious that John's description of the "works" and unprofitable occupations that consumed the person before this state of loving union is one of a person living outside him- or herself in other people, alienated from their deeper center and living to please others in an inordinate manner.[37]

Secondly, the loving person is a zealous and active soul. Like the love between husband and wife, the love of God demands total commitment and thus expression. The loving person is truly committed to the kingdom of God. She expresses her love by a life of service and thus proves her love by her deeds. In this sense, she is a missionary of love.[38]

The loving person is lost to collective expectations. That is, she is free from the fear of what others will think about her works of charity; she is not afraid to confess Jesus Christ before others. John says that few spiritual persons have such daring and determination in their works. Some do reach this freedom, but they never lose themselves entirely in some matters and execute their works for Christ selflessly; they worry about what others will think or how they will appear. They are not lost to themselves.[39]

This loving person is now free from fear; she is courageous. Because the love of God is the source of her dignity, worth, and emotional and spiritual happiness, she is no longer dependent upon others. She is not threatened by the fears of the "world"—that is, the fear of what others will think and say about her and of losing their favor.[40]

Thirdly, this loving person is truly committed to and concentrated on loving Christ the Beloved without self-interest.

---

[37] John, *CW*, *The Spiritual Canticle*, Stanza 28, no. 7.
[38] John, *CW*, *The Spiritual Canticle*, Stanza 29, no. 7.
[39] John, *CW*, *The Spiritual Canticle*, Stanza 29, no. 8.
[40] John, *CW*, *The Spiritual Canticle*, Stanza 3, nos. 7–10.

> Aware of the Bridegroom's words in the Gospel, that no one can serve two masters but must necessarily fail one [Mt. 6:24], the soul claims here that in order not to fail God she failed all that is not God, that is, herself and all other creatures, losing all these for love of him.
>
> Anyone truly in love will let all other things go in order to come closer to the loved one. On this account the soul affirms here that she lost herself. She achieved this in two ways: she became lost to herself by paying no attention to herself in anything, by concentrating on her Beloved and surrendering herself to him freely and disinterestedly, with no desire to gain anything for herself; second, she became lost to all creatures, paying no heed to all her own affairs but only to those of her Beloved. And this is to lose herself purposely, which is to desire to be found.[41]

Genuine love implies commitment, which means fidelity to relationships regardless of feelings. For John, the truly loving person loves for the sake of Christ, not for selfish motives. She is not motivated by likes or dislikes, pleasure or displeasure. She simply loves for the sake of loving, not to receive something in return.[42]

John provides an evocative metaphor to describe the genuinely loving personality. Their love is like "old wine." Their love is not based on sensible delights as it is for new lovers, but it is "fermented" through fidelity, dryness, and sufferings. Like old wine, their love has lost the early effervescence of new wine; now it is aged and solid with a rich flavor that fortifies. They are like old lovers who hardly ever fail God. "And their wine of love is not only fermented and purged

---

[41] John, *CW*, *The Spiritual Canticle*, Stanza 29, no. 10.

[42] "Lovers are said to have their heart stolen or seized by the object of their love, for the heart will go out from self and become fixed on the loved object. Thus their heart or love is not for themselves but for what they love. Accordingly, the soul can know clearly whether or not she loves God purely. If she loves him her heart or love will not be set on herself or her own satisfaction and gain, but on pleasing God and giving him honor and glory. In the measure she loves herself, that much less she loves God" (John, *CW*, *The Spiritual Canticle*, Stanza 9, no. 5).

of lees, but even spiced, with the perfect virtues that do not let it go bad as does the new wine."[43]

Genuine committed love is also attentive to the Beloved. The loving person is concentrated on the Beloved. She is attentive to him and engaged in the continual exercise of love for him.[44]

Psychologists like Rollo May, Erich Fromm, and M. Scott Peck tell us that the principal form of love is attention to the one we love.[45] Peck writes:

> The principal form that the work of love takes is attention. When we love another we give him or her our attention; we attend to the person's growth. When we love ourselves we attend to our own growth. When we attend to someone, we are caring for that person. The act of attending requires that we make an effort to set aside our existing occupations and actively shift our consciousness. Attention is an act of the will, of work against the inertia of our minds.[46]

Attention to the Beloved implies being present to and listening to the other with all one's being. Therefore, the loving person is one who is truly present to the one he or she loves, present to the moment and listening to the Beloved. She is not fragmented and dispersed, nor is she self-preoccupied and imprisoned by her own needs; rather, she is totally present to the moment. In this sense, she is present to life as it is and to the needs of the kingdom. Loving attention brings about an emptiness of self that leads to the fullness of life in Christ and freedom to proclaim the kingdom of God. It leads us to lose ourselves in order to be seized by Christ's love which surpasses all understanding. In being lost this way, we find our true self in Christ Jesus and thus come to know true peace, harmony, and health of mind and heart.

---

[43] John, *CW*, *The Spiritual Canticle*, Stanza 25, no. 11.
[44] John, *CW*, *The Spiritual Canticle*, Stanza 29, no. 1.
[45] See Rollo May, *Love and Will* (New York: Delta Books, 1969); Erich Fromm, *The Art of Loving* (New York: Harper and Brothers, 1956), 111–15; M. Scott Peck, MD, *The Road Less Traveled* (New York: Simon & Schuster, 2002).
[46] Peck, *The Road Less Traveled*, 120.

Love in the Midst of Suffering

It would be erroneous to think that the life of the person who reaches this state of love is free from suffering. The loving soul about whom John writes lives in the midst of trials and difficulties that are part of human existence. We catch a glimpse of this in the following prayer: "My Beloved, all that is rough and toilsome I desire for your sake, and all that is sweet and pleasant I desire for your sake."[47]

The healthy personality is like a bee that sucks honey from all the wildflowers—that is, she is able to transform everything that happens to her, good or bad, pleasant or unpleasant, into love. She has a positive attitude toward life, even in the midst of trials. She finds meaning in all that happens to her and is spiritually and psychologically healthy enough to respond with faith, hope, and love in all situations of life. "Like the bee that sucks honey from all the wildflowers and will not use them for anything else, the soul easily extracts the sweetness of love from all the things that happen to her; that is, she loves God in them."[48]

We have no better example of a healthy personality than John of the Cross. His last days and illness are a living illustration of a healthy and loving person. His final years were marked by persecution and suffering because he stood up for what he believed was a just cause.[49] In June 1591, he was relieved of his charge as superior in Segovia and was sent back to Andalusia. When a Carmelite nun wrote to him expressing her distress over the persecution launched against him, he reacted in this way:

> Do not let what is happening to me, daughter, cause you any grief, for it does not cause me any. What greatly grieves me is that the one who is not at fault is blamed. Men do not do these things, but God, who knows what is suitable for us and arranges things for

---

[47] John, *CW, The Spiritual Canticle*, Stanza, 28, no. 10.
[48] John, *CW, The Spiritual Canticle*, Stanza 27, no. 8.
[49] Federico Ruiz, *Dios habla en la noche* (Madrid: Editorial de Espiritualidad, 1990), 335–37.

> our good. Think nothing else but that God ordains all, and where there is no love, put love, and you will draw out love.[50]

John embraced the persecution in faith, hope, and love. He didn't respond to his persecutors with bitterness, anger, or revenge. He didn't play the victim or martyr's role. He looked at the situation with the eyes of faith. "Think nothing else but that God ordains all." He sought to put love into an unjust situation to draw out love.

John's reaction reveals his loving and healthy personality. Even though he died a year later from a tumor on his leg and fevers due to infection, his mind and heart were healthy and full of love, for he was free from disorders of the mind and heart such as anger, bitterness, and vengefulness. The wounds of violence, hatred, bitterness, and injustice are only healed by forgiveness, love, and compassion. John lived Jesus' teaching: "I say to you: Do not resist an evildoer. But if anyone strikes you on the right cheek, turn the other also" (Matt 5:39). "I say to you: Love your enemies and pray for those who persecute you, so that you may be children of your Father in heaven, for he makes his sun rise on the evil and on the good and sends rain on the righteous and on the unrighteous. For if you love those who love you, what reward do you have? Do not even the tax collectors do the same?" (Matt 5:44-46). Of course, to love this way is only possible through an infusion of God's love that comes to us through purgative contemplation.

> A soul enkindled with love is a gentle, meek, humble, and patient soul. A soul that is hard because of self-love grows harder. O good Jesus, if you do not soften it, it will ever continue in its natural hardness.[51]

Love is the only reality that ultimately heals the pathologies of the mind and heart. John expressed this belief in a letter to a Carmelite nun who was suffering from difficulties in community life.

---

[50] John, *CW*, *Letters*, no. 26.
[51] John, *CW*, *The Sayings of Light and Love*, nos. 29-30.

Have a great love for those who contradict and fail to love you, for in this way love is begotten in a heart that has no love. God so acts with us, for he loves us that we might love by means of the very love he bears toward us.[52]

Paradise Regained

In chapter 2, we read that John of the Cross gives us an insight into the integral health to which we are called in those texts where he refers to original justice.[53] In the state of original innocence the whole person—body-soul-senses-spirit—was harmoniously directed toward God and in harmony with themselves and creation.

However, as we said in chapter 2, we must not understand the grace of Paradise as an expression of a perfect human being before original sin. The return to "original justice" is best understood as God's gift of divine life given to human beings from the beginning of their appearance on earth, manifested in Christ, and coming to fullness only at the end of time. It expresses symbolically that "from the beginning of time we were created with a supernatural vocation to be children of God, and harmoniously and completely oriented toward God."[54] As children of God, we were created out of love and for love, to share in divine life. Therefore, we function healthily only in relationship to God and to the extent that we reach the fullness of our humanity as beings created for an intimate friendship with God and with one another.

Original justice expresses our call to share in divine life. As we saw in an earlier chapter, one theologian described Paradise as the symbol of the incarnate Word. The incarnation of Jesus Christ not only restored humanity to our original nature but gives us the possibility of

---

[52] John, *CW*, *Letters*, no. 33.
[53] In the following texts, John refers to "original justice": *CW*, *The Ascent of Mount Carmel*, Book 3, chap. 26, no. 5; *The Dark Night*, Book 2, chap. 24, no. 2; *The Spiritual Canticle*, Stanza 26, no. 14.
[54] Juan L. Ruiz de la Peña, *El don de Dios: Antropología teológica especial* (Santander, Spain: Editorial Sal Terrae, 1991), 160–64.

realizing the fullness of life for which God predestined us from all eternity; it is a mystery of divinization. In Jesus Christ, God entered into creation and shared fully in our human existence in all things but sin. In becoming one with us to this extent, Christ not only communicated divine life to us, but also revealed the deepest meaning of our humanity. Now the possibility exists for us to know in "flesh and blood" what it means to resemble God and to participate in divine life.

For John, our human destiny is profoundly shaped by the mystery of the incarnation. "He who resembles you most, satisfies me most, and whoever is like you in nothing will find nothing in me."[55] We were created in the image and likeness of Christ. By the incarnation and resurrection of Jesus Christ, we bear within us a sketch of the Beloved.

> It should be known that love never reaches perfection until the lovers are so alike that one is transfigured in the other. And then the love is in full health. The soul experiences within herself a certain sketch of love, which is the sickness she mentions, and she desires the completion of the sketch of this image, the image of her Bridegroom, the Word, the Son of God, who, as St. Paul says, *is the splendor of his glory and the image of his substance* [Heb. 1:3]; for this is the image referred to in this verse and into which the soul desires to be transformed through love. As a result she says: For the sickness of love is not cured except by your very presence and image.[56]

The grace of original justice is life in Jesus Christ, transformation into Jesus Christ. Jesus Christ reveals God's original plan in creating us and the meaning of the grace of original justice: a life of loving dedication to the Father and others. Jesus of Nazareth was a man totally directed toward the Father and dedicated to his brothers and sisters in a life of loving service. Jesus was the man of radical self-

---

[55] John, *CW, The Romances*, no. 2.
[56] John, *CW, The Spiritual Canticle*, Stanza 11, no. 12.

giving love. This is the "sketch of the Beloved" that we are called to complete. Herein lies the health of the human person: union with Jesus Christ, loving as Jesus loves—with a love equal to God's Son, a life totally directed toward God—living the great commandment of love: "You shall love the Lord your God with all your heart and with all your soul and with all your mind. . . . You shall love your neighbor as yourself" (Matt 22:37-39).

Conclusion

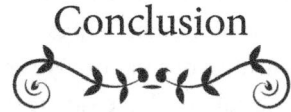

Contemplative Love

IN THE INTRODUCTION to this book, I noted that there is a growing interest in the United States in the relationship between faith, spirituality, and healing. This reflects the search for healing in our culture and a growing consciousness of the holistic nature of healing and the spiritual nature of human beings. The World Health Organization now recognizes that healing is more than an absence of physical illness. Health is a state of well-being experienced on the psychological, moral, and physical levels. Health care professionals such as medical doctors, psychologists, psychiatrists, nurses, and social workers recognize the curative power of faith. Prayer and meditation can bring about psychological and physical healing to help people manage suffering and dysfunctional behavior. Consequently, health care professionals are looking to world religions for enlightenment on the meaning of health and how we can grow toward integral health.

This growing awareness of and interest in the relationship between spirituality and healing and the desire to learn from the great world religions, as well as my own journey of healing within the Carmelite tradition, inspired me to study the writings of St. John of the Cross through the lens of healing. John's doctrine concerns the transformation of the human person created by God out of love and for love, created to share in divine life. Because John of the Cross is a mystic and doctor of the church, and mystics are paradigms of the Christian life, he has something important to offer to the contemporary search for healing.

The theme of healing is an important and universal one. It concerns the health and wholeness of human beings. We all long to love and be loved. Love is the heartbeat of creation. We are wired for love. John of the Cross says that we suffer a "love sickness," and this sickness is only cured by God's love.[1] In one way or another, we all suffer from a "love sickness." We carry a love wound that only God can heal.

We see this "love sickness" in our world that is severely wounded by wars. We witness the plight of poor immigrants searching for a secure home and country. Violence has reached pandemic proportions in our world. An archetypal rage seems to fester deep within the psyche of both young and old and erupts into violence. Racism continues to breed violence and segregation.

Furthermore, we witness this "love sickness" due to addictions. We might look for love in all the wrong places—food, drugs, sex, and alcohol, and in more unnoticed places—work, prestige, power, control, wealth, or comfort. Social media has become a major source of enslavement in our highly technological culture. Just think of the addictive power of the internet: surfing from one site to another to purchase books, clothes, or electronic equipment. Pornography, the dark side of social media, has become a powerful addiction for so many people who hunger for love and seek to assuage their hunger in a dark world, void of true love and relationship.

We also experience our own "sickness of the soul" on a more personal level. We tend to follow our own selfish desires instead of placing the love of God at the center of our lives and relationships. We displace our desires for God with substitutes that can never satisfy us. We may struggle to overcome our deeply rooted egotism manifested by selfish ambition and pride, jealousy, envy, anger, impatience with ourselves and others, and judgment and criticism of others. We may be conditioned by painful past memories from our childhood

---

[1] John, *CW*, *The Spiritual Canticle*, Stanza 11, nos. 11–12.

that undermine healthy self-esteem and trusting relationships with others. We may struggle to forgive and reconcile with our parents or siblings because of past emotional hurts that linger in our memory and prevent us from moving on in life peacefully. Depression is definitely a psychological and emotional suffering that some people bear heroically in daily life.

St. John of the Cross has a therapeutic remedy for the "love sicknesses" in our personal and collective lives, for all who are seeking healing, whether physical, emotional, or spiritual. His therapy is putting God's love at the center of our lives.

For John of the Cross, our understanding of health depends upon our concept of the human person. We were created for an intimate relationship with God that John defines as "union with God through love."[2] God created us out of love and for love, to be completely directed toward God with our whole being. "Love is the end for which we were created."[3] In the words of the English poet William Blake, "We are put on this earth a little space, / That we may learn to bear the beams of love."[4] In other words, we are put on this earth to be bearers of God's love, that is, to know God's love, to receive God's love, and to radiate the very love of God to others. Our intimate relationship with God is meant to be the source of interior harmony and integration that is reflected in our relationship with others and creation.

However, we often find it hard "to bear the beams of love." Due to the effects of original sin and our personal history, we are divided, fragmented, and dispersed. We do what we do not want to do, as St. Paul expressed it.[5] We tend to pour ourselves out into created things that will never ultimately satisfy our longing for love, meaning, and happiness. A deeply rooted egotism is embedded within our spirit

---

[2] John explains our divine vocation to union with God through love in *The Ascent of Mount Carmel*, Book 2, chap. 5.

[3] John, *CW*, *The Spiritual Canticle*, Stanza 29, no. 3.

[4] William Blake, *Poems and Prophecies* (New York: Everyman's Library, 1991), 10.

[5] "I do not understand my own actions. For I do not do what I want, but I do the very thing I hate. . . . For I do not do the good I want, but the evil I do not want is what I do" (Rom 7:15, 19).

like an old stain on a piece of cloth.[6] The sickness of soul about which John writes is deeper than just moral, emotional, or physical illness; rather, it is a sickness that has its origin in the ontological level of the human person. Fundamentally, our sickness of soul is the inability to love authentically as God has created us to love, a love equal to God's.[7] This lack of love comes from separating ourselves from the divine Source of all love and meaning who dwells in the depths of our being. Choosing to center our lives on created things, hoping to find ultimate satisfaction of heart in them rather than in God, locks us in a world of egotism that leads to dysfunctional behavior and suffering. Because we carry a wound on the ontological level of our being, only God can heal us.

Healing and transformation come from opening ourselves more and more to God self-communicating love through prayer and contemplation. "The love of God is the soul's health. In the measure that love increases she will be healthier, and when love is perfect she will have full health."[8] God's love heals us through contemplative prayer, which is an inflow of God's love in our psyche and spirit. It is the experience of being loved by God and of loving at ever deeper levels of our being. God's healing love is a progressive and gradual process

---

[6] John, *CW*, *The Dark Night*, Book 2, chap. 2, no. 1.

[7] We will only know perfect love, as God loves, in eternal life. However, our divine vocation is to become transformed little by little in order to share in divine life, and thus to love as God loves. There are degrees of love in this life, degrees of transformation. God's love is like an abyss of love in which we can always venture further within. "We speak of the highest degree of perfection one can reach in this life (transformation in God), these stanzas treat of a love deeper in quality and more perfect within this very state of transformation. Even though it is true that what these and the other stanzas describe is all one state of transformation, and as such one cannot pass beyond it; yet, with time and practice, love can grow deeper in quality, as I say, and become more ardent. We have an example of this in the activity of fire: Although the fire has penetrated the wood, transformed it, and united it with itself, yet as this fire grows hotter and continues to burn, so the wood becomes much more incandescent and inflamed, even to the point of flaring up and shooting out flames from itself" (John, *CW*, *The Living Flame of Love*, Prol. no. 3).

[8] John, *CW*, *The Spiritual Canticle*, Stanza 11, no. 11.

that takes place in stages through the dark night of sense and spirit. This transformation is a work of the Holy Spirit, who uproots, purifies, and heals the disorders of the personality and dysfunctional manner of loving. Contemplation heals the mind and heart of selfish, unloving attitudes and unconscious debris that negatively influence our relationship with God, others, and creation. It is empirically proven that unloving attitudes and unconscious negative emotions in our psyche can cause mental and physical illness.[9] Purgative contemplation, therefore, heals the psyche and spirit of those thoughts, emotions, memories, and attitudes that prevent the psychological and spiritual well-being of the person. It brings about harmony within the person and orders the person toward the love of God and neighbor.[10] God's self-communicating love through contemplation teaches us how to love and transforms the deepest structures of the human person so that we can love God, others, and creation with "the strength of the Holy Spirit," and radiate God's compassionate and merciful love to a broken world.[11] It is worth reading this remarkable text:

> It should be noted that the soul does not say that there he will give her his love—although he really does—because she would thereby manifest only that God loves her. She states rather that there he will show her how to love him as perfectly as she desires. It is precisely by giving her his love there that he shows her how to love as she is loved by him. Besides teaching her to love purely, freely, and disinterestedly, as he loves us, God makes her love him with the very strength with which he loves her. Transforming her into his love, as we said, he gives her his own strength by which she can love him. As if he were to put an instrument in her hands and show her how it works by operating it jointly with her, he shows her how to love and gives her the ability to do so.[12]

---

[9] Bill Moyers and B. S. Flowers, eds., *Healing and the Mind* (New York: Doubleday, 1993), 177–239.

[10] See John, *CW*, *The Spiritual Canticle*, Stanza 28, nos. 1–2.

[11] John, *CW*, *The Spiritual Canticle*, Stanza 38, no. 3.

[12] John, *CW*, *The Spiritual Canticle*, Stanza 28, no. 4.

As we shall see, John's theory has much to offer health care professionals who are looking to the mystics of world religions for enlightenment on faith and healing.

Putting God at the Center of Our Life

First of all, John reminds us that we are healthy only when we are related to God. Because we are structured toward God by our very being, created for an intimate relationship with God, our relationship with God is a determinant factor in the integration of the human person. When we separate ourselves from the Source of all love and meaning, there is disorder, fragmentation, and dispersion, a breakdown in the well-being of the person. The physical healings of Jesus were signs of the deeper healing of one's relationship with God. More and more, John's theory, as well as the Gospel's, seems to have the empirical support of medical doctors and psychologists.[13]

Contemplative Prayer and Healing

The second area of contribution John can offer to health care professionals concerns the therapeutic quality of contemplative prayer. There is widespread interest and extensive literature on the therapeutic effects of meditation. There is enough evidence to support the theory that meditation can have therapeutic effects on the mind and body. Studies by Herbert Benson, MD, Jon Kabat-Zinn, PhD, and

---

[13] See Herbert Benson, *Timeless Healing: The Power and Biology of Belief* (New York: Fireside, 1996), 171–91. Also, Kevin Culligan, OCD, writes: "In general, John's theory has enough empirical support to argue against, on the one hand, a position in contemporary psychology which a priori reduces religion to a negative detriment of human behavior and, on the other hand, to corroborate the growing acknowledgement that a person's perceived relationship with the Transcendent is always a significant variable in determining human behavior and therefore ought openly and without prejudice to be examined in psychodiagnosis and explored psychology" (Culligan, "St. John of the Cross and Modern Psychology: A Brief Journey into the Unconscious," in *A Fresh Approach to St. John of the Cross*, ed. John McGowen [Middlegreen, England: St. Pauls, 1993], 45).

Larry Dossey, MD, exemplify medical research on the power of prayer and meditation as a path of healing.

Professor Herbert Benson, a cardiologist and associate professor of medicine at Harvard Medical School, became a pioneer in the field of the therapeutic effects of meditation when he introduced it into patient care. Dr. Benson founded the Benson-Henry Institute for Mind Body Medicine, which studies the inseparable connection between the mind and body and the complicated interactions that take place among the thoughts, the body, and the external world.[14]

Dr. Benson developed what he calls the "Relaxation Response," which is a physical state of deep rest that changes the physical and emotional response to stress. It decreases heart rate, blood pressure, the rate of breathing, and muscle tensions. The Relaxation Response can be found in the context of some of the great religious traditions: Christian, Buddhist, Hindu, Jewish, and Muslim. Among the Christian mystics that Dr. Benson and his colleagues studied are St. Augustine, the unknown author of *The Cloud of Unknowing*, Francisco de Osuna, and St. Teresa of Jesus. They discovered that there exists in all major religious teachings (mystical literature) on prayer and meditation three basic elements: (1) A quiet environment such as a room or place of worship, or even nature. (2) An object to dwell on. This can be a single word, sound, or phrase. Focused concentration helps eliminate all other thoughts. (3) A passive attitude, that is, the emptying of all thoughts and distractions of one's mind.[15]

Dr. Benson's research has taken him and his colleagues a step beyond the medicinal effects of the Relaxation Response to what he calls the "faith factor." This faith factor is the combination of the Relaxation Response and an individual's belief system. Although his research confirms that committed meditators without religious affiliation reap

---

[14] See https://www.massgeneral.org/psychiatry/treatments-and-services/benson-henry-institute.

[15] Henry Benson, MD, *The Relaxation Response* (New York: William Morrow, 1975), 110–11. See his further edition: Henry Benson, MD, *Beyond the Relaxation Response* (New York: Times Books, 1984).

the same physical and emotional benefits as religiously oriented meditators, a person's deepest personal beliefs can provide a strong motivation to meditate and help the person reach enhanced states of health and well-being.[16]

Dr. Jon Kabat-Zinn, PhD, is another leader in the area of meditation and healing. He is professor of medicine emeritus of the University of Massachusetts Medical School and founder of the Stress Reduction Clinic at the University of Massachusetts Medical Center and Center for Mindfulness Medicine and Health Care. Dr. Kabat-Zinn is internationally known for his work teaching mindfulness meditation to help medical patients suffering from chronic pain and stress-related medical disorders, and psychological and emotional disorders, especially depression.[17]

Another trailblazer in the field of mind-body medicine is Dr. Larry Dossey, MD. Dr. Dossey is a physician in internal medicine and past president of the Isthmus Institute of Dallas, Texas, an organization dedicated to exploring the possible convergences of science and religion. His scientific research into the power of prayer to influence healing and the importance of spirituality in medicine has earned him great respect by physicians, health care professionals, and scientists.

Whereas Drs. Benson and Kabat-Zinn teach methods of meditation that have an Eastern background, Dr. Dossey comes from a

---

[16] "Religious commitment is consistently associated with better health. The greater a person's commitment, the fewer his or her psychological symptoms, the better his or her general health, the lower the blood pressure, and the longer the survival. I believe that humans are wired for faith and there is a healing generated by people who rely on faith" (Herbert Benson, MD, *Timeless Healing: The Power and Biology of Belief* [New York: Fireside, 1996], 157). Also regarding the healing power of faith, see Harold G. Koenig, MD, *The Healing Power of Faith: How Belief Can Help You Triumph Over Disease* (New York: Simon and Schuster, 1999).

[17] Mindfulness meditation is a Buddhist practice that cultivates an "open-hearted, moment by moment, non-judgmental awareness" and acceptance of each moment of experience, good, bad, pleasant, or unpleasant (Jon Kabat-Zinn, *Coming to Our Senses: Healing Ourselves and the World through Mindfulness* [New York: Hyperion, 2005], 24).

Protestant Christian background and understands prayer less as a technique, but as something that arises from our unconscious, from the depths of the human person. He recognizes the mystery of prayer and that there are many forms of prayer; essentially, "prayer is an attitude of the heart, a matter of being, not doing. Prayer is the desire to connect with the Absolute, however it may be conceived."[18] Dossey understands prayer as primordial; it comes from a profound level of our spirit. "Prayer starts without words and often ends without them."[19]

Dossey maintains that the primary reason to focus on the role of prayer in healing is deeper than to prove its effectiveness scientifically—although this can be done—but because prayer reveals who we are and what our destiny may be. "The most important reason for examining the effects of prayer, however, has little to do with its healing effects in illness. The fact that prayer works says something incalculably important about our nature, and how we may be connected to the Absolute."[20] Prayer reveals that the human person is a "spark of the divine"; we are a dwelling place of God. In this sense, prayer connects us with the Divine within us and it is our connection with the Divine that is the source of healing. It is also the Divine within us that connects us with other people and allows us to be channels of healing for others by our prayer.[21] Like many other health care professionals, Dossey recognizes that love is intimately related to healing. The power of love to heal may be the key to unlock the mystery of how prayer works. "When one person prays for the welfare of another, the person is extending compassion, empathy and love."[22]

---

[18] Larry Dossey, MD, *Prayer Is Good Medicine* (San Francisco: HarperCollins, 1996), 83.

[19] Larry Dossey, MD, *Healing Words: The Power of Prayer and the Practice of Medicine* (San Francisco: HarperCollins, 1993), 5.

[20] Dossey, *Healing Words*, 6.

[21] Dossey, *Healing Words*, 6–7.

[22] For instance, a survey of ten thousand men with heart disease found a 50 percent reduction in frequency of chest pain (angina) in men who perceived their wives as supportive and loving. Dossey demonstrated the power of love to make the body healthier in what he called the "Mother Teresa effect." He showed

Christian Prayer: A Personal Relationship with God

The goal of Christian prayer is not primarily therapeutic. The aim of Christian prayer and meditation is a personal relationship with God who transforms the human person. John's doctrine reminds health care professionals and meditation seekers that Christian prayer is not about lowering one's blood pressure and feeling relaxed; rather, prayer opens us to a personal loving relationship with God. This loving relationship with God is the source of healing. John's theory that "the love of God is the soul's health" is particularly important today because the search for healing, peace, and relaxation in a stressful world can lead people to think that a simple meditation technique heals. Meditation techniques can be physically and mentally beneficial for disposing one for deeper prayer because of the quiet, passive nature of prayer; ultimately, however, it is opening ourselves to the inflow of God's unconditional love that heals.[23]

Although John of the Cross speaks about the passive and tranquil quality of contemplative prayer, contemplative prayer may not always result in tranquility and peace. On the contrary, contemplative prayer may become stressful because it may incite an interior war.[24] The fire of God's love brings to consciousness all the dark and unconscious debris of the psyche in order to be seen and felt.[25] In this way true peace can be restored. Therefore, although silent and tranquil contemplative prayer may heal, both physically and emotionally, we usually have to engage in an intense interior battle before we experience

---

a documentary to students on Mother Teresa of Calcutta ministering lovingly to the sick. He then tested the students' immunoglobulin A (Ig A). (Ig A is an antibody active against viral infections such as colds.) Ig A levels rose significantly after seeing the documentary, even in those students who found Mother Teresa too religious. See Dossey, *Healing Words*, 110–11.

[23] According to William Johnston, SJ, the secret to the therapeutic dimension of meditation lies in passive concentration and passive energy. In quiet meditation one goes beyond discursive reasoning and yet one remains alert and aware. See William Johnston, *Silent Music* (London: HarperCollins, 1974), 118.

[24] John, *CW*, *The Dark Night*, Book 2, chap. 9, no. 6.
[25] John, *CW*, *The Living Flame of Love*, Stanza 1, no. 21.

peace and spiritual wholeness. In other words, there is no shortcut to healing. Healing is a process of death and resurrection. It involves entering into the paschal mystery of Jesus Christ.

The Christian Mystical Tradition

The third contribution follows the one about the therapeutic quality of meditation. In many parts of the Western world, especially in the United States and Europe, more people, especially young people, are drawn to Buddhism and Hinduism to learn Eastern methods of meditation. Furthermore, as we have discussed, doctors and other health care professionals in the United States are drawing upon Eastern methods of meditation as a path toward greater healing and wholeness. Undoubtedly, the East has an ancient tradition of the psychology of meditation and techniques that can deepen and broaden our understanding of the contemplative path, and these methods can have therapeutic effects. However, it is unfortunate that we don't always draw from the treasures of our own Christian mystical tradition. Therefore, without undermining or denying the wisdom of the East and Eastern techniques of meditation, the writings of St. John of the Cross, and his doctrine on contemplative prayer, has much to contribute to the ongoing dialogue with non-Christian religions regarding spirituality and healing. John's writings can benefit Christians who are searching Eastern mysticism for healing and transformation yet remain unaware of the riches of his doctrine.[26]

Integral Healing

A fourth aspect of John's doctrine relates to the contemporary interest in spirituality and healing in regards to integral healing. John

---

[26] I refer readers to the following article: William Johnston, "The Third Millennium: St. John of the Cross and Interreligious Dialogue in Asia," in *A Better Wine: Essays Celebrating Kieran Kavanaugh, OCD*, Carmelite Studies 10, ed. Kevin Culligan, OCD (Washington, DC: ICS Publications, 2007): 317–36.

affirms the substantial unity of the human person. He describes the dark night of sense and spirit as a progressive purification of the totality of the human person: sense-spirit-body-soul. The dark night gathers and unifies the totality of the person so that the person is in harmony with God, self, and others, and directed toward God.[27]

John's doctrine, therefore, supports the contemporary understanding of health as defined by the World Health Organization. Health is more than the absence of physical illness; rather, health is a state of well-being experienced on the psychological, moral, and physical levels and spirituality is an integral part of the healing process. Contemplation leads to wholeness because it heals the disordered attitudes of the psyche and spirit; it purifies and heals the unconscious and the memory, the contents of which can have a debilitating effect on the body. However, there are four implications to the idea of integral health we need to briefly clarify.

First of all, John's teaching confirms the truth that contemplation is not just an ethereal experience dissociated from the body and other dimensions of our life. Contemplation leads to the integration of the whole person.

Secondly, this does not mean, as we have previously noted, that just because one is physically ill, one is unhealthy. The essence of health is much deeper than physical illness. Health is a matter of the heart that is open, loving, and free from negative attitudes such as pride, anger, greed, lust, avarice, and sloth. In this sense, John's doctrine points to the quality of a person's life: the quality of love, service, openness, and abilities to forgive others and to let go of attachments that prevent wholehearted love and service of God and others.

The third implication relates to the mind-body connection. John of the Cross does not write about the mind-body connection in the way modern science and medicine now recognize, yet he is conscious of the unity and inter-causality of sense and spirit in a way that con-

---

[27] Nothing of the human person is excluded; even the body is directed toward loving and serving God. See John, *CW*, *The Dark Night*, Book 2, chap. 11, no. 4; *The Spiritual Canticle*, Stanza 28, nos. 2–4.

firms the findings of doctors and psychologists. This is an area of his doctrine where much study and reflection is necessary.

A fourth area where John's theory of healing can be of assistance concerns his doctrine on the theological virtues of faith, hope, and love, which is one of his richest contributions to mystical theology. He offers a path of healing and transformation through the active exercise of the theological virtues. The theological virtues both purify us and unite us to God. They are the attitudes of heart we need to nourish and practice as we live through the purifying dark night journey. We have to rise from our "bed of comfort" and go in search of the Beloved by the practice of the virtues.[28] John's teaching on the theological virtues is rich in psychological insight and contains an authentic therapy for the intellect, the memory, and the will. Healing involves more than passive reception; healing also requires our participation by actively striving to maintain positive attitudes of trust (faith), hope (keeping our eyes fixed on God's love and providential care for us), and love, endeavoring daily to transcend selfishness, to put God's love at the center of our life, and to love and serve others in the spirit of Jesus Christ.

"To love," Thomas Merton said, "you have to climb out of the cradle where everything is 'getting' and grow up to the maturity of giving, without concern for getting anything in return."[29] To move beyond disordered selfish desires, to forgive others, to open our hearts to those around us and with whom we live regardless of our natural feelings of like and dislike, and to put love as the motivating force of our life pave the way for transformation. "Have a great love for those who contradict and fail to love you, for in this way love is begotten in a heart that has no love. God so acts with us, for he loves us that we might love by means of the very love he bears toward us."[30] And

---

[28] John, *CW, The Spiritual Canticle*, Stanza 3, no. 2.

[29] Quoted by Ilia Delio, *The Unbearable Wholeness of Being: God, Evolution, and the Power of Love* (Maryknoll, NY: Orbis Books, 2013), 186.

[30] John, *CW, Letter* 33, November 1591. This letter was one of the last letters John wrote at a moment in his life when he was undergoing a persecution from some friars.

again, "Think nothing else but that God ordains all, and where there is no love, put love and you will draw out love."[31]

John's belief that the love of God is the soul's health has implications for all areas of pastoral ministry, such as the proclamation of the word of God, the sacraments, spiritual direction, pastoral care of the sick, and counseling. The image and experience of God in John's mysticism is one of God as a nourishing Father or Mother who enfolds us, cares for us, nourishes us, heals us, and transforms us into divine life.

In this interior union God communicates himself to the soul with such genuine love that nothing else is comparable to it. There is no friendship like God's friendship; there is no love of a brother like God's love; there is no affection of a mother, who tenderly caresses her child, like God's affection.[32] John impresses upon us that in the history of humanity there is no love like God's love. God's tenderness and transforming love is for everyone.

> It should be noted for an understanding of this that just as God loves nothing outside himself, he bears no love for anything lower than the love he has for himself. He loves all things for himself; thus love becomes the purpose for which he loves. He therefore does not love things because of what they are in themselves. With God, to love the soul is to put her somehow in himself and make her his equal. Thus, he loves the soul within himself, with himself, that is, with the very love by which he loves himself. This is why the soul merits the love of God in all her works insofar as she does them in God.[33]

If God loves nothing outside himself, it is as though we exist in the love of God as a fetus lives enveloped in the womb of his or her mother. We are like fish swimming in the ocean of God's love.

The good news of God's love for us revealed in Jesus Christ is the heart of our Christian life, and to come to know God's love opens the

---

[31] John, *CW*, *Letter* 26, July 6, 1591.
[32] John, *CW*, *The Spiritual Canticle*, Stanza 27, no. 1.
[33] John, *CW*, *The Spiritual Canticle*, Stanza 32, no. 6.

door to our well-being, spiritually, psychologically, and even physically. The more we open to God's self-communicating love through contemplative prayer and the practice of the theological virtues, the more profoundly we will experience God's healing and transformative love.

John's belief that God's love is the health of the soul also has implications for political and social structures. When political and social structures reject Gospel values such as peace, justice, concern for the poor and the marginalized, and the dignity of human life from conception to natural death—when political and social structures become self-serving in their desire for power, dominance, and wealth—then the consequence is suffering and a breakdown in the well-being of society. People suffer, and it is usually the poor, especially the innocent and defenseless. John of the Cross has much to offer in the political and social domain that remains untapped. When we are separated from God, there is pathology, personally, collectively, and socially. When we are centered in God and Gospel values, there is wholeness, unity, harmony, peace, health, and well-being.

God's healing love transforms us into vessels of love for humanity. We are not healed and transformed for ourselves alone, but for the transformation of our world.[34] God created us for intimate union with God through love, to participate in the outpouring love of the Trinity, that is, to become bearers of "conscious love," to radiate God's compassionate love in our world.[35] By our self-giving conscious love, we become healers in our beautiful world marred by so much sin, poverty, and suffering.

St. Teresa of Jesus expresses it well in the seventh dwelling places of *The Interior Castle*. All the graces of prayer are to "fortify our weakness" in order to imitate Christ crucified, that is, Christ's self-giving,

---

[34] *Lumen Gentium* reminds us that "the church, in Christ, is a sacrament—a sign and instrument, that is, of communion with God and of the unity of the entire human race" (*Lumen Gentium*, no. 1, in Austin Flannery, ed., *Vatican Council II: Constitutions, Decrees, Declarations; The Basic Sixteen Documents* [Collegeville, MN: Liturgical Press, 2014]).

[35] I have borrowed the expression "conscious love" from Ilia Delio in *The Unbearable Wholeness of Being*, 179–82.

compassionate love.[36] The imitation of Christ crucified is lived most profoundly in Jesus' commandment: "This is my commandment, that you love one another as I have loved you. No one has greater love than this, to lay down one's life for one's friends. You are my friends if you do what I command you" (John 15:12-14).

John of the Cross tells us that "the love of God is the soul's health," and the more we grow in love through friendship with Jesus Christ in prayer, the healthier and more whole we become. The image of Jesus Christ we bear within us becomes more complete and we radiate in our very lives the beauty and love of Christ and reach the fullness of life for which God created us. We become bearers of Christ's beauty in a world longing for meaning, love, and healing.[37]

> Let us rejoice, Beloved,
> and let us go forth to behold ourselves in your beauty,
> to the mountain and to the hill,
> to where the pure water flows,
> and further, deep into the thicket.[38]

---

[36] "It will be good, Sisters, to tell you the reason the Lord grants so many favors in this world. Although, if you have paid attention, you will have understood this in learning of their effects, I want to tell you again here lest someone think that the reason is solely for the sake of giving delight to these souls; that thought would be a serious error. His Majesty couldn't grant us a greater favor than to give us a life that would be an imitation of the life His beloved Son lived. Thus I hold for certain that these favors are meant to fortify our weakness, as I have said here at times, that we may be able to imitate Him in His great sufferings" (Teresa of Jesus, *The Interior Castle*, Dwelling Places 7, chap. 4, no. 4, in *The Collected Works of St. Teresa of Avila*, vol. 2, trans. Kieran Kavanaugh and Otilio Rodriguez [Washington, DC: ICS Publications, 1980]).

[37] "It should be known that love never reaches perfection until the lovers are so alike that one is transfigured in the other. And then the love is in full health. The soul experiences within herself a certain sketch of love, which is the sickness she mentions, and she desires the completion of the sketch of this image, the image of her Bridegroom, the Word, the Son of God, who, as St. Paul says, *is the splendor of his glory and the image of his substance*; for this is the image referred to in this verse and into which the soul desires to be transformed through love. As a result she says: For the sickness of love is not cured except by your very presence and image" (John, *CW*, *The Spiritual Canticle*, Stanza 11, no. 12).

[38] John, *CW*, *The Spiritual Canticle*, Stanza 36.